"Win the war" cook book

Reah Jeannette Lynch

I am very happy indeed, to endorse the "Win the War" Cook Book now being compiled by the St. Louis County Woman's Committee.

In addition to being a very great boon to the homemakers of this generation, this book will be of great interest and value from a historical viewpoint and as a souvenir of this period.

Yours cordially,

Mrs. B. F. Bush.

Chairman Woman's Committee
Council of National Defense
Missouri Division

"WIN THE WAR"
COOK BOOK

Published by
ST. LOUIS COUNTY UNIT
Woman's Committee
COUNCIL OF NATIONAL DEFENSE
Missouri Division

Sold for War Work or War Relief Only

PRICE FIFTY CENTS

·

Compiled by
REAH JEANNETTE LYNCH, B. S.
1918

To
The Mothers
of our Soldier and Sailor
Boys

GO *back* to the *simple* life, be contented with *simple* food, *simple* pleasures, *simple* clothes. Work hard, pray hard, play hard Work, eat, recreate and sleep. Do it all courageously.

We have a victory to win.

—HOOVER

HER 1918 COOK BOOK

SAVE WHEAT
SAVE MEAT
DON'T OVER EAT
DON'T WASTE

GREATER CONSERVATION OF FOODSTUFFS WILL HELP WIN THE WAR

AMERICAN HOUSEWIFE

COURTESY
ST LOUIS TIMES

Preface

The only principles of public conduct worthy a man or gentleman are to sacrifice ease, estate, health, applause and even life to the sacred call of country.　　JAMES OTIS, 1761.

We here highly resolve that the dead shall not have died in vain—that this nation under God shall have a new birth—freedom—and that government of the people, by the people and for the people shall not perish from the earth.

ABRAHAM LINCOLN, 1863

We dedicate our lives and our fortunes, everything that we are, and everything that we have.　　WOODROW WILSON, 1917.

The great light of liberty, justice and equality that burst upon the world in 1776 is today threatened to be put out with a hand of blood and iron

Women of America, awake! We have a definite part to play in this, the greatest tragedy in the world's history. We need not form ourselves into BATTALIONS of death, but into BATTALIONS of life Save food and we save life!

We are unwilling to believe that the women of America are slackers, in other words, traitors to our beloved country and its beautiful emblem, within whose folds are wrapped all that makes existence worth while. A woman, if there be such, who says, "I will not use corn in place of wheat," who says, "I will not save ꓹ teaspoonful of sugar each day," who says, "I will eat beef, mutton and pork daily," is as truly a traitor to her country as was Benedict Arnold or Aaron Burr.

The object of this War Cook Book is to place within one cover all that which has been printed in manifold forms of the best thought of those capable of telling us how to use intelligently the substitutes which our Government has asked us to use.

Ours is the splendid burden of feeding the world. It can be done in but one way· The way of voluntary and larger resolution and action of the whole people in every shop and every kitchen and at every table in the land.

The Woman's Committee Council of National Defense have published this book with no other idea or purpose than to help our fellow-women do the little part which old Uncle Sam has asked us to **do.**

So let us substitute food value for food value.

We send our book forth with a prayer that it may play its little part in bringing liberty, justice and peace not only to our own country, but to the world.

ACKNOWLEDGMENTS

We have been greatly assisted in the compilation of this book by the National and State Food Administration, to whom we extend our cordial thanks.

We are particularly indebted to the Domestic Science Instructors of the State University and of the Preparatory Schools of the city of St. Louis and St Louis County, for their advice and generous help

For encouragement and material assistance, we are especially grateful to Mr T B Boyd and Mr. J Hal Lynch.

Woman's Committee Council National Defense,

St. Louis County Unit

ENDORSEMENTS

The United States Food Administration, in returning our manuscript, writes:—

We thank you for submitting the matter to us and regret the delay in its return to you May we take this opportunity also of expressing our deep appreciation of your obviously sincere and effective effort to aid the vital work of Food Conservation

It is becoming increasingly evident day by day that food will win the war, and it is largely through the work of women like yourself and your associates that food will be effectively used to sustain the health and efficiency of our allies and our own people

U S Food Administration,

States Division Department.

Dr. Anna Howard Shaw, Chairman Woman's Committee Council National Defense, says in her letter from Washington:—

I think your plan a good one. It should be carried out without delay because more and more we are going to be restricted as to the quality and kinds of food we can use. The sooner we obtain definite information with good recipes, the better it will be for us all.

Mrs. George Gellhorn. Chairman Woman's Central Committee on Food Conservation and State Chairman Woman's Committee, says:—

It is with the greatest interest that I have heard of your plan for a conservation cook book. The ability with which your Committee is handling this matter justifies me in the belief that the work will be a real contribution to food conservation in this state and trust throughout the country. I congratulate you and assure you every sort of co-operation in my power as State and City Chairman of Foods and give you my hearty endorsement and congratulations.

The Food Administration of St Louis, in writing says —

The Food Administration of St Louis heartily endorse your "Win the War" Cook Book. This should be a very valuable medium for informing the housewife how she can demonstrate her patriotism in her home.

F. B. Mumford, Federal Food Administrator for Missouri, writes to the Chairman of the Committee:—

This war will not be won by the last 500,000 fighting men but by the last 500,000 bushels of wheat. We are under the impelling necessity of conserving wheat, meat, fat and sugar

Any educational movement which will result in saving any of these vital war food products has the full endorsement of the United States Food Administration. Enclosed I am sending you some recipes which are authorized by the United States Food Administration.

Mrs. Geo. A. Still, President of the Missouri Federation of Woman's Clubs, says:—

It gives me great pleasure to add my name to the distinguished number of men and women who have endorsed the "Win the War" Cook Book. I hope the book may have the sale it deserves

ST. LOUIS COUNTY UNIT

Woman's Committee Council of National Defense

Mrs. J. Hal Lynch, Chairman_____Clayton, Mo

Mrs. W T Donovan, Vice-Chairman_____Normandy, Mo

Mrs. William H Davies, Secretary_____Clayton, Mo.

Mrs. R. E Eggebrecht, Chairman of Finance____Webster Groves

Mrs. Emil Laun, Chairman Courses Instruction_____Clayton, Mo

Mrs. Walter M. Langtry, Chairman Red Cross_____Clayton, Mo

Mrs L W Lacy, Chairman Speakers_____Webster Groves

Miss Marion Griffin, Chairman of Child Welfare and
     Maintenance of Existing Social Agencies__St. Louis County

Town Chairmen (Executive Council)

Mrs Robt. H McMath_____
     Webster Groves

Mrs P. O Bruno_____Wellston

Mrs Warren McGinnis _____
     Wellston

Mrs. W. H Allen_____
     University City

Mrs. E S Sieber____Kirkwood

Mrs F. P. Knabb__Valley Park

Mrs. Marie Reine F Penaloza_
     Ferguson

Mrs. H Von Schrink_____
     Florissant

Mrs Chas C. Craft_____
     Florissant

Mrs Thomas F. Shields_____
     Eureka

Mrs. Wm. D Buchannan_____
     Pine Lawn

Mrs. B F Tate_____
     Hancock S Dist

Mrs. Geo Eades ___ Midland

Mrs A E Wiedmer_____
     Maplewood

Mrs Wm. Davidson __ _____
     Normandy

Mrs. B. J Buss_____Jennings

Mrs. R. J. Winters_____
     Richmond Heights

Mrs. H. Woerther _____
     Baldwin and Manchester

Mrs John Phelan ____Allenton

Mrs. W. W. Henderson_____
     Bridgeton

Mrs D E Horton__Bridgeton

Miss Ruth Nolte ___Black Jack

Mrs Lewis S Doyle_____
     Creve Coeur

Mrs. H C Harwood_____
     Des Peres

Mrs H G Koerber_____
     Hampton Park

Mrs Paul D Walsh__Overland

Miss Ida Post_____Pattonville

Miss Cora Schall _____
     Rock Hill S. Dist.

Mrs A. Blanner___Shrewsbury

Mrs F. J Gould___Vinita Park

Mrs T L Fitzwilliams_____
     Lincoln S. Dist.

Miss Elsa Bruenjes___Glendale

MEASUREMENTS

Level measurements make exact recipes possible because the quantity measured is uniform, the same table may be used for solids and liquids, and measures can be easily divided.

A spoonful is a spoon level full. Use a straight-edged knife or the spatula to obtain a level surface. Half a spoonful is a spoonful divided lengthwise One-fourth of a spoonful is a half spoonful divided crosswise, the division line a little nearer the handle end of the bowl.

A cupful is a cup level full. Fill the cup and level the top with a spatula knife.

Do not shake or press down dry material, as flour or sugar Measure flour after sifting once To measue a fat, as butter, by the cupful, pack solidly and level. To measure less than one-half cupful, use a tablespoon. Pack solidly into the spoon and level.

A speck is that which may be held on the tip of a vegetable knife.

TABLE OF EQUIVALENTS

3	tsp.	1	tbsp
16	tbsp.	1	c
2	c	1	pt
2	pts.	1	qt
4	qts	1	gal.
2	gal	1	pk
2	c. sugar	1	lb
4	c. flour	1	lb
2	c solid fat	1	lb
1	pt. liquid	1	lb
1	tbsp liquid	½	oz
1	tbsp butter	½	oz
1	rounded tbsp. of flour	½	oz.
3	c. corn meal	1	lb.
1½	pt corn meal	1	lb.
1	solid pt chopped meat	1	lb.
1	rounded tbsp. flour	½	oz
*10	eggs	1	lb.
1	pt. gran sugar	1	lb
1	pt brown sugar	13	oz
2½	c. powdered sugar	1	lb
Butter size of an egg		2	oz
Butter size of ½ egg		1	oz

One medium-sized lemon contains from four to four and one-half tablespoons of juice.

One medium-sized orange contains from five to eight tablespoons of juice.

One egg contains about three tablespoons unbeaten yolk and white

When using oil to replace butter or lard use one-third less.

When using syrup to replace sugar subtract the liquid in the syrup from the liquid in the recipe.

*Approximately

ABBREVIATIONS

c._____cupful
tbsp _____tablespoonful
tsp._____teaspoonful
spk _____speck
lb _____pound
qt._____quart
pt _____pint
gal _____gallon
pk._____peck

"A LESSON IN BUYING"

Yet another method of studying food value is to be found in a consideration of weight, cost and measure Such a common commodity as potatoes, of course, are always purchased by weight, but it is very important to realize that there are 15 pounds of potatoes in a peck and that these 15 pounds also represent about 50 medium-sized potatoes In other words, if the housekeeper buys a pound of potatoes she will get three medium-sized potatoes, and a little one thrown in for full weight A pound of prunes may be ordered without any special interest by the woman buyer, and she may get either large or small prunes, depending upon the grocer's wishes, while a wise buyer would stipulate the size wanted because she would know that in a pound of small prunes she would get about 40 prunes, while if they were large there would be about 28

The following table shows the relation of weight and measure and also brings about the difference in the weight of contents of the cans of different sizes. In the case of canned pork and beans, the No 1 can, cost 15 cents, weighs 11 ounces, while the No 2 can, cost 20 cents, weighs 21 ounces. In the latter can, the cost of the additional 10 ounces is 5 cents. If the housekeeper used condensed milk in quantity it is better for her to buy the 16 ounce can, as the cost per ounce is much less than if she purchases the 6 ounce can. Of course, it may be better economy for the woman to buy the No. 2 can of vegetables, but this is true only when the No. 2 can gives her exactly enough for one meal for her family. If there is a serving left over, it is evidently wiser for her to buy the No 3 can, because then she has enough for two meals and with different methods of preparation, will run no risk of monotony.

It seems clear, then, that several elements enter into intelligent buying of food. One who enlists in that service ought to have a clear conception of the relation of these units of weights, cost and measures.

TABLE OF WEIGHTS AND MEASURES

Material	Weight	Measure
Apricots	1 lb.	75 pieces
Bananas	1 lb	3 large
Beans, Navy	1 lb.	2⅓ cups
Beans, canned		
String, No. 2	1 lb. 2 oz	1⅔ cups, drained
Lima, No 2	1 lb. 4 oz.	1⅔ cups, drained
Bread:		
Graham	12 oz.	14½ in. slices
Rye, Ward's	1 lb.	21½ in. slices
White, Ward's	1 lb 2 oz	16½ in slices
Whole wheat, Ward's	1 lb. 4 oz.	15½ in. slices
Butter	1 lb	48 squares
Milk, condensed	6 oz.	⅔ cup
" "	16 oz	1 7/9 cups
Molasses, No 2½	2 lbs. 6 ozs	2¾ cups
Pineapple:		
No. 1 flat	9 oz	5 slices
No 2 tall	1 lb 3 oz.	10 slices
Prunes:		
Small	1 lb.	40 prunes
Large	1 lb	28-30 prunes
Tapioca		
Instant	10 oz.	1 3/7 cups
Minute	10 oz	1 3/7 cups
Pearl	1 lb.	2 1/7 cups

1   ounce of sugar measures 2 level tablespoons.
⅓ ounce of butter measures 2 level tablespoons.
2   ounces of flour measures ¼ cup

U. S Food Administration

MEAL PLANS

Study your meals. Plan them for at least three days in advance This helps you to buy to better advantage, gives variety in material and preparation.

Ask yourself the following questions about your meal:

Does this plan mean—

1. The use of home-grown products and thus allow the railroads to be hauling supplies for the army instead of food for my family?

2. The exchange of milk, cheese, eggs, fish, game and partial exchange of beans, nuts and peas for beef, mutton, pork? Beans, nuts and peas are not meat substitutes, but meat savers. Soy bean is an exception.

3. The use of barley. buckwheat, corn, oats, potatoes and rye instead of wheat?

4. Plenty of whole milk for the children and, if possible, for adults?

5. Twelve ounces of fat per adult per week and six ounces per child per week?

6. The substitution of honey, molasses, corn syrup or other syrup for sugar, so as to reduce the amount of sugar used to three pounds or less per person per month?

7 Meals adapted to the season and pocketbook?

U. S. Food Administration

FOLLOW THESE DIRECTIONS

The Food Administration asks everyone to maintain rigidly a minimum of at least:

ONE WHEATLESS day each week and one WHEATLESS MEAL each day; the wheatless day to be Wednesday. By wheatless we mean eat no wheat products.

ONE MEATLESS day each week which shall be Tuesday, and one MEATLESS MEAL each day By meatless we mean to eat no red meat—beef, pork, mutton, veal, lamb, no preserved meat—beef, bacon, ham, or lard

SUGAR—You can materially reduce sugar by reducing the use of candy and sweet drinks. We will make every endeavor to see that the country is provided with a supply of household sugar on the basis of three pounds of sugar for each person per month Do not consume more.   U. S. Food Administration.

CALENDAR OF PATRIOTIC SERVICE

SUNDAY—One wheatless meal, one meatless meal

MONDAY—Wheatless day, one meatless meal

TUESDAY—Meatless day, porkless day, one wheatless meal

WEDNESDAY—Wheatless day, one meatless meal.

THURSDAY—One meatless meal, one wheatless meal

FRIDAY—One meatless meal, one wheatless meal.

SATURDAY—Porkless day, one wheatless meal, one meatless meal.

EVERY DAY—Save wheat, meat, fats, sugar to create provision for our armies and the allies.

Temporarily to save wheat, Food Administration asks you to observe beefless and porkless Tuesday, but not meatless meals and porkless Saturday

STUDY THESE FIVE FOOD GROUPS
(Sources.)

1   Carbohydrates:
>   Commercial and metabolised products.

>   Sugars:
>>   Glucose, Dextrose—Grapes, sweet corn, onions.
>>   Fructose, Fruit sugar—Fruits, honey, hydrolysis of sucrose.
>>   Sucrose, Cane sugar—Fruits, sugar beet, sugar cane, sorghum canes, palm sugar, sugar maple, pineapples, carrots.
>>   Lactose, Milk sugar—Milk of all mammals.
>>   Maltose, Malt sugar—By diastatic action on germinating seeds, malt and malt products

>   Starches:
>>   Starch—Grains, roots, tubers, bulbs, stems, leaves.
>>   Dextrin—Brown flour—By heating flour.

2   Proteins:

Meats.	Milk.
Fish.	Cheese.
Poultry	Beans
Game.	Peas
Rabbits	Cereals
Eggs	Nuts.

3   Fats:

Commercial products	Vegetable fats:
Animal fats:	Troco
Butter	Crisco.
Lard.	Vegetable oil:
Part animal fat:	Cottonseed oil.

Oleomargarine   Corn oil.
Cottolene.   Olive oil
Snow Drift   Peanut oil

4   Mineral (chiefly in vegetables, fruits, milk, eggs):
Salts·

Calcium   Iron.   Sodium.   Sulphur.
Phosphorous   Potassium   Chlorine.   Magnesium.

5   Water.
6.   Vitamines: Fat soluble.   Water soluble

COMPOSITION OF CEREALS.

	Protein	Fats	Carbo	Ash	Water
Barley:					
Pealed barley	8 5	1 1	77.8	1.3	11.3
Barley, entire grain	10 5	2 2	72 8	2.6	11.9
Patent barley flour	8 0	1.7	79.35	0.65	10.3
Buckwheat					
Entire grain	10.7	2 0	62 8	1.8	12 3
Flour	8.7	1 6	76 2	1.0	11 9
Maize (Indian Corn):					
Whole	10 0	4 3	71 8	1 5	10.7
Corn meal (old process)	9 0	4 3	72.5	1.3	11 6
Corn meal (new process)	7 8	1 3	78 5	0 6	12.0
Hominy	8.3	0.6	79 0		11 8
Oats:					
Oatmeal	16 1	7 2	67.5	1.9	7.3
Rolled oats	16 7	7 3	66 2	2 1	7.7
Rice:					
Cured rice	8 02	1.96	76.05	1 15	11.88
Polished rice	7.18	0 26	79.36	0 46	12 34
Rye:					
Flour	6 8	0 9	78 7	0 7	12.9
Meal	13 6	2 0	71.5	1.5	11.4
Wheat:					
Whole wheat flour	12 26	2 24	73 67	1.02	10.81
Graham flour	13 3	2 2	71.4	1.8	11.31
Shorts	12 65	2.44	74 58	1.72	8.61
Bran	14 02	4 39	65 54	6.06	9 99

Sherman.

Note: Use whole wheat flour instead of white flour because it has more food value, and helps in the conservation value of the whole grain.

Use graham flour with white flour to restore food value to white flour.

However, the use of whole wheat and graham flours is not regarded as saving wheat

Note· The changes which take place in the foodstuffs after they have been absorbed from the digestive tract are included under the general term "metabolism."

Wheat Substitutes

Housekeepers are asking why they are requested to substitute corn for wheat flour. Because of the countries allied with us only Italy raises corn and is accustomed to its use. War time is not a good time to try to introduce a new product. Besides, there is practically no corn-milling machinery in Europe except in Italy, and corn meal can not be shipped in large quantities owing to the fact that it spoils readily The whole problem can be met if our loyal housewives will substitute one pound of corn or other cereal flour per week per person. We all like corn; a very trifling change in our diet will release for our Allies millions of bushels of wheat.

HERBERT HOOVER.

Note: Subject to change, just now we are required to buy with every pound of flour one pound of other cereal

Modify Your Own Recipes

If you have good recipes for bread of any kind make them conform to food conservation by omitting sugar (using substitutes) and animal fats (using vegetable fats) and by using one-fourth wheat substitute.

Try for yourself with your own recipe.

Many people think milk is necessary for good bread, but it is not, although it, of course, adds to the food value, and is therefore advisable when it can be afforded. Water, milk and water, whey, potato water or rise water may be used for the liquid.

Use white potatoes, sweet potatoes, rice, squash and pumpkin as substitutes for the wheat flour.

Those who can save more than the one-fourth will help make up for those who cannot, or are not willing to do their share.

A fair bread can be made on a 50-50 basis

YEAST BREAD

You must know that in using substitutes in the making of War Bread that about two-thirds of the mixture should be wheat or rye flour These are the only two of the cereals which contain gluten, which is a protein substance, which gives strength to the dough, and holds the expansion made by the use of leavening. The gluten which is in the dough retards the escape of the carbon dioxide and the tension of the warm gas, produced by the action of the yeast, expands the cells, then the dough is puffed up and becomes light and spongy.

In the raising of bread, the conditions should be favorable, first, for the breaking of starch by the diastase into a variety of sugar, and second, by the action of the yeast, a part of the sugar is changed into carbon dioxide and alcohol.

In the manipulation of the dough, extreme cleanliness is necessary. The dough should be a smooth, uniform, well aerated mixture, which may be obtained by thorough beating, light, firm kneading. It should be kept at the temperature most favorable to the growth of the yeast plant (77-95° F.; 25-35° C.) until the gas produced by the yeast in growth has leavened the mixture double its bulk. Kneading down occasionally will, by stretching the gluten, increase the feathery appearance of the crumb.

It is then molded into loaves to fit an individual loaf tin (9½x4½x3½) and carefully pressed into the corners of the tin to assure straight edges. The loaves are set in a warm place till the expansion of the gas has raised them double their bulk, and then baked in an oven heated to the temperature of 350-570° F. The oven should not be too hot at first until the crust is set, which should take the first 15 minutes. During this time the heat should be gradually diminished to prevent too thick and too brown a crust before baking is accomplished. This will take 50 to 60 minutes to cook the starch and destroy the yeast in the center of the loaf.

On taking from the oven, the bread should be cooled in currents of air and then put away, without wrapping, in a closed tin or earthen jar.

BARLEY BREAD

1 cup liquid,
1 tsp. salt,
2⅓ cups white flour,

⅓ to ¼ cake yeast softened in
¼ cup lukewarm water,
1⅙ cups barley flour.

Long Process—Scald the liquid, cool to lukewarm, add the salt, the softened yeast and half the flour. Beat thoroughly, cover and let rise until very light. Then add the remainder of the flour. Knead, cover and let rise again until double in bulk. Shape into a loaf, cover and let rise again until double in bulk. Bake.

Short Process—Follow the directions as given above, but add all the flour at once

U S Food Administration.

BUCKWHEAT BREAD

1½ cups milk,
¼ cup molasses,
2½ cups buckwheat flour,
1½ cups white flour,

1 tsp salt,
2 tbsp fat,
½ yeast cake,
½ cup lukewarm water.

Add yeast to lukewarm water. Scald milk and put in mixing bowl with fat and salt When lukewarm add molasses and yeast. Knead in the flour slowly and let rise until it doubles in bulk. Beat it down and put in greased pan Let rise until almost double in bulk, bake one hour in a moderate oven.

Jennie W. Gilmore,
Domestic Science Instructor, McKinley High School

BRAN BREAD

4 cups bran,
2 cups wheat flour,
½ cup molasses,
2 cups milk or water,

1½ tsp salt,
3 tbsp. fat,
½ yeast cake,
¼ cup lukewarm water

Prepare and bake as any light bread.

Jennie W Gilmore,
Domestic Science Instructor, McKinley High School.

COTTONSEED MEAL BREAD

2 cups milk or water,
2 cups cottonseed meal,
4 cups flour,
½ yeast cake,

1½ tsp. salt,
2 tbsp. fat,
2 tbsp. sugar,
¼ cup lukewarm water.

Prepare and bake as shorts bread.

Jennie W Gilmore,
Domestic Science Instructor, McKinley High School

CORN MEAL YEAST BREAD

1½ cups liquid,
⅛ to ¼ yeast cake,
1½ tsp salt,
More if needed

2½ cups flour,
⅔ cup corn meal, white or yellow.

Note: One-fourth cup of liquid yeast may be used in place of the ¼ yeast cake, and ¼ cup of liquid when making bread by the short process. For the long process sponge method, ⅛ cake of compressed yeast or 2 tbsp. of liquid yeast is sufficient For the short process use more yeast.

Long Process—1 Soften the yeast in ½ cup of lukewarm water. Add ¾ cup of white flour Beat thoroughly, cover, and if the sponge is to stand over night, let rise at room temperature (about 65° to 70° F) and at 80° F , if the time is to be shortened. When this sponge is so light that the slightest touch causes it to fall it is ready for the addition of the ingredients

2. Stir the corn meal into the remaining cup of salted water and heat to the boiling point over the direct flame. Cook 20 minutes in a double boiler or over hot water. Cool until it feels warm to the hand (about 90° to 95° F.).

3. Beat the cooked corn meal into the light sponge prepared as directed above Add gradually sufficient flour to make a dough somewhat stiffer than for ordinary bread. It is impossible to give the quantity of flour exact because different samples of flour may not absorb the same amounts of liquid Knead a few minutes until the dough is smooth and elastic

Continue according to general directions for making yeast bread

Short Process—Cook the corn meal in 1¾ cups of liquid, cool to about 90° F., add the yeast softened in the remaining ¼ cup of liquid (or the liquid yeast) and flour to make a stiff dough. Proceed from this point as directed above

U. S. Food Administration.

(The long process usually produces better results in this bread)

GRAHAM BREAD

1 cup boiling water,	1½ tsp. salt,
1 cup milk,	½ yeast cake,
¼ cup molasses,	¼ cup lukewarm water,
⅔ cup graham flour	⅓ white flour

Prepare and bake as entire wheat bread

Jennie W. Gilmore,
Domestic Science Instructor, McKinley High School.

DATE BREAD

2 cups warm corn meal mush,	2 tbsp fat,
¼ cup brown sugar,	1 tsp. salt,
¼ cup lukewarm water,	½ yeast cake.
1 cup dates, stoned and cut,	

Mix mush, sugar, salt and fat, add yeast mixed in lukewarm water and flour to knead, cover and let rise till double in bulk, while kneading add dates. Shape, let rise in pan and bake in a moderate oven.

Jennie W Gilmore,
Domestic Science Instructor, McKinley High School

HOMINY BREAD

1 cup warm cooked hominy,	¾ tbsp. sugar,
¼ cup fat,	1 tsp salt,
1 cup scalded milk,	½ cake yeast,
Flour to make dough,	¼ cup lukewarm water.

Scald milk, add sugar and fat, when lukewarm add dissolved yeast cake and flour enough to make a sponge When light add hominy and salt, also enough flour to make soft dough, knead well. When light shape into loaves and let rise twice its size Bake in hot oven.

Miss J Crowder,
Domestic Science Instructor Central High School.

NUT BREAD

1 tsp. shortening,	1 yeast cake,
2 tsp molasses,	½ cup white flour,
½ tsp. salt,	2¾ cups whole wheat flour,
1 cup milk or water, or ½ of each,	1 cup chopped nuts

Same as for white bread. When mixture has risen first time add the nuts before the rest of the flour

Miss Ella D. Rode,
Domestic Science Instructor Patrick Henry School

PEANUT BREAD

1 cup lukewarm liquid,	1 or 2 tbsp. syrup,
1 tsp. salt,	⅛ to ¼ cake yeast softened in
3 cups flour (more if desired),	¼ cup lukewarm water
1 cup peanut meal or flour,	

Long Process—Follow the directions given for the long process under Corn Meal Bread, making the sponge with part of the liquid and flour, salt and yeast. When light add the rest of the liquid, the syrup, the peanut meal and the remainder of the flour. Knead until smooth and elastic, adding more flour if necessary to secure the proper consistency Cover and let rise until double in bulk. Shape into a loaf, cover and let rise 2½ times the original bulk, and bake.

Short Process—Dissolve the salt and syrup in the cup of luke-warm liquid, add to the softened yeast and add all to the mixture of the flour and peanut meal Knead until smooth and elastic From this point follow the directions as given for long process

Peanut meal may be prepared by shelling roasted peanuts, removing red skin and crushing the nuts with a rolling pin

U. S. Food Administration.

POTATO BREAD

1¼ cups mashed potatoes (packed solid),	⅛ to ¼ yeast cake softened in 2 tbsp lukewarm water
1½ tsp. salt,	2¼ cups flour (more or less flour may be needed),

Note: Mashed sweet potato or cooked cereal or squash may be used in the same way as the Irish potato. In using any substitute which has a marked flavor it is better to try the bread first with less than 1¼ cups and add more liquid Squash rolls are very good

Long Process—Cool the mashed potatoes to lukewarm, add the salt and the yeast softened in the warm water and about ¼ cup of flour Mix well, cover and let rise until very light. To the well-risen sponge, add the remaining flour, kneading thoroughly The dough should be very stiff, as it softens considerably in rising Cover and let rise until double in bulk. Shape into a loaf cover, let rise again until it has increased 2½ times in bulk, and bake

Short Process—Follow the directions as given above, but add all the flour at once The dough in this case is so stiff that it is difficult to work in all the flour.   U S Food Administration

OATMEAL BREAD

3 cups hot oatmeal mush,	1 yeast cake,
3 tbsp. Crisco,	½ cup lukewarm water,
2 tsp salt	7 cups whole wheat flour,
¼ cup molasses,	1 cup corn meal.

Mix the Crisco, salt, molasses and mush; when cooled to luke-warm add the yeast dissolved in the water Add the corn meal and one-half of the flour, beat thoroughly, cover and set to raise until double its bulk; add balance of flour, knead until elastic Place in greased pans, let rise until double its bulk. Bake in moderate oven 50 to 60 minutes   Miss Mary Nicholson

ROLLED OATS AND ENTIRE WHEAT FLOUR BREAD

2½ cups boiling water,
½ cup molasses,
1 tsp salt,
1 tbsp fat,
½ yeast cake,
¼ cup lukewarm water,
2 cups rolled oats.

Whole wheat flour to make a soft dough, add boiling water to oats, let stand one hour, add molasses, salt, fat, yeast and flour, beat thoroughly, let rise to double its bulk again, beat well, turn into greased pans, let rise again, and bake.

Jennie W. Gilmore,
Domestic Science Instructor McKinley High School.

SHORTS BREAD

2 cups milk or water,
1 cup shorts.
2 cups flour,
1½ tsp salt,
2 tbsp. fat,
2 tbsp. sugar,
½ yeast cake,
¼ cup lukewarm water.

Make a sponge, using flour; when this is light add shorts

SQUASH BREAD

1 cup steamed squash,
¼ cup brown sugar or molasses,
1 tsp. salt,
Flour to knead,
1 cup scalded milk,
¼ cup fat,
½ yeast cake,
¼ cup lukewarm water.

Scald milk, add fat and sugar or molasses; when lukewarm add dissolved yeast cake and enough flour to make a sponge. When light add salt and squash and enough flour to knead, let rise, shape into loaves and when twice the size bake in hot oven.

Miss J. Crowder,
Domestic Science Instructor Central High School.

YEAST

Because of the high price of yeast it may be economical when bread is made frequently and in large quantities to prepare yeast

In making the bread the amount of yeast used, of whatever kind, will depend upon the time in which the process is to be carried through

LIQUID YEAST

4 medium-sized potatoes,
1 qt hot water,
1 tsp salt,
1 cake dry yeast softened in ¼ cup warm water, or 1 cake of compressed yeast,
¼ cup sugar.

Wash, pare and cook the potatoes in the water, drain, mash, and return to the water, make up to one quart. Add the sugar and salt and allow the mixture to cool When lukewarm add the yeast. Keep at room temperature (65° to 70° F) for 24 hours before using If kept for a longer time it should be poured into a sterilized jar and put in a dark, cool place

BREAD TESTS

(1)   Will your dough stick to the board without the use of flour?

If it does, then more flour must be kneaded into the dough to make it the right consistency

(2)   Does your dough have blisters on the surface?

If so, you have kneaded it enough.

(3)   Cut the dough to see if the air is evenly distributed throughout the mass.

If it is not, continue the kneading

(4)   Knead for about 15 to 20 minutes the first kneading. The last kneading must be of short duration, otherwise you will drive off the gas formed in the raising of the dough.

HOW TO CONSERVE WHEAT

Cut the loaf on the table, and only as required.

Do not have stale bread

If any breads, muffins, gems are left from meals, toast and use with creamed fish or left over bits of meat, fish or vegetable

If there are bits of bread left, dry and grind, put in cheese cloth bag, using the crumbs in scalloped dishes, croquettes and as substitute for wheat flour in breads and puddings.

Do not use crackers made from wheat (or graham) flour

Do not use breakfast cereals made from wheat.

If you use macaroni, spaghetti, any Italian paste or noodles, remember that it is made of wheat and do not serve bread at the same meal.

Use corn starch or rice flour for thickening sauces and gravies and in puddings (use half as much as you would of flour)

Remember—bread made of mixed flours is better body building material than that made from one grain alone.

"Have at least one wheatless meal a day Use corn, oats, barley, or mixed cereal rolls, muffins and breads in place of white bread certainly for one meal and, if possible, for two Eat less cake and pastry As to white bread, if you must buy from a baker, order it a day in advance; then he will not bake beyond his needs Use stale bread for toast and cooking."

Substitute potatoes when they are plentiful for all bread in two meals a day.

U. S. Food Administration

A COMPARISON OF BATTERS AND DOUGHS

Kind	Proportion	Appearance	Use
Pour batter	1 flour to 1 water	Thin pastry	Griddle cakes, waffles
Drop batter	2 flour to 1 water	Thicker	Gems, muffins.
Soft batter	3 flour to 1 water	Soft sticky mass	Cakes, biscuit, doughnuts.
Stiff batter	4 flour to 1 water	Not sticky	Breads

CHIEF PROTEINS OF WHITE FLOUR

Gliaden gives elasticity to the dough

Gluten gives strength to hold up the expansion made by the use of leavenings

QUICK BREADS AS WHEAT SAVERS

Many processes have been devised for making dough light without the use of yeast; the object of these is to shorten time and labor.

PROCESS OF LEAVENING

1 By air—expansion with heat and moisture.
   Ex —Eggs beaten to a froth
2. By steam—expansion of dough by application of sudden heat in oven.
   Ex.—Popovers.
3. By chemical reaction (formation of carbon dioxide gas)
   1—Soda (alkali) and molasses (acid)
   2—Soda (alkali) and sour milk (lactic acid)
   3—Soda (alkali) and cream of tartar (acid)
4 Commercial baking powder (three classes)
   1—Cream of tartar powders or tartrate powders
   2—Phosphate powders
   3—Alum powders

Note. The carbon dioxide gas which is formed in the above reactions expands with heat and moisture, making the bread light

CORN MEAL BISCUITS

1½ cups flour,
½ cup corn meal,
½ tsp. salt,
¾ cup sour milk,

3   tsp baking powder,
½ tsp soda,
2   tbsp. veg fat.

Mix and sift dry ingredients. Add the fat, mix thoroughly, then add one-half the milk, then add more gradually to make a soft dough, mixing with a knife; when smooth turn dough on to a flour board; toss until coated with flour; roll out ¼ inch thick and cut out   Bake in hot oven 12 to 15 minutes

Miss Winnetta H Grady,
Domestic Science Instructor

GRAHAM BISCUITS

1   cup white flour,
1   cup graham flour,
3   tsp. baking powder,
⅔ cup milk,

2   tbsp sugar,
1   tsp salt,
¼ cup veg fat

Mix and sift all dry ingredients, cut in vegetable fat and moisten dough evenly. Put dough on slightly floured board, pat out ½ inch thick and cut with biscuit cutter   Bake in a hot oven

Miss E. Rode,
Domestic Science Instructor, Patrick Henry School

SHORTS BISCUITS

1   cup shorts,
1   cup flour,
3   tsp baking powder,

½ tsp. salt,
2   tbsp shortening,
about ¾ cup milk

Sift together dry ingredients, chop in shortening with a knife until fine. Add milk gradually, mixing with a knife. Roll out dough ½ inch thick and cut with a biscuit cutter. Handle dough as little as possible   Bake in a hot oven about 15 minutes

Hilda Z Rollman,
Domestic Science Instructor, Cote Brilliante School.

MUFFINS

BUCKWHEAT MUFFINS

1   cup buckwheat,
1   cup wheat flour,
4   tsp baking powder,
¾ tsp salt,

1¾ cups milk,
1   egg,
1   tbsp melted veg fat,
2   tbsp molasses

Sift together the dry ingredients Combine the milk, beaten egg, melted fat and molasses Add the liquid to the dry ingredients. Mix well and bake one-half hour in a moderately hot oven.

Rye flour or 1 cup of barley and 1 cup of wheat may be used in this recipe if the liquid is reduced to 1 or 1¼ cups The buckwheat flour absorbs more liquid than other flours

If you can get flour, barley flour, rye meal, peanut flour, soy bean meal, a great variety of muffins can be made. Combinations of one-third barley flour, one-third corn flour and one-third wheat flour, or one-half rye meal, one-fourth corn meal and one-fourth wheat flour have been found satisfactory.

U. S. Food Administration

1.—CORN MUFFINS

1 cup milk,	1½ tbsp. veg. fat or oil,
1 cup corn meal,	1 tsp. salt,
1 egg,	2 tsp. baking powder

Beat egg till light, add milk, then corn meal to which baking powder and salt have been added. Melt fat and add to batter This should be a drop batter. Fill hot molds three-fourths full and bake in a hot oven   Elizabeth Mount Walker,
Domestic Science Instructor, University City School.

2.—CORN MUFFINS

2 cups corn meal,	¼ tsp soda,
1 cup hot water,	1 tsp. salt,
1 dessert spoon molasses,	1 tbsp melted Troco (short-
2 tsp. baking powder,	ening).

Pour hot water over corn meal to which has been added baking powder, soda and salt. Add molasses, melt Troco and whip into the mixture and put in hot muffin rings Mrs Haydock.

GRAHAM AND CORN MEAL MUFFINS

1 cup graham flour,	3 tsp. baking powder
1 cup meal,	1 tsp salt,
1¼ cups milk,	1 tbsp. sugar,
1 egg,	1 tbsp. veg fat

Beat the eggs, add the milk, sugar, salt and fat Add sifted flour, corn meal and baking powder Pour into greased pans, bake in moderate oven 20 to 30 minutes.

Miss Mary Nicholson,
Domestic Science Instructor.

COOKED CEREAL MUFFINS (10-12 muffins)

1½ cups flour,	1 cup cooked rice,
4 tsp. baking powder,	½ cup milk,
¾ tsp. salt,	1 egg,
	1 tbsp. melted fat

Sift together the dry ingredients Add the milk, beaten egg and melted fat to the cooked rice Beat thoroughly. Finally add the sifted dry ingredients. Mix well. Bake in greased muffin tins about one-half hour in a moderately hot oven

Other cooked cereals or mashed potatoes may be used in this recipe If the dough is too soft, add a little more flour, if too thick, a little more liquid

U. S. Food Administration

SOUTHERN RICE BREAD

2 cups white corn meal,	2 tbsp. veg oil,
3 eggs,	½ tsp salt,
1¼ pt milk,	4 tsp baking powder.
1 cup cold boiled rice,	

Beat the eggs until light without separating, add the milk, meal, salt, rice and melted vegetable oil Beat thoroughly for two minutes, add the baking powder and mix again Grease three deep pie dishes, turn in the mixture, and bake in a hot oven thirty minutes.

BARLEY AND WHOLE WHEAT MUFFINS

2 eggs,	2 cups whole wheat flour,
3 tbsp sugar,	1 tsp baking soda,
2 tbsp olive oil,	1 tsp. salt,
1 qt sour milk or buttermilk,	2 tsp baking powder
2 cups barley meal,	

Mix and beat well for five minutes. Bake in well greased muffin tins for twenty minutes in a moderate oven

BARLEY SCONES

1 cup barley meal,	2 tsp. baking powder,
1 cup whole wheat flour,	¾ cup sour milk,
¼ tsp. salt,	2 tbsp. veg. oil.
½ tsp. soda,	

Mix and sift the dry ingredients. If coarse whole wheat flour is used, do not sift it. Add sour milk and vegetable oil and blend the mixture well. Turn that soft dough thus formed on to a floured board, knead slightly, roll to one-half thickness, cut into fancy shapes and bake in a hot oven.

BARLEY PONE

1 cup freshly cooked hominy grits,
2 cups milk,
3 tbsp. butter,

½ tsp salt,
1 cup barley meal,
2 tsp. baking powder

Add to the cooked hominy grits the milk and butter. Cool and add salt, barley meal and baking powder sifted together, then the well beaten eggs Pour into a round, shallow, buttered baking dish and bake in a moderate oven forty-five minutes Cut in triangular pie-shaped pieces and serve hot from the dish in which it was baked

CORN AS BREAD

Corn bread is especially good made with sour milk and soda; but sweet milk and baking powder are satisfactory. Eggs improve the flavor and add to the food value, but may be omitted if too expensive

CORN BREAD

(1.)
2 cups corn meal,
2 cups sweet milk (whole or skim),
4 tsp. baking powder,
1 tbsp. sugar,
2 tbsp fat,
1 tsp salt,
1 egg (may be omitted).

(2.)
2 cups corn meal,
2 cups sour milk,
1 tsp. soda
1 tbsp. sugar,
2 tbsp. fat,
1 tsp. salt,
1 egg (may be omitted)

Mix dry ingredients Add milk, well-beaten egg and melted fat. Beat well. Bake in shallow pan for about 30 minutes

CORN DODGERS

2 cups corn meal,
1 tsp salt,

2 tsp. fat,
1¾ cups boiling water.

Pour the boiling water over the other materials. Beat well When cool form into thin cakes and bake ½ hour in a hot oven These crisp biscuits are good served hot with butter or gravy Eat them with your meat and vegetables

U S Food Administration

AN OLD SOUTHERN RECIPE

Here is an old-fashioned soft spoon bread that Southerners like With milk or syrup it makes a satisfying meal.

SPOON BREAD

2 cups water,   1 tbsp fat,
1 cup milk (whole or skim),   2 eggs,
1 cup corn meal,   2 tsp. salt

Mix water and corn meal and bring to the boiling point and cook 5 minutes. Beat eggs well and add with other materials to the mush Beat well and bake in a well greased pan for 25 minutes in a hot oven Serve from the same dish with a spoon. Enough for six.

U S Food Administration.

STEAMED CORN BREAD

2 cups yellow corn meal,   2   tbsp   sugar (4 tbsp. mo-
1 cup flour,   lasses),
1 tsp. salt,   1¼ tsp. soda,
                         ½ tsp. baking powder.

Sift these ingredients together and then add 2½ cups sour milk. Beat well, pour into a buttered mold with a tight fitting cover and steam for two hours Remove and brown in oven.

BANANA FLOUR BREAD

1 cup banana flour,   ½ tsp. salt,
1 cup bread flour,   3   tbsp sugar,
2 tsp baking powder,   2   tbsp. veg. fat
1 cup milk,

Mix the dry ingredients, cut in fat, then add milk, put into greased loaf pan; bake in a moderate oven.

PEANUT AND RAISIN BREAD

1   qt. whole wheat flour,   1   tbsp fat,
¼ cup sugar,   4   tsp. baking powder,
1   tsp. salt,   1   cup chopped peanuts,
1   cup milk,   ½ cup chopped raisins.

Mix the dry ingredients, cut in fat, add nuts, raisins and milk. Put into a greased loaf pan. Bake in a moderate oven.

PRUNE BROWN BREAD (Steamed)

1   cup corn meal,   1 tsp. soda,
1   tsp. salt,   1 cup sour milk,
2   cups whole wheat flour, 1 cup prunes chopped fine
½ cup molasses,

Mix dry ingredients, add molasses, milk and prunes. Fill greased molds two-thirds full. Grease the cover and cover tightly Steam three hours.

OATMEAL MUFFINS

1½ cups milk,	1 tbsp. melted fat,
2 cups rolled oats,	1 cup flour,
1 egg,	4 tsp baking powder,
2 tbsp. molasses,	¾ tsp. salt

Pour hot milk over the oats and let soak about one-half hour Add the beaten egg, molasses and melted fat. Finally add dry ingredients which have been sifted together Bake in greased muffin tins one-half hour in a moderately hot oven.

BOSTON BROWN BREAD

1 cup rye flour,	3 cups milk,
1 cup graham flour,	¾ cup molasses,
1 cup corn meal,	6 tsp. baking powder,
½ tsp salt,	1 cup raisins if desired

Sift the dry ingredients into the liquids, mix quickly, pour into greased cups, cover the top and steam 2 to 3 hours

Miss E. D. Rode,
Domestic Science Instructor, Patrick Henry School

BAKED BROWN BREAD

⅓ cup corn meal,	1 cup sour milk,
2½ cups graham flour,	1 cup molasses,
1½ tsp. soda,	1 cup water
1 tsp. salt,	

Mix the dry ingredients; mix the wet ingredients; pour the wet into the dry and beat well Pour the batter into three oiled pound baking powder cans; leave uncovered and bake in a slow oven for 1½ hours. It is well to use an asbestos mat under the cans while baking so as to avoid burning the bread.

Miss Leigh Harris,
Domestic Science Instructor, Yeatman High School.

GRIDDLE CAKES

CORN MEAL GRIDDLE CAKES

2 cups corn meal,	1 egg,
1½ cups milk or water,	3 tsp baking powder,
1 tbsp. fat,	

Miss Alice Waugh,
Domestic Science Instructor Ritenour School.

GRIDDLE CAKES

1 cup milk,	½ cup flour,
1 egg,	¾ tsp salt,
1 tbsp. melted fat,	4 tbsp. baking powder
1½ cups cooked oatmeal,	

Combine the milk, beaten egg and melted fat. Beat this into the cooked oatmeal. Add the flour, salt and baking powder which have been sifted together. Bake on a hot greased griddle

Other cooked cereals, mashed Irish potatoes, sweet potatoes, etc., may be used in the place of the oatmeal. When rice is used, ¼ cup more flour is necessary.

Griddle cakes may also be made by using one-half or more of corn meal or buckwheat flour.

If desired, sour milk may be substituted in these recipes for the sweet In doing this the quantity must usually be increased a little Use ½ teaspoonful of soda for each cup of sour milk. For each ½ teaspoonful of soda the quantity of baking powder can be reduced by 2 teaspoonfuls.

U S Food Administration.

BATTER CAKES

1 cup corn meal,	2 tsp. baking powder,
1 cup bran,	½ tsp soda,
1 cup hot water,	1 tsp salt,
1 dessert sp. molasses,	1 tbsp. melted Troco

Sift corn meal, baking powder, soda and salt, add bran, pour over this the hot water Add molasses and lastly the melted Troco whipped in.

Mrs. Haydock.

Note Use stale bread crumbs to replace part of flour in making muffins, gems and griddle cakes, also in steamed puddings.

Steam a vegetable, cornbread, and rice in steamer at one time to conserve fuel

CEREALS

Corn meal, oatmeal, rice, hominy (grits) These are much cheaper than the "ready-to-eat" breakfast foods A "ready-to-eat" breakfast food may cost 15 cents for a big package, but if the package contains only one-quarter pound—60 cents a pound for cereal! This is eight or ten times as expensive as corn meal at 6 or 7 cents a pound. Look for the weights printed on the package and get the most for your money.

Corn meal mush and oatmeal are good only when well cooked. Many people use too little salt and don't cook them long enough.

All cereals should be cooked in a double boiler; one can be improvised by setting a pail or pan into a kettle of water. Cereals for breakfast may be cooked the day before, but should not be stirred while reheating. A tablespoonful or two of cold water on top will prevent a hard skin from forming while standing. All prepared cereals are better if cooked for a longer time than the package directions indicate. It is hardly possible to cook any grain too long. The fireless cooker is especially valuable for cooking cereals, but a longer period of time must be allowed than for cooking in a double boiler.

GENERAL DIRECTIONS

Kinds.	Quan. to 1 c. water.	Time of Cooking.
Whole or cracked	¼ cup	3-12 hrs., except rice
Flaked	½ cup	½-3 hrs.
Granular	3 tbsp.	1-4 hrs.

Use ½ teaspoonful of salt to each cup of water. Have water boiling hot. Add cereal gradually. Let mixture cook directly over the flame 5 minutes. Place over boiling water or in fireless cooker to cook slowly for a long time, without stirring, and covered. Fruit may be cooked with the various cereals, raisins, figs and dates being most acceptable. (Use water.) For hot weather, cereals may be cooked the day before, molded and served cold.

Gruels are prepared from flaked or granular cereals, using 1½ times the proportionate amount of water. Gruels after cooking should be strained and reheated.

EXAMPLES OF CEREALS

Whole	Flaked.	Granular.
Barley Rice Macaroni	Rolled oats	Vitos Corn meal

CEREALS

Cereals act as fuel to let you do your work, much as the gasoline burning in an automobile engine makes the car go. This you can think of as their chief business. And they are usually your cheapest fuel. Besides they give your body some building material.

U. S. Food Administration.

CORN MEAL AND MILK

Do you use corn meal mush for a breakfast food? It is both cheap and good. Cooked in skim milk instead of water it is extra fine and the food value of the dish is nearly doubled.

CORN MEAL MUSH

To cook corn meal mush for five people use 1½ cups corn meal, 2 teaspoonfuls salt (level), 5 or 6 cups water. Bring salt water to a boil. Stir in the corn meal slowly. Don't let it lump. Cook it at least 30 minutes. It is better when cooked for three hours, or over night. Use a double boiler or a fireless cooker.

CORN MEAL MUSH WITH CHEESE

Prepare the mush as in the foregoing recipe and pour into a flat, wet pan to cool. When cold, turn out and cut in half-inch slices with grated cheese and paprika and bake in a hot oven to a delicate brown. This dish possesses all the supplies of a well-balanced food. The meal supplies carbohydrates; the cheese, the protein and some fat. It is a tempting dish, too, which cannot be said of all wholesome foods.

Caroline B. King, G. H. K.

OATMEAL

For oatmeal use 2½ cups rolled oats, 2½ teaspoonfuls salt, 5 or 6 cups water. Bring the water to a boil, stir the rolled oats slowly into the boiling water and cook for one hour, or over night. Eat the cereal with milk or syrup or butter or butter substitutes.

TO BOIL HOMINY

Soak one cup of hominy in the evening, let it stand over night then put on to boil with six cups boiling water, one teaspoonful salt, and boil slowly all day, stirring occasionally, or put in top of double boiler or fireless cooker. The best thing during the cold weather is to always have a crock of cold boiled hominy on hand; it keeps a week or more in cold place, and is a great help to the housekeeper, taking the place of potatoes and bread, besides being very wholesome. This serves five adults.

HOMINY CAKES

1 cup cracked corn or pearly hominy,
7 cups boiling water,
2 tsp. salt,
3 tbsp fat

Boil the corn and water for ½ hour, add seasonings, place vessel over water and cook from six to eight hours. Serve in place of potatoes. For the second day put the left over cold hominy through the meat grinder, add a beaten egg, a tablespoonful sugar and ½ teaspoonful vanilla; make into cakes, flour and cook in a frying pan until delicately browned on both sides. Serve these cakes instead of potatoes.

Miss Mary Evans,
Domestic Science Instructor, Yeatman High School.

STEAMED RICE

Cook rice as any whole cereal. The time is 20 minutes, or until kernels are soft. Uncover, that steam may escape. When rice is steamed for a simple dessert use one-half the quantity of water Steam until rice has absorbed water, then add scalded milk for remaining liquid.

BOILED RICE

Pick over and wash rice. Add gradually to a large quantity of rapidly boiling salted water. Stir at first with a fork to prevent any grain from sticking to the bottom of kettle. Let it boil rapidly 20 minutes, or until tender. Drain in strainer, pour over it cold water, reheat in oven. Serve plain as a vegetable, or use for croquettes, etc. One cupful of rice when cooked will measure nearly 4 cups.

BOILED MACARONI

Break macaroni in two-inch pieces and cook as boiled rice.

SAUTED MUSH

Pack hot corn meal mush in wet molds. Cool, and cover to prevent crust forming. Remove from mold, cut in ½-inch slices and saute. If slices are dipped in flour or corn meal sauteing should be made thicker, using 4 tablespoonfuls granular cereal to 1 cup of water.

UNPOLISHED RICE

The hull which is removed in polishing rice is very rich in mineral content. It is said that armies fed on polished rice without this mineral being supplied by other foods, quickly contract scurvy, while those fed on brown or unpolished rice do not have the disease. It seems that this most valuable part of the rice is being sold as waste stock feed. If this can be bought at 2½ cents or 3 cents per pound, it should be used in large quantities everywhere. If this cannot be obtained, then every woman should ask her grocer for brown or unpolished rice.

BARLEY MUSH.

½ cup barley meat,   ½ level tsp salt
2   cups boiling water,

Method: Add the barley meal to the boiling salted water, stirring constantly. Cook over the fire for 5 minutes, then over hot water for one hour. Serve with sugar and cream.

FRUITED CEREALS

Note: Oats are among the highest in caloric values of all the cereals.

Figs and dates and raisins are conceded the highest in caloric or food value of all the fruits.

The combination of these cereals and fruits therefore offers more nutrition for the money expended than any other staple food.

When cereal is about half cooked, add fruit whole or chopped.

Meat Savers

"Use more poultry, rabbits, and especially fish and sea food in place of beef, mutton and pork"

U. S. Food Administration

Poultry:
  Chicken
  Turkey
Game:
  Duck
  Goose
  Squab
  Quail
  Rabbits
Nuts:
  Almonds
  Walnuts
  Pecans, etc.
Peanuts
Beans
Peas
Lentils
Cheese:
  Cottage cheese
  Whole milk cheese
Milk:
  Whole milk
  Skimmed milk
  Sour milk
Eggs

Fish:
  Base
  Bluefish
  Crab
  Cod
  Catfish
  Clams
  Haddock
  Halibut
  Herring
  Lobster
  Mackerel
  Oyster
  Shadroe
  Shrimp
  Smelt
  Trout
  Tripe
  Tuna
  Salmon
Cereals:
  Oatmeal
  Corn meal

Note: Use beans, they have nearly the same food value as meat if used with milk. Do not use either beef, mutton or pork more than once daily, and then serve smaller portions. Use all left-over meat cold or in made dishes. Use soup more freely Cereals contain much protein. A combination of cereals is better than one alone Milk is most important. Use much of it.

U. S. Food Administration.

Note: New kinds of fish, especially recommended by Bureau of Fisheries· Bowfin, Burbot, Whiting, Sable fish, Eulachion.

WHY YOU SHOULD USE MEAT SUBSTITUTES

Meat is bound to be dear. It was scarce and high before the war.

For years the number of people in this country has been increasing faster than the number of meat animals Much of the open country out West where cattle used to range by hundreds of thousands has been fenced into farms.

Then came anthrax, foot and mouth disease, hog cholera, one plague after another.

Four years ago our government began a great campaign for more livestock, just to feed us in peace times.

War doubles and trebles the demand for our meat. We must provide meat for the boys in the trenches. We must stretch our meat supply. We must Save Meat to Save Ourselves.

We can eat fish, it's as hearty as meat Eat poultry, it does not make army rations. Use milk, eggs and cheese, they are almost the same as meat.

Peanut butter and vegetable oils are good fats Dried beans, peas and grains take the place of meat if milk is used with them, or cheese or eggs or plenty of green vegetables.

One ounce of meat a day for every one in the country amounts to the meat from 4,400,000 animals in a year Save your ounce It's a little thing to do to save your country.

U. S. Food Administration

THE EFFECT OF HEAT ON PROTEIN

Egg albumin or meat albumin serve as good examples to show the effect of heat on protein. If heat is applied a gradual process of hardening begins at the outer edge of the albumin, and continues toward the center in thin lines or fibrils until the transparent albumin becomes dense and leathery. This change is known as coagulation, and is typical of the change in all protein foods as the result of the application of heat. A few simple experiments will show the effect of the different temperatures on protein. At 134 .... F the egg ..... of a semi solid white substance .... At 160 degrees F it changes to a tender jelly-like substance. At 180 degrees F. it becomes dense and white Boiling temperature changes it into a tough, leathery substance. Therefore, the higher the temperature the tougher and harder the protein; consequently all protein foods are best if cooked at as low a temperature as will render them palatable.

LEGUMES AS MEAT SUBSTITUTES

Dried peas and beans are rich in muscle making principle and for this reason are often called the "poor man's beef," of very poor quality, about ¼ as good in quality as animal protein, but because they are somewhat difficult of digestion, they should not replace animal protein altogether, but should be used with discretion as meat substitutes. Soy beans are an exception to this. Cereal protein is about two times as valuable for growth as beans. No matter how dried legumes are to be cooked, they must first be soaked over night in cold water, that they may absorb moisture to replace that lost in evaporation; after soaking dried legumes may be cooked in almost any of the ways which fresh ones are cooked. It is then necessary to drain and wash them thoroughly, cooking gently until tender in water containing a very little common baking soda. This tends to soften the water and hastens the cooking process; it also aids in removing excess sulphur.

There is nothing in all cookery that needs more careful seasoning than dried legumes; salt and pepper, lemon rind, nutmeg, onion, celery salt, celery leaves, mustard in the right proportions may be used. As these legumes are deficient in fats, they should be combined with some fatty ingredients to preserve the balance—salt pork and beans.

SOY BEANS

Soy beans are excellent substitutes for meat. They contain almost twice as much protein as beefsteak, and more fat than any other of the legumes except the peanut. The protein of the soy bean is more nearly like animal protein in value than that of other plant foods as far as is now known. The fat contains the important growth-promoting fat soluble vitamine. The yellow or green varieties are best for eating purposes, the darker varieties having an unpleasant strong taste.

Green soy beans, when three-fourths grown, may be cooked and seasoned like the lima bean; change the water once during the cooking.

Dried soy beans should be soaked in 5 per cent salt water 12-16 hours Drain, put on to cook in hot water and cook slowly until tender (6-8 hours), changing the water often while cooking in order to remove the strong flavor.

1 lb. of meat costs $0.35, contains 224 calories.
1 lb. soy beans costs $0.05, contains 1970 calories.
1 lb. navy beans costs $0.20, contains 1605 calories

SOY BEAN CROQUETTES

2 cups cooked soy beans
    (chopped),
1 cup chopped onions,
2 tbsp. oleo,
Salt,

1 cup cooked rice,
1 tbsp chopped pickle,
1 beaten egg,
Pepper.

Combine as for soy bean loaf. Form into croquettes, roll in egg and cracker crumbs, and fry in deep fat or bake in oven

SCALLOPED SOY BEANS

Alternate layers of beans and white sauce Cover with buttered crumbs and grated cheese Brown in oven.

BAKED SOY BEANS

2   cups soy beans, parboiled,
1/3 cup molasses,

Cayenne pepper,
Salt pork.

Place in baking dish parboiled soy beans, in the midst of which is buried 2 pieces of salt pork one inch square, add molasses, salt, cayenne and a little mustard and onion if desired Bake with cover until tender, then remove cover to brown.

SOY BEAN LOAF

2 cups cooked soy beans
    (chopped),
1 cup cooked rice,
1 chopped onion,

1 tbsp. chopped pickle,
2 tbsp. oleo,
1 beaten egg,
Salt, pepper.

Serve with tomato or brown sauce.
Put soy beans through a meat chopper, combine with other ingredients and form in a loaf Brown in the oven

SOY BEAN SOUFFLE

1 cup soy beans,
2 tbsp. veg. oil,
4 tbsp. flour (rice flour if you have it),

1 cup milk,
1 tsp salt,
⅓ tsp. pepper,
2 or 3 eggs.

Cook beans until tender (4 hours), drain and rub through strainer. Heat oil, add flour and milk, boil 1 minute, add 2 cups bean pulp, cool and add beaten egg yolks and seasoning. Beat white of eggs until stiff and fold into bean mixture Bake in buttered casserole in moderate oven 30 minutes.

SOY BEAN AND TOMATO STEW

2 tbsp fat,
1 medium onion,
1 small green sweet pepper,
2 cups cooked soy beans,

1½ cups cooked tomatoes,
1 tbsp. flour,
Salt,
Pepper

Melt the fat in a frying pan and add the chopped onion and pepper. When these are tender add the soy beans, stirring until they are slightly browned in the fat. Add tomatoes and cook ten minutes. Thicken with the flour mixed with a little water or tomato juice.

Patriotic Food Show,
St. Louis, Mo.

JUNGLE STEW (SOY BEANS)

1 qt. water,
3 small onions (chopped fine),
1 can kidney or
1 cup soy beans (dry),

½ lb. macaroni,
1 pt. tomatoes,
2 tbsp. butter sub.,
Salt, pepper.

Fry onion in fat, add tomatoes and water, allow to come to boiling point, add macaroni, cook twenty minutes. Add beans which have been cooked Let simmer, serve hot.

Oswego (Kansas) College.

BAKED BEANS (NAVY)

2 cups beans,
2 tbsp. molasses or brown sugar,

¼ tsp. mustard,
1 tsp salt,
2 oz. salt pork or bacon

Wash and soak beans over night, add a little baking soda and cook until the skins easily slip from the bean (easily determining by taking a bean on tip of spoon and blowing on it). Add the seasoning and the pork which has been previously scraped and scored (cut in strips just through rind). Cover and bake slowly 6-8 hours; uncover the last hour of the cooking so that the rind of the meat may become brown and crisp. If less seasoning is preferred the amount of molasses or sugar may be cut down

BEAN TIMBALES

2   cups beans,
1   egg,
⅔ tsp. salt.

1   tbsp catsup,
⅛ tsp cayenne pepper,
Few drops of onion juice.

Put beans through a sieve, add seasoning. egg and catsup Cook in pan of hot water in a moderate oven Serve with tomato sauce.

Miss J. Crowder,
Domestic Science Instructor, Central High School.

PEANUT LOAF

2 cups bean pulp,
1 cup strained tomato,
2 eggs (beaten),
2 cups peanuts (chopped fine),

1 cup or more bread crumbs,
Season with minced celery, onion
        and salt.

Mix in order named. Make into loaf, and bake in a moderate oven until stiff enough to slice. Good hot or cold (8 servings).

Jesse Cline,
St. Joseph, Mo.

MOCK CHICKENS

2   cups beans,
⅓ loaf bread,
¼ cup fat,

½ tsp. sage,
Salt, pepper.
½ cup hot water.

Wash beans, soak over night in cold water, drain and cook in boiling water, simmer till tender, but not broken, drain and mash Make a stuffing of bread crumbs, melted fat, sage and seasoning. Arrange in a baking dish, alternating mashed beans and dressing. Cover with buttered crumbs and bake 20 minutes Serve with tomato sauce or white sauce flavored with parsley.

Anna Jensen,
Domestic Science Instructor, St. Joseph, Mo.

HORTICULTURAL LOAF (BEAN LOAF)

Mix two cups of beans with three chopped pimentos, one cup of bread crumbs cooked to a paste with half a cup of tomato puree. Season with pepper, a teaspoonful of salt, grated lemon rind, and a few drops of onion juice. Beat the yolks of two eggs well, add to the mixture and fold in the stiffly beaten whites, pile into a well-oiled bread tin, set in a moderate oven and cook until firm. Serve with tomato sauce.

COWPEAS

In composition cowpeas are similar to navy beans, and the uses and methods of preparation are much the same. Cowpeas are low in fat, but when this is added in the process of cooking they may well take the place of meat in the meal.

Cowpeas should be soaked in water several hours or over night Simmer until tender and season well. Pork fat or vegetable oils, cheese, onion, green pepper, celery or tomatoes will combine well as seasonings with cowpeas.

BOILED COWPEAS

Soak the cowpeas and cook half done. Add the pork, cut into small squares. Cook until tender, allowing most of the water to evaporate.

2 cups cowpeas,   ¼ pound salt pork or 3 tbsp.
                                        drippings.

1.—BAKED COWPEAS

Cover with water and bake slowly several hours.

1   qt. parboiled cowpeas,   Salt,
 ¼ lb. salt pork,   Pinch of cayenne pepper,
 ½ tsp. mustard,   ⅓ cup sorghum molasses.

2.—BAKED COWPEAS

Bake as above, substituting for the molasses

1 onion,   ¼ cup vinegar,
2 cups tomato juice,   1   tbsp. sugar.

SCALLOPED COWPEAS

2 cups cooked cowpeas,   1 cup cheese sauce

Place in baking dish alternating layers of peas and sauce. Cover with buttered crumbs and brown in oven.

DRIED PEAS WITH RICE AND TOMATOES

1½	cups rice,	1	tbsp. salt,
2	cups dried peas,	¼	tsp pepper,
6	onions,	2	cups tomatoes (fresh or canned)

Soak peas over night in two quarts of water, cook until tender in water in which they soak, add rice, onions, tomatoes and seasoning and cook 20 minutes

SAUCES

Especial attention must be given to the seasoning of dishes which have as their foundation beans, rice, or other foods having little flavor of their own

Use peppers, onions, garlic, leek, celery, catsup, Worcestershire sauce, etc., for increasing flavor. Bean and nut loaves should be served with highly seasoned sauces

ITALIAN TOMATO SAUCE

2	cups cooked tomatoes,	2	tsp. salt,
½	cup finely cut onion,	½	cup cut green peppers,
½	cup grated or cut turnip,	4	tbsp. butter sub. or vegetable drippings,
½	cup grated or cut carrot,	2	tbsp. flour.

Cook vegetables (except tomatoes) in the fat until tender. Add tomato and salt, cook 5 minutes Put through strainer, return to fire, add flour mixed with 2 tablespoonfuls cold water, boil 5 minutes.

PIMENTO SAUCE

Force canned pimento through a strainer Add 2 cups of this puree to 1 cup of white sauce

BROWN NUT SAUCE

2	tbsp drippings or vegetable oil,	1½	cups meat or vegetable stock or milk,
2	tbsp. peanut butter,	½	tsp. salt,
3½	tbsp. flour,		Few grains pepper

Brown the fat, add peanut butter and when well mixed add flour and continue browning Pour in the stock gradually, stirring constantly. Bring to the boiling point and add salt and pepper.

TOMATO SAUCE

2 tbsp. veg. fat,	1 tsp onion juice,
2 tbsp flour or 1 tbsp. corn starch,	½ tsp. salt,
	1 spoonful of salt and pepper.
½ pt. strained tomatoes,	

Rub the vegetable fat and flour together; add the water and onion juice; stir until boiling and add the salt and pepper.

U. S. Food Administration.

CAPER SAUCE

Make a plain white sauce, take from fire and add capers.

BROWNING OR KITCHEN BOUQUET

This can be purchased at any grocer's or may be made at home. Put 1 cup of sugar in an iron frying pan over the fire, shake and stir until it melts and turns a dark brown and smokes. Add 12 cups water, stir until boiling, add a chopped onion, six whole cloves, 1 teaspoonful salt, saltspoonful black pepper and a dash of Tabasco sauce. Simmer twenty minutes, strain and bottle for use This will keep for months.

BROWN SAUCE

2 tbsp. vegetable fat,	1 tsp. Kitchen Bouquet or Browning,
2 tbsp. flour,	½ tsp. salt,
½ pt. stock or water,	Saltspoonful black pepper.

Rub the vegetable fat and flour together, add the stock or water and stir until boiling. Add the Kitchen Bouquet or Browning, salt and pepper.

BROWN MUSHROOM SAUCE

1 forty cent can French mushrooms,	2 tbsp. flour,
	4 tbsp. butter,
2 cups of stock,	Salt, pepper.

Melt the butter, add the flour and stir until a very dark brown, then gradually add the stock; when this boils up, add the liquor from the mushrooms. Season and simmer twenty minutes. Skim off any fat that may rise to the top; add the mushrooms and simmer 5 minutes longer. Too much cooking toughens the mushrooms. This sauce is to be served with any kind of roasted, broiled or braised meats. It is especially nice with beef.

Nuts as Meat Substitutes

Nuts vary considerably in composition, some as chestnuts being starchy, others as cocoanut and walnuts being especially rich in fat, while many as almonds, Brazil nuts, butternuts and peanuts are rich in protein and fat.

The protein of nuts as far as known at present has not the value of animal protein. When used with some cheese, milk or meat they make an excellent meat substitute. When used without these they make good meat savers. With the constant tendency toward higher cost of meat and the necessity of shipping meat to our allies and our own soldiers (for they in their exposed life need the blood producing elements of meat) and with the growing knowledge of nut culture we may look for a much larger use of nuts as "meat substitutes."

10c spent for beefsteak will buy about 400 calories with almost 30 gms. protein.

10c spent for peanuts would buy about 1800 calories with 90 gms. protein.

10c spent for peanut butter would buy about 750 calories with 35 gms. of protein.

Thus nuts are plainly a more economical food from standpoint of food value.

Sherman.

PEANUT CROQUETTES

1 cup mashed potatoes,
¼ cup ground peanuts,
½ tsp. salt,
½ tsp. butter sub.,

Celery salt,
Paprika,
1 egg,
½ tsp. chopped parsley.

Add seasoning, butter and beaten egg to potatoes, also ground peanuts. Shape, roll in crumbs, then egg and crumbs, fry in deep fat. Serve with white sauce or tomato sauce.

Miss J. Crowder,
Domestic Science Instructor, Central High School.

BAKED OATMEAL AND NUTS

2 cups cooked oatmeal,
1 cup crushed peanuts,
½ cup milk,

1 tsp. vinegar,
½ tsp pepper,
1½ tsp. salt.

Mix together and bake in a greased pan 15 minutes. This is

enough for five people. Instead of meat, cook this appetizing dish for your family.

U. S. Food Administration.

BAKED RICE AND PEANUTS

2   cups cooked rice,   ½ cup shelled peanuts,
                                        1   cup white sauce.

Butter a casserole or baking pan. Place in a thin layer of cooked rice, then some peanuts, and next, white sauce. Arrange all ingredients in layers, having white sauce on top. Cover with bread crumbs and place in a hot oven for 20 minutes, having the top slightly browned.

Hilda Z. Rollman,
Domestic Science Instructor, Cote Brilliante School

PEANUT ROAST

1½ cups shelled peanuts,   1 tsp. baking powder,
1½ cups dried bread crumbs,   1 egg,
Milk to moisten crumbs,   Salt, pepper.

Cover bread crumbs with milk and soak until soft. Chop peanuts fine, mix with baking powder, beat the egg. Mix thoroughly all ingredients, turn into oiled baking pan. Bake 25 minutes in moderate oven. Serve hot with tomato sauce.

SCALLOPED ONIONS AND PEANUTS

5   medium onions,   1 cup milk,
 ¾ cup peanuts,   1 tbsp. flour,
1   tbsp. fat,   Salt.
4   cups bread crumbs,

Boil onions, drain and slice, melt fat, add flour, and cook 3 minutes. Add milk and cook till it thickens. Season with salt and pepper. In a greased baking dish, alternate layers of bread crumbs, onions, peanuts and cover with white sauce. Brown in a hot oven. The top layer should be bread crumbs.

Anna Jensen,
Domestic Science Instructor, Central High School,
St. Joseph, Mo.

WALNUT ROAST

⅓ cup cooked rice,
½ cup bread crumbs,
1   cup ground walnuts,
1   cup solid tomatoes,
1   pt. mashed potatoes,

1   egg,
1   small onion,
½ tsp. salt,
⅛ tsp. pepper,
Parsley.

Anna Jensen,
Domestic Science Instructor, Central High School,
St. Joseph, Mo.

NUT AND CHEESE LOAF (University of Ill.)

1 cup grated cheese,
1 cup nuts,
1 cup dry bread crumbs,
2 tbsp. water,

1   tsp salt,
½ tsp. pepper,
2   tbsp. onion,
1   tbsp. oil.

Cook onion in cooking oil and water until tender. Strain into mixture of cheese ground nuts and crumbs. Add seasoning. Bake in a loaf until brown. Garnish with lemon points.

Patriotic Food Show,
St. Louis, Mo

NUT SURPRISE

Parboil six medium onions in salt water. Hollow out centers of onions, chop centers and mix with one cup of ground nuts ½ cup bread crumbs and ½ cup standard cream sauce. Fill onions with this mixture, cover with buttered bread crumbs and let brown in oven.

Patriotic Food Show,
St. Louis, Mo.

Cheese as a Meat Substitute

Cheese is one of the most valuable of meat substitutes. Whole cheese contains about 25 per cent protein and cottage cheese about 20 per cent. U. S. Food Administration urges the larger manufacture and use of cottage cheese, utilizing the skim milk.

Cheese is a concentrated form of food. It is rich in both protein and fat. In combination with starchy food it may be used as a substitute for meat. Experiments have proved that cheese does not ordinarily cause indigestion and neither is it a frequent cause of constipation.

A recent compilation describes no less than 350 varieties of cheese.

Cheese is divided into two main types:

Hard Cheeses: Chedder, Edam, Emmental (or Swiss), Parmesan and Roquefort.

Soft Cheeses: Brie, Camembert, Gorgonzola, Limberg, Neufchatel and Stilton.

FOOD VALUE AS COMPARED TO MEAT

1 lb. chedder cheese=2,079 calories
1 lb. beef tenderloin=1,290 calories
1.24 oz. of beef=.77 oz. cheese=100 calories
3½ to 5½ oz. raw meat=usual serving.

COTTAGE CHEESE

Cottage cheese is one of the important meat substitutes, say specialists of the U. S. Department of Agriculture. It contains a larger percentage of protein than most meats and furnishes this material at a lower cost. In every pound of cottage cheese there is about one-fifth of a pound of protein, nearly all of which is digestible. Meats, on the other hand, usually contain less protein and, besides, have a certain waste, such as bone and other inedible material. A pound of cottage cheese daily would supply all the protein required by the ordinary adult engaged in a sedentary occupation.

CHEESE ON TOAST

1   tbsp. butter substitute,   1   cup milk,
1½ tbsp. flour,   ¾ cup grated cheese,
1   tsp. salt,   1   egg
⅛ tsp. pepper,

Mix the dry ingredients. Melt butter and add dry ingredients. Add milk gradually and stir well, cooking for five minutes. Add cheese and cook until dissolved Add to slightly beaten egg and cook until egg begins to thicken. Serve on hot toast.

Hilda Rollman,
Domestic Science Instructor, Cote Brilliante School.

COTTAGE CHEESE ON TOAST

1½ cups cottage cheese,   4 tbsp. flour,
1   cup milk,   1 egg,
1   cup tomato juice,   1 tbsp. fat.

Make white sauce of flour, fat, milk and tomato, stir in cottage cheese and beaten egg and serve on toast.

CHEESE FONDU

1⅓ cups hot milk,   1⅓ cups soft stale bread crumbs,
1   tsp. butter substitute,   4   eggs
⅓ lb. of grated cheese,   ½ tsp. salt.

Mix the milk, bread crumbs, salt and cheese, add the yolks thoroughly beaten; into this mixture cut and fold the whites of eggs beaten until stiff. Pour into a buttered baking dish and cook 30 minutes in moderate oven. Serve at once.

The protein value of this dish is equal to that of one and one-eighth pounds of potato and beef; the calculated cost, 22 cents.

CHEESE CUSTARD

4   eggs,   2 cups milk,
½ tsp. salt,   ½ cup grated cheese.
⅛ tsp. pepper,

Beat eggs slightly, add seasoning, cheese and hot milk. Pour into a buttered pudding dish or custard cups and set in a pan of hot water. Bake about one-half hour, or until the handle of a spoon can be run into it and will come out clean.

1.—STEAMED CHEESE SOUFFLE

4 tbsp. oleo,	¼ tsp. mustard,
4 tbsp. flour,	3 eggs,
1 cup milk,	½ lb cheese cut fine,
4 tsp. salt,	3 egg whites.

Melt fat, add flour and stir smooth, then add milk. Cook directly over the fire, stirring constantly, until it boils, for 1 minute. Remove from fire, add condiments, then egg yolks (beaten smooth), the cheese, and lastly cut and fold in the egg whites, beaten stiff, and dry. Smooth the top cover immediately, place the vessel over boiling water and cook without lifting the lid for 30 minutes. This dish should be made either in a double boiler or a chafing dish.

Miss Mary Evans,
Domestic Science Instructor, Yeatman High School.

ASPARAGUS WITH CHEESE

Drain liquor from one can of asparagus tips, arrange the stalks on squares of toast and pour over a sauce made as follows: Melt two tablespoons of butter substitute, with this blend two tablespoons of flour, add one cup of hot milk and cook until it thickens; season with salt and pepper Now stir in a half cup of grated cheese. When cheese is melted pour over asparagus.

BAKED STUFFED CUCUMBERS

Wipe and peel cucumbers, cut in two-inch pieces, crosswise, and remove seeds. Mix four tablespoons of bread crumbs, two tablespoons of finely chopped cooked ham and two tablespoons of grated Parmesan cheese. Moisten with tomato sauce and season with salt and pepper. Put cucumber cups in shallow pan Fill with mixture, surround with chicken stock, and bake thirty minutes. Remove, cover with buttered crumbs, and bake until crumbs are brown.

BAKED HOMINY AND CHEESE

1 tbsp. of oleo. or drippings,	½ tsp. paprika,
1 tbsp. cornstarch or	½ to 1 cup cheese, grated or
2 tbsp. of flour,	cut fine,
1 cup milk,	2 cups cooked hominy,
1 tsp. salt,	½ cup bread crumbs.

Make a sauce of the fat, cornstarch, salt and milk, add the cheese and paprika to the sauce, arrange the hominy in baking dish and pour the sauce over it. Cover with crumbs and bake 20 minutes in a moderate oven. The hominy and cheese may be arranged in layers and the white sauce poured over it if desired.

CHEESE AND COWPEA LOAF

2 cups cooked cowpeas, mashed or run through sieve,
½ cup grated cheese,

1 tbsp. butter substitute,
1 tbsp. chopped green pepper,
1 small onion, chopped

Cook the vegetables in the fat, mix with the peas and form into a loaf. Bake, basting with butter substitute and water. Use as a meat substitute, either hot or cold.

BOSTON ROAST

1 lb. beans (cooked),
½ lb. cottage cheese,

Bread crumbs,
Salt.

Run beans through food grinder, add cheese and enough crumbs to form a stiff roll. Bake in a moderate oven, baste with butter or some fat. Serve with tomato sauce.

Miss Anthony,
Instructor Domestic Science, Maryville, Mo.

CORN AND CHEESE

Cook corn, cut from cob,
2 cups corn,

½ cup cheese.

Make as macaroni and cheese, using white sauce No. 4, cayenne pepper. Pimento and cottage cheese with fish, good substitute for meat.

Miss Anthony,
Domestic Science Instructor, State Normal School,
Maryville, Mo

2.—CHEESE SOUFFLE

3 eggs,

1 cup cheese (grated).

Make white sauce, using 2 tbsp. fat, 2 tbsp. flour and one-half cup milk. Add yolks to sauce, add cheese, cool. Add stiffly beaten egg whites. Pour in buttered baking dish   Set in hot water, bake 10 minutes in moderate oven.

Miss Anthony,
Domestic Science Instructor, State Normal School,
Maryville, Mo.

CHEESE OMELET

4 eggs,
4 tbsp. cheese, grated,
Salt and pepper to taste,

2 tsp. chopped parsley (may be omitted).

Beat eggs, add other ingredients, turn into hot omelet pan well greased with veg. oil, fold, serve on hot dish

NEUFCHATEL CHEESE BALLS

To be served on luncheon plate.

2 Neufchatel cheeeeses,
A little cream,

Salt, pepper, red or white,
Ground or chopped pecans.

Mix ingredients, form in balls, roll in the nuts.

BAKED CHEESE WITH EGG

6   tbsp cheese (grated),
½ pt. milk,
3   egg yolks,
A little mustard,

2½ tbsp. veg. oil,
Whites of 2 eggs,
3 slices of bread,
Salt and red pepper.

Put milk and bread on to boil, stir, add cheese and fat. Place over fire and stir for one minute; add seasoning and yolks of eggs, also whites beaten stiff, stir gently, pour into greased casserole, bake a light brown.

CHEESE BALLS

1½ cups of cheese, grated,
¾ cup fine bread crumbs,
1   egg, well beaten,

A few drops of Worcestershire sauce.

Roll into balls one inch in diameter, just before serving drop into hot fat to brown. Serve hot with salads.

CHEESE STRIPS

1   cup flour,
1   tbsp. Troco or oleo,
¼ cup grated cheese,

½ tsp. baking powder,
½ tsp. salt,
A dash of cayenne.

Mix with water as for biscuits, roll out thin, cut in strips, bake in moderate oven.

CHEESE STRAWS

1½ lbs. grated cheese,
1   cup white flour,
1   cup white corn meal,
 ½ cup veg. oil,

1   tsp. salt,
2 tbsp. cream,
Dash of cayenne

Mix well as for biscuits, make a very stiff dough, roll out to ¼ inch in thickness, cut in strips 4 inches in length, ¾ inch wide, and bake golden brown.

Note: Cheese should be wrapped in a slightly damp cloth or in paraffin paper and then in wrapping paper. It should be kept in a cool place. Never cover cheese in a dish from which the air has been wholly excluded, as it molds more readily.

COTTAGE CHEESE AND NUT LOAF

1 cup cottage cheese (or grat-
 ed cheese),
1 cup nut meats,
1 cup stale bread crumbs,
Juice of ½ lemon,

1   tsp. salt,
¼ tsp. pepper,
2   tbsp. chopped onion,
1   tbsp oleo, meat drippings
 or table oils.

Mix the cheese, ground nuts, crumbs, lemon juice, salt and pepper. Cook the onion in the fat and little water until tender. Add to the first mixture the onion and sufficient water or meat stock to moisten. Mix well, pour into a baking dish and brown in the oven. Variations: two cups of cooked oatmeal may be substituted for the cheese and bread crumbs. One pound of beans cooked and put through a sieve may be substituted for the nuts. American cheese, grated or cut fine, may be used in place of cottage cheese. The amount of liquid added will vary in each case. The seasoning may be varied to suit the taste.

U. S. Food Administration

Note: Especial attention must be given to seasoning of dishes which have as their foundation beans, rice or other foods, having little flavor of their own. Use peppers, onion, garlic, catsup, Worcestershire sauce, etc, for increasing flavor. Beans and nut loaves should be served with highly seasoned sauces.

Note: Rinds and bits of cheese may be scalded, dried and ground for use in any dishes requiring cheese

Fish as a Meat Substitute

Eat more fish and sea food to save meat, is the request of our Government. The fish products, as estimated by the Bureau of Fisheries, amount to 2,169,000,000 pounds in weight.

Fresh Fish—10 per cent to 14 per cent protein.

Buying of Fish:

1 Find the varieties recommended by the United States Government and ask for them Insist that your dealer carries them Look up their food value and the best methods for their preparation.

2. In winter use frozen fish Frozen foods are best cooked before thawing them. It is becoming a common practice to preserve fruits and vegetables by freezing, but they must be used before thawing if the quality of the food is to be preserved. Frozen fish cooked at once is as delicious as fresh fish, providing the fish was originally fresh.

3. Use fish all the week, so that the demand will be extended and it will be possible to get it on other days than Friday.

4 A large number of perfectly good fish are being wasted each year because there is no demand for them We are too conservative and cling to the use of certain well-known varieties, while others equally good are not used

5. If possible, buy local fish, to avoid shipping. This rule does not hold in winter, when it is almost impossible to get river fish.

POINTS TO BE REMEMBERED IN THE PREPARATION OF FISH

1. Fish is tender; therefore long cooking is not necessary

2 Flavor should be retained and added.

3. Most fish lack fat; therefore the addition of it is desirable from the standpoint of food value as well as flavor.

A fish to be eatable must be perfectly fresh. Nothing else in the line of food deteriorates so rapidly. Fresh fish may be preserved frozen by the best cold storage process for at least two years, but if once heated and allowed to stand, nothing will bring back the delicious flavor of a fish just caught. Fresh fish will be

COURTESY DONNELL ST.LOUIS GLOBE DEMOCRAT

firm and the skin and scales bright. When a fish looks dim and limp do not buy it. Fish should be washed quickly in only one cold water. Wash whole and cut up for frying after, if fish is to be cut in pieces.

Fish may be baked, broiled, boiled, fried or sauted. Fresh cod, lake trout, red snapper, haddock are good boiled.

TO BOIL FISH

Pin the fish in a piece of strong white cotton cloth and plunge into boiling salt water, let simmer gently for 30 minutes, longer or shorter time according to size of fish. Boiled fish may be served with a great variety of sauces.

BOUILLON

If fish is boiled in the following bouillon it will add greatly to its flavor.

4 qts. of water,
1 onion,
1 slice of carrot,
2 cloves,
2 tbsp. salt,

1 tsp. pepper,
1 tbsp. vinegar,
Juice ½ lemon,
Some herb may be used.

Tie all spices in muslin bag. Cook all together, simmering slowly for one hour. Put in the fish and cook as directed for one hour.

BAKED FISH

Make a dressing of rolled crackers (fine), salt, pepper and chopped parsley, a small quantity of chopped salt pork (or butter substitute will do).

After fish has been carefully cleansed, rub well with salt, put in dressing and sew up the fish Cut gashes in the sides of fish about 1 inch deep and 2 inches long. Fill gashes with strips of fat salt pork. Now put the fish into the baking pan, dredge well with flour, salt and pepper, cover the bottom of the pan with water and put into moderate oven. A five-pound fish should bake in about one hour. The fish should be basted about every 15 minutes Water must be renewed often as only the bottom of pan should be kept covered. Do not allow the pan to burn. When done carefully slip the fish into center of hot platter, pour over

any kind of sauce desired, garnish and serve. It is well to place
fish on tin sheet before putting in baking dish; it will then slip
easily onto platter without breaking.

SAUTED FISH

All small fish like brook trout, smelts, perch, cat, are best
fried.

When thoroughly cleaned they should be rolled in a mixture of
flour and Indian meal, thoroughly mixed, salted and peppered
Fry brown on one side in shallow vegetable fat or salt pork drippings, turn carefully, brown and serve on hot platter. Sliced
fish may be fried in the same manner. Do not burn the fish.

CREAMED COD FISH

Buy the large white, boneless steaks of cod, break into small
pieces, let stand ½ hour in water, drain

Make cream sauce, 2 to 1

Add fish, let stand over very slow fire until heated through, do
not boil after fish is added. A beaten egg makes the dish richer.

1   cup cod fish,   1   egg
1½ cup cream sauce (2 to 1).

COD FISH BALLS

2 pts. raw potatoes,   Pepper,
1 pound cod fish,   1 tbsp. veg. fat.
Salt,

Boil cod fish picked in pieces with potatoes until latter are done,
mash, beat, add beaten eggs, salt, pepper and fry light brown in
vegetable oil or butter substitute.

BAKED SALT FISH

2 cups salt (flaked),   2 eggs,
2 cups cold mashed potatoes,   2 to 3 tbsp. of drippings.
1 pt milk,

Soak the flaked fish in cold water over night Freshen the
fish by boiling up several times in fresh water (usually three
times is sufficient). Then simmer until tender. Drain off the
water, mix the potatoes with the milk, eggs, fat and seasoning. Add the fish, turn into a greased baking dish and bake one-
half hour.

U. S. Food Administration.

SALMON CROQUETTES

Other fish may be substituted.

1½ cups thick rich cream sauce,
1 small can good brand salmon,
1 tsp. onion juice or finely chopped onion,
¼ tsp. pepper,
1 tbsp parsley.

Remove bones, skin and oil from salmon, mix salmon into cream sauce, add other ingredients, shape into balls, dip in egg and fine cracker crumbs and fry in hot fat a light brown. Serve with sauce.

SALMON LOAF

Mince a can of salmon; add one cup stale bread crumbs, two beaten eggs and ½ cup milk. Season to taste with salt, pepper, parsley and lemon juice. Put in a buttered mold and steam or bake for thirty minutes Turn from mold and serve hot with white or Hollandaise sauce Remnants of a baked fish and its stuffing may be used in place of the salmon and bread crumbs

May Secrist,
H. E. Dept., Cal Polytechnic.

SALMON AND MASHED POTATOES

1 can of salmon,
2 cups of mashed potatoes,
Onion,
Pepper—salt to taste.

Mix all and form in cakes and fry. Serve hot

C. L Bruno,
Wellston.

HOMINY AND FISH LOAF

1 cup hominy grits,
2 cups water,
2 cups skimmed milk,
1 tsp salt.

Cook the hominy, milk, water and salt in a double boiler for 6 hours. Serve as a vegetable or cereal For the second day line and oil bowl with the cold hominy, fill the center with flaked salmon, cover with hominy and steam for one hour. Turn onto a hot platter and serve with a sauce made from the liquor that was in the salmon as a base.

Miss Mary Evans,
Domestic Science Instructor, Yeatman High School.

BAKED TUNA FISH

1 can Tuna fish, No. 2,　　　½ cup fine bread or cracker
6-10 crackers,　　　　　　　　crumbs.
1½ cups cream sauce, thick,

Break up Tuna fish with fork, butter baking dish or casserole.
Alternate the layers of fish, cream sauce and crackers, put
small bits of butter substitute and fine crumbs on top. Juice of
lemon may be used over all if desired. Serve with baked potatoes
and a relish

Tuna fish has been called the chicken of the sea.

HALLENDEN HALIBUT

Arrange 6 slices salt pork or bacon, 2½ inches square, and a
bay leaf. Place on this 2 pounds sliced halibut Cover with 3
tablespoonfuls oil or butter substitute, creamed and mixed with
3 tablespoonfuls flour. Cover with oiled bread crumbs and lard
with thin strips of salted pork. Cover with oiled paper and bake
in moderate oven 50 minutes Remove the paper last 15 minutes,
garnish with lemon and chopped parsley

PLANKED WHITEFISH (Whitefish or Shad Preferred)

Select a 1 to 2-pound fish. It should be cleaned by opening
down the front. Start at the tail end and loosen the backbone
by running the finger or a sharp knife underneath. Break off
where it joins the tail fin. Follow the bone up, loosening as you
go Most of the bones will come out with the backbone. Any
small bones that are left may be picked out later

Soak a plank well to prevent burning Lay fish on plank skin
side down and place either in main part of oven or in the broiler
until tender and slightly browned. Serve with Maitre d'Hotel
butter

BAKED SPANISH MACKEREL

Clean and wash well. Fill with a stuffing prepared from the
following ingredients: 2 cups bread crumbs, ¼ cup corn oil, a
small onion sliced, ½ teaspoonful of sage, chopped celery and
parsley Lay in pan, cover witth strips of salt pork and bake 20
to 30 minutes. Any other fish may be prepared in this same way.

BROILED EULACHON

Dress without splitting and wipe dry. Score across the back, broil slowly over a clear fire, turning once. No fat need be used. Serve on a hot platter with a seasoning of salt, pepper and lemon juice.

Broiled fresh whiting, prepared in same way as the Eulachon.

BAKED SABLE FISH

Cut fish in slices about an inch thick. Have a hot baking pan ready with just enough fat to prevent the fish from sticking. Dip the fish steak in a mixture of one egg and two tablespoonfuls of milk. (The soaked fried egg may be used for this.) Place in baking pan and put in moderate oven until both sides are browned. This is a very acceptable substitute for fried fish. Serve with lemon.

CORN MEAL FISH BALLS

2 cups cold white corn meal mush,
1 cup shredded codfish,
1 egg,
1 tbsp. butter.

Pick over the codfish and soak it to remove salt if necessary. Combine the ingredients and drop by spoonfuls into hot fat. Drain on porous paper. These codfish balls compare very favorably in taste with those made with potatoes and are prepared more easily and quickly. The mush must be as dry as possible. This make 12 fish balls.

Farmers' Bulletin 565.

JELLIED FISH

1½ cups flaked fish,
2 tbsp. chopped capers,
1 tbsp. gran. gelatine,
1 cup boiling water,
2 tbsp. lemon juice,
¼ tsp. salt,
2 tbsp. cold water.

Mix the fish and capers. Arrange in a mold. Soak the gelatine in two tablespoonfuls of cold water. Add the boiling water and stir until the gelatine dissolves, then add the lemon juice and salt. Pour this jelly carefully over the fish and set in a cool place to harden. Cut into portions and serve on lettuce with salad dressing. If desired celery to hard boiled eggs cut in slices may be added to the fish.

U. S. Food Administration.

CREOLE TOMATOES

Wipe six medium-sized tomatoes, remove a slice from the top of each, scoop out some of the pulp, sprinkle insides with salt, invert and let stand one hour. Melt one and one-half tablespoonfuls of vegetable fat, add one tablespoonful of flour and stir until well blended; then pour on gradually, while stirring constantly, ½ cupful of milk. Bring to the boiling point and add one cup of crab meat, one tablespoonful of green pepper (from which the seeds have been removed) finely chopped, ½ teaspoonful of salt, ¼ teaspoonful of paprika, and a few grains of pepper. Fill tomatoes with mixture, sprinkle tops with coarse, buttered bread crumbs, put in buttered pan and bake in a moderate oven 15 or 20 minutes.

CREAMED TUNA FISH

A nice breakfast or luncheon dish. Try Tuna fish salad (sea chicken salad), substituting Tuna for chicken.

1 can Tuna fish, broken into pieces with silver fork),

1 cup cream sauce, A little parsley.

Add broken fish to hot cream sauce; do not cook but let stand on slow fire until very hot. Serve on squares of buttered toast.

FINNAN HADDIE (Smoked)

Remove skin carefully.

Let fish come to boiling point in clear water; remove to tin shallow baking pan, cover with bits of butter substitute, dredge with flour, pour over 1 pint of cream. Place in the broiler of gas stove, let it brown slightly, serve on hot platter. This makes a nice meal when served with baked potatoes.

BROILED SALT MACKEREL

Freshen the fish by soaking 10 to 12 hours with the skin side up. Change the water several times. Simmer until tender (15 to 20 minutes) in water to which 1 teaspoonful vinegar, a bay leaf, one slice of onion and a sprig of parsley have been added. Drain, rub the fish with a little salt and margarine or other fat; grease the hot broiler and lay the fish on it. Brown on both sides quickly, garnish with slices of lemon and parsley.

OYSTERS, FRIED

2 doz. large oysters,	4 tbsp. fine cracker crumbs,
2 tbsp. fat, butter or veg fat,	Salt, pepper

Heat fat. stir in the flour, put in oysters, then boil up once, add the hot cream and pour over toast.

OYSTER PATTIES

2 tbsp. fat (veg. oil),	1 pt. liquor from oysters,
2 heaping tbsp flour,	1 qt. small oysters (drained).
1 pt. cream,	

Make cream sauce of fat, flour, liquor, cream, salt, pepper; put in the oysters and let come to a boil or until edges of oysters curl. Make shells of rich paste, fill and cover with rounds of same paste, set in oven a few minutes, serve on hot plates.

SCALLOPED OYSTERS

1 can corn,	1 tbsp. veg. oil,
1 pt. oysters,	1 tbsp. flour,
1 cup liquor from oysters or milk,	½ tsp. salt,
	¼ tsp. pepper.

Melt butter, add flour, salt and pepper, mix until smooth, add warm liquor, cook until slightly thickened.

Put corn and oysters in two layers in large baking dish, add sauce. Sprinkle top with crumbs, bake 30 to 45 minutes in moderate oven.

Miss Mary Sherzer,
St. Louis Public Schools.

OYSTER COCKTAIL

24 small raw oysters,	¼ tsp. salt,
3 tbsp. tomato catsup,	3 tsp. chopped celery,
1½ tbsp. lemon juice or vinegar,	1½ tsp. Worcestershire sauce,
6 drops of Tabasco sauce,	3 tsp grated horse-radish.

Mix all the ingredients except oysters and chill thoroughly. Place oysters on cracked ice in cocktail glasses, and just before serving add the sauce.

DEVILED CRABS

1 cup chopped crabs,	⅔ cup white stock,
¼ cup mushrooms finely chopped,	Yolks 2 eggs,
2 tbsp veg. oil,	1 tsp. chopped parsley,
2 tbsp. flour,	Salt and pepper.

Make a sauce of vegetable oil, flour and stock; add yolks of eggs, seasonings (except parsley), crab meat and mushrooms; cook 3 minutes, add parsley and cool mixture. Wash and trim crab shells, fill rounding with mixture, sprinkle with bread crumbs mixed with small quantity of vegetable oil. Grease on top with a case knife, having three lines parallel with each other across the shell and three short lines branching from outside parallel lines. Brown crumbs and serve hot with a sauce.

Elizabeth Walker,
Domestic Science Instructor, University City, Mo.

SAUCES

MAITRE D'HOTEL BUTTER

¼ cup butter substitute,	½ tsp. finely chopped parsley,
½ tsp. salt,	¾ tsp. lemon juice.
⅓ tsp. pepper,	

Cream in a bowl with small wooden spoon. Add salt, pepper and parsley, then lemon juice very slowly.

HOLLANDAISE SAUCE

½ cup veg. oil,	½ tsp. salt,
2 eggs (yolks only),	A few grains cayenne pepper,
1 tbsp. lemon juice,	⅓ cup boiling water.

Put ⅓ vegetable oil in a sauce pan with the yolks of the eggs and lemon juice. Place over hot water and stir constantly. Add slowly as it thickens the last of the vegetable oil; add the water and cook one minute. Season with salt and cayenne.

DRAWN BUTTER SAUCE

Mix to a smooth paste two tablespoonfuls of butter substitute, and one of flour; put bowl in pan of boiling water on the fire, adding gradually ½ pint of boiling water or stock; stir until it thickens, add ½ teaspoonful of salt, cook until flour is done and smooth; if it is to be used for fish put in chopped eggs and capers. If wanted acid, use a little venegar or lemon juice.

SAUCES

REURRE NOIR

Two tablespoonfuls of butter substitute, one of vinegar, one of chopped parsley, one teaspoonful of lemon juice, ½ teaspoonful of salt, ¼ quarter of a teaspoonful of pepper. Put the butter substitute in the frying pan and when very hot add the parsley and then the other ingredients Boil up once. This sauce is for fried and broiled fish, and it is poured over the fish before sending to the table.

AURORA SAUCE

Aurora sauce for fish is prepared by adding to 1 pint of thick tomato sauce ½ of a cup of chopped canned mushrooms, two tablespoonfuls of mushroom liquor, and one tablespoonful of butter substitute cut into bits and stirring until the butter substitute is absorbed.

Poultry as a Meat Substitute

"Eat poultry; it does not make army rations."

U. S. Food Administration.

Poultry (unless frozen) deteriorates very rapidly and so must be eaten near the place of production.

STUFFING FOR FOWLS

3   cups of cornbread crumbs,
1   cup Liberty bread crumbs,
1   onion minced,
1   tbsp. chopped parsley,
½   cup chopped celery,

½ cup fat from the fowl,
2   tsp. sage—enough stock or milk to mix to the right consistency.

Melt or fry out fat to mix with the crumbs, add seasoning and liquid to bring to the right consistency.

POTATO STUFFING

2   cups hot mashed potatoes,
1¼ cups bread crumbs,
1   tsp. sage,
1   chopped onion,

3   tbsp. fat from fowl,
1   egg,
1½ tsp. salt.

Clean and stuff fowl, place in roasting pan in moderate oven Bake until tender and a knife inserted at the joint will show that it may be easily separated. For a tougher fowl, place in fireless cooker 4 hours or over night, then stuff and brown in oven

ROAST CHICKEN OR OTHER FOWL

Dress, clean, stuff and truss a fowl, lay on back on rack of roasting pan. Rub breast well with fat (salt pork in strips may be used) after the war, put into oven until it begins to brown, lower temperature and cook until tender, about 3 or 4 hours

SAUTED FRIED CHICKEN

Cut up young chicken, season with salt and pepper, dredge with flour, brown on both sides in generous quantity of vegetable fat, add a bit of water, cover tightly and steam 30 minutes.

MARYLAND CHICKEN

Dress, clean, and cut up fowl, sprinkle with salt and pepper, dip in egg and fine bread crumbs, place in well-oiled roaster and bake until tender in hot oven; baste after first 5 minutes with melted fat or cream. Prepare either brown or cream sauce with dripping in pan and serve with chicken

JELLIED CHICKEN

1 chicken cooked until tender,   Olives or pickles,
4 hard cooked eggs,   Celery or celery salt,
2 tbsp. gelatine,   Salt and pepper.

Reduce the liquor in which the chicken was cooked to 1 pint, add the diced or minced chicken, sliced eggs, the celery salt and pepper and pickles and olives, add the gelatine soaked in ½ cup of cold water and dissolved over hot water   Put into wet molds and chill thoroughly. The jelly and the food may be added one layer at a time, arranging the food in a design if desired

CHICKEN PIE

Dress, clean and cut up a plump fowl, put in a stew pan with one onion, salt and pepper, add boiling water to cover. Let simmer until done, remove the chicken, strain the stock, skim off the fat and thicken with a paste of flour and water   Invert a small cup in the center of baking dish, dispose the chicken about it after having removed some of the larger bones   Add bits of butter and the thickened gravy. Cover with a baking powder biscuit crust ½ inch thick in which incisions have been made to allow the escape of steam. Bake until the crust is well done and nicely browned.

CHICKEN AND CORN MEAL CROQUETTES

1 cup white corn meal mush,   Salt and pepper,
1 cup chopped chicken,   Few drops of onion juice.
1 egg,

Combine the ingredients and drop by spoonfuls into hot fat. White corn meal may be combined very satisfactorily with other kinds of cold meat to make croquettes. In general, corn meal croquettes need not be egged and crumbed like ordinary croquettes, for the hardening of the corn meal on the surface of the mixture forms the necessary crust. This serves three people.

Farmers' Bulletin 565

Meat Sparers

USE SAVORY STEWS AND MEAT PIES

Do you know how good they are? They may be so varied that you can have a different one every day in the week, and all of them delicious. It needs only a small piece of meat to give flavor to a hearty dish.

Don't think that you must eat a lot of meat to be strong. Meat is good to help build up the body, but so are many other foods

In these dishes, part of your building material comes from the more expensive meat and part from the cheaper peas, beans, hominy and barley. The little meat with the vegetables and cereals will give your body what it needs.

U. S. Food Administration

TAMALE PIE

Another good way to use a little meat. Have you ever used rice, corn meal mush, or hominy for a crust? This is less work than a pastry crust and saves wheat.

4 cups cooked corn meal, rice, or hominy,	⅛ tsp. pepper,
1 onion,	1 tbsp. fat,
2 cups tomato,	1 pound raw meat or left over meat cut up small.

Melt the fat, add the sliced onion, and, if raw meat is used, add it, and place over fire until red color disappears Add the tomato and seasoning. If cooked meat is used, add it with the tomato and seasoning after the onion is browned, and heat through. Grease a baking dish, put in a layer of the cereal, add the meat and gravy, and cover with the cereal, dotted with fat. Bake for half hour.

SHEPHERD'S PIE

This is the name of a meat pie with a mashed potato crust browned in the oven.

HOT POT OF MUTTON AND BARLEY

1 pound mutton,	3 onions,
½ cup pearled barley,	Celery tops or other seasoning
1 tbsp. salt,	herbs.
4 potatoes,	

Cut the mutton in small pieces, and brown with the onion in fat cut from meat. This will help the meat tender and improves the flavor. Pour this into a covered sauce pan. Add 2 quarts water and the barley. Simmer for 1½ hours. Then add the potatoes cut in quarters, seasoning, and cook one-half hour longer

SCRAPPLE

2 lbs. (meat) pork, game, poultry, etc.,
½ lb. liver (beef or pork).

Cook together till very tender, remove from liquor and grind. To liquor add enough water to make 2 quarts, make corn meal mush with those 2 quarts, using about 2 cups of meal (must be rather thick). When done, add ground meat, salt, pepper, sage, allspice to taste. Pour into greased mold. In frying be sure to have pan thoroughly heated. Slice pieces from the mold and fry.

Mrs. F. W. Shipley

SPAGHETTI A L'ITALIENNE

An excellent dish containing all the food elements necessary for substantial meal may be varied. Use left over gravy, bits of meat of any kind, rice or vegetables, always using common sense (the best ingredients) in cooking.

1 cup grated cheese,	1 tsp. salt,
½ can tomatoes,	½ tsp. pepper,
1 large onion,	¼ lb. ground beef,
2 tbsp Mazola or veg. oil,	1 cup hot water or milk,
½ bay leaf,	Bit of parsley.

Cook spaghetti 30 minutes, cut onion fine, fry in the oil till golden brown, add tomatoes and all other ingredients except cheese. Let simmer slowly for 30 minutes or while spaghetti is cooking; have baking dish ready. Place alternate portions of spaghetti. sauce and cheese, cover with bread crumbs and bake 15 minutes.

SPAGHETTI, CHEESE AND MUSHROOMS

1 box spaghetti,
1 can tomatoes,
1 can mushrooms,
1 small onion,
3 tbsp. butter,

Salt, pepper to season highly,
¼ lb. cheese,
1 egg,
Paprika.

Boil spaghetti ¾ of an hour, cut onion and brown in 1 table-spoonful butter, cut mushrooms into pieces or purchase the broken mushrooms, which are cheaper. Beat egg well and mix all ingredients, turn into two baking dishes and bake until mixture becomes rather thick (about 1½-2 hours). This makes an amount sufficient for several meals, but it keeps well and gets better as it is reheated.

Elizabeth Mount Walker,
Domestic Science Instructor, University City.

POTATOES AU GRATIN

Cream sauce No. 2 (butter sub. used),
Potatoes sliced (raw),
Cheese (grated).

Put ingredients into baking dish in alternate layers with bread or cracker crumbs on top. Bake 30 minutes. For six people.

CASSEROLE OF RICE AND MEAT

1 cup cooked rice,
2 cups cooked meat,
Spk. cayenne,
¼ tsp. celery salt,
Few drops onion juice,
1 tsp. chopped green peppers,

¼ cup crumbs,
1 tsp. lemon juice,
1 egg,
1 tsp. salt,
¼ tsp. pepper,
¼ cup tomato juice.

Chop the meat fine and add the other ingredients, except the rice, mixing well. Line a casserole or individual ramekin with rice. Add meat mixture. Bake 20 minutes, serve hot with to-mato sauce. This may be steamed in a mold 30 to 45 minutes and turned onto a platter to serve.

JELLIED MEAT LOAF

2 cups cooked meat,
1 cup stock,
1 tbsp. catsup,
1 bay leaf,

2 cloves,
½ tsp. celery salt,
Spk. salt,
Spk. pepper.

Add seasonings to stock and bring to boiling point, swell gelatine in cold water, and dissolve in hot stock. Strain, add meat and mold, serve garnished with hard cooked eggs

STUFFED MUSHROOMS A LA BRADFORD

Select a dozen large mushrooms, peel them and remove the stems. Make a forcemeat from the following ingredients: Use the mushroom stems and three whole mushrooms Chop fine and saute in butter for three minutes. Add one-half cup of bread crumbs which have been moistened with chicken stock. Season with salt, pepper and 1 tbsp. of tomato catsup Fill the large mushrooms with this mixture. Crumb, and bake about fifteen minutes. Serve on toast surrounded by a brown sauce, flavored with sherry.

BEEF STEW

1 lb. beef,	¼ peck green peas or 1 can,
4 potatoes,	1 cup carrots cut up small.
1 tsp. salt,	

Cut meat in small pieces and brown in the fat from the meat Simmer in 2 quarts of water for 1 hour. Add the peas and carrots and cook for one-half hour, then add the potatoes. If canned peas are used add them 10 minutes before serving. Serve when potatoes are done.

Variations —1 The meat —This may be any kind and more or less than a pound may be used. Use the cheap cuts, the flank, rump, neck or brisket. The long, slow cooking makes them tender; game and poultry **are** good.

2. Potatoes and barley may be used or barley alone or rice, hominy or macaroni.

3. Vegetables—carrots, turnips, onions, peas, beans, cabbage, tomatoes are good canned or fresh. Use one or more of these as you wish.

4. Parsley, celery tops, onion tops, seasoning herbs or chopped sweet peppers add to the flavor

5. Many left-overs may be used, not only meat and vegetables, but rice or hominy.

U. S. Food Administration.

The fireless cooker may well be used, the meat and the vegetables being put in at the same time. Left-overs or canned vegetables need only to be heated through. Add them 15 minutes before serving.

SWEETBREADS EN CREME

Put sweetbreads in bowl, cover with cold water, let stand an hour, drain, remove the fat and membranes. Cook in boiling acidulated water 20 minutes, allowing ½ tsp each of salt and vinegar to a pair of sweetbreads, then drain again and plunge into cold water. Cut parboiled sweetbreads in ½-inch cubes, to ⅓ cup cubes add ¼ cup white sauce.

BROILED SWEETBREADS

After parboiling as above, split crosswise. Season with salt and pepper and broil eight minutes. Serve with lemon, butter made by creaming 4 tbsp oil, and adding slowly 2 tbsp. of lemon.

STUFFED HEART

Remove veins and arteries Wash carefully. simmer for 1 hour Stuff, sprinkle with salt and pepper (1 tbsp. of salt to 1 pound; pepper to taste), dredge with flour, bake in stock in which it was stewed, thicken liquid with corn starch to the thickness of sauce for creamed dishes, and serve hot.

BOILED TONGUE

1 tongue,	1 tbsp. vinegar,
4 cloves,	1 tbsp salt,
4 pepper corns,	½ tsp. pepper.

Wipe the tongue and place in boiling water to which the seasoning has been added. Boil for 10 minutes, then draw to a cooler part of the range and simmer until tender, ¾ hours, partially cool in the liquid; take the tongue from the water and remove the skin and roots If pickled tongue is used and is very salty, it should be soaked in cold water several hours or over night before cooking.

ASPEC JELLY

2 cups white or brown stock,	Lemon juice,
1 tbsp. gelatine,	Salt,
½ cup cold water,	Pepper,
Bay leaf,	Celery salt.
Worcestershire sauce,	

(If the stock does not form a soft jelly itself when cold, use 1½ tbsp of gelatine)

Soak gelatine in cold water and dissolve over boiling water

Put seasoning to taste into stock and heat together, clarify, stir in dissolved gelatine and strain. Mold and decorate with meat and vegetables as desired.

TONGUE IN ASPEC

1 cup diced tongue,	1 hard cooked egg and pimento or parsley for decoration.
1½ cups liquid aspec jelly,	

Prepare according to directions for decorating gelatine molds, add tongue. Let stand until firm and molded.

BRAISED TONGUE

1 beef tongue,	⅓ cup onion, diced,
⅓ cup carrots, diced,	¼ cup celery, diced
1 sprig parsley,	

Place tongue in fireless cooker vessel and heat to boiling. Place in fireless cooker with hot plate. Leave two to three hours. Take out and remove skin and roots. Place back in fireless cooker pan and surround with vegetables. Add **four cups of sauce** made according to the next recipe Cover closely, reheat stone and return to fireless cooker. Bake two to three hours longer.

SAUCE FOR BRAISED TONGUE

Melt one-fourth cup oleo, add one-fourth cup corn flour and stir together until well browned. Add gradually four cups of hot water in which the tongue was cooked. Season **with salt,** pepper and one teaspoon Worcestershire sauce. One and one-half cups strained tomatoes may be substituted for **part of the water.**

SAUTED LIVER

Cut liver in slices ½ inch thick and cover with boiling water, let stand 5 minutes to draw out the blood, drain, wipe and remove outer skin and veins, sprinkle with salt and pepper, dredge with flour and saute in bacon fat (if you have it).

Note· Make gravies to conserve food values of the extractives and fats from meats.

Note: Nourishing soups can be made from scraps of meat from vegetables that are usually thrown away

Soups That Save

An Overlooked Economy

Many housekeepers throw away the water in which vegetables have been boiled, unmindful of the fact that somewhat less than a third of the contained mineral matter and about the same amount of starchy and protein substances are dissolved out into this water, which may well be utilized for soup. For instance, the water in which cabbage has been cooked requires only the addition of a little milk, butter and thickening to furnish an agreeable thin soup

In this connection it may be noted that much nutriment is also lost in the water in which vegetables are soaked in order to restore them to freshness, an excellent reason why wilted products should not be bought, and for the same reason vegetables should be covered with boiling water, not tepid, and the cooking started without delay. While such vegetables are thought to taste better if cooked in a large amount of water, they should be just scalded or parboiled, this water thrown away, and the cooking concluded in a small quantity of water or by steaming.

Since one of the great ends of cooking is the production of flavor, we should place high in our list those cheapest of all flavors which result from browning. Toasted bread or croutons is a favorite addition to soups, but many housekeepers do not seem to know that toasting or parching gives a new flavor to rice, or if applied to the highly flavored vegetables used to season soups, results in new and delicious flavoring substances as carmelized onion, carrot, celery, green pepper, etc

Cream soups are in place only at luncheon or at supper because they are so heavy that they partly satisfy the appetite. To this end they should be recognized as having actual food value, while the clear soup that appears at dinner is used more as a stimulant to the appetite. A cream soup is always bland in taste and should be followed by some strong flavored dish of firm texture. Creamed chicken is too similar to harmonize with cream soup; croquettes or salads would give a better effect. Cream soups are in place at dinners if used as a meat substitute.

SOUP MADE FROM LEFT-OVERS

Put bones and pea pods in water and boil until all of the flavor has come out into the water, remove bones and water. Put through meat grinder any small amount of left over food which does not contain bananas or is very sweet. Add to the above stock, cook thoroughly, strain and season.

CORRECT PROPORTIONS FOR A WHITE SAUCE FOR SOUPS

1 tbsp fat,   1 tbsp flour.
1 cup milk or soup stock,

Soups can be thickened with stale bread, which makes it possible to utilize still another food, sometimes thrown away. Half a slice of bread, or about ¼ ounce of bread, is enough to thicken one cup of soup

THE FOLLOWING IS A TYPICAL RECIPE

1 head lettuce,   1 large slice stale bread,
1 small sliced onion,   Veg fat if desired,
2 qts. skim milk,   Salt and pepper.

Put the lettuce and onion through the meat chopper with the bread to save the juice. Put into a double boiler with the skim milk and cook until the lettuce is soft. Add fat (if desired) and the salt and pepper.

U. S Bulletin 871.

CREAM OF CHEESE SOUP

Put three pints of milk into a sauce pan, add ¼ pound of grated cheese, salt, pepper and paprika to taste. Add one heaping tablespoonful flour to the cheese mixture and stir until smooth and thick. Beat the yolks of three eggs with a little of the soup mixture and then add the rest of the soup. A thin slice of green pepper may be added to each plate

PEANUT SOUP

In the upper part of a double boiler put ¼ cup ground peanuts, ¼ cup dried bread crumbs or 2 tablespoonfuls flour, 2½ cups skim milk, or 1¼ cups vegetable soup stock and 1¼ cups skim milk. Cook over hot water one-half hour, season with salt, pepper and onion juice if wished Always beat a cream soup well before serving.

MEATLESS VEGETABLE SOUP

Fresh Vegetables

⅓ cup carrots,	½ onion,
⅓ cup turnips,	1 qt. water,
½ cup celery,	4 tbsp. fat,
1½ cups potatoes, or ¼ cup cereal,	½ tsp. finely chopped parsley, Salt and pepper.

Wash and cut up into small pieces, without peeling, carrots, turnips, celery and potatoes. Measure. Place fat in sauce pan, add carrots, turnips, celery and onion; cook ten minutes, stirring constantly. Add potatoes (or cereal) and water, boil gently until vegetables are very tender. Beat with fork or spoon to break vegetables. Add parsley and season.

1.—LENTIL SOUP

1 cup lentils,	2 tbsp. cornstarch,
2 pts. milk,	Seasoning of salt,
1 tbsp. of butter,	Pepper

Wash the lentils, cover them with cold water and soak over night. Bring them to boiling point and boil until they mash easily. Drain and put them into a sauce pan. Add gradually the milk, butter, seasoning of salt and pepper, and the cornstarch moistened with half a cup of water or milk. Stir till it boils up, when it is ready for serving.

2.—LENTIL SOUP

Soak the dry lentils over night, pour off water, put on stove with enough water or milk to make a desired quantity of soup. When nearly done add butter in which a little flour has been browned, and let it all boil about 10 minutes. Season to taste and serve with small cubes of roasted stale bread.

Miss Ella D. Rode,
Domestic Science Instructor, Patrick Henry School

PEA SOUP

½ lb split peas,	½ tbsp. butter or dripping,
1 onion,	A little dried mint,
1 stack celery,	1 qt. stock,
1 small carrot,	Seasoning of salt and pepper,
1 small turnip.	3 thin slices of bacon

Soak the peas in cold water for several hours; melt the butter or drippings in a sauce pan, drain the peas and put them into the pan with the onion and the vegetables cut into small pieces; stir over the fire for 5 minutes, taking care that they do not brown, then add the stock, and season with salt and pepper. Boil up gently and skim well, let it simmer slowly until the peas are tender, rub the soup through a sieve and add the bacon, previously fried and cut into small dice. Reheat, add the mint and serve.

SOY BEAN SOUP

1 cup cooked soy beans, rubbed through a sieve,	2 tbsp. butter or butter sub, 1 chopped onion,
1 qt. water,	½ cup tomato catsup
4 tbsp flour,	

Melt the butter and add the onion. Stir in the flour and add the water. When thickened add the bean pulp. If the catsup is used it may be added just before serving.

FOR CREAMED SOUP SEE WHITE SAUCE
SCOTCH SOUP

With bread and dessert it is enough for lunch or supper.

2½ qts. water,	2 onions, sliced,
1½ cups rolled oats,	2 tbsp. flour,
5 potatoes cut in small pieces,	2 tbsp fat.

Boil the water and add the oatmeal, potatoes, onion, ½ tablespoonful salt and ½ teaspoonful pepper. Cook for one-half hour. Brown flour with the fat (vegetable oil) and add to the soup. Cook until thick. One cup of tomato adds to the flavor. Serves five people.

U. S. Food Administration.

LIMA BEAN CHOWDER

¼ lb. salt pork,	1 pt. or ½ lb. green shelled lima beans,
1 onion,	
1 green pepper,	4 small potatoes,
3 cups skim milk,	Salt and pepper

Put the pork, onion and pepper through the grinder. Cook carefully for 2 or 3 minutes, being careful not to burn; add either the beans or the potatoes with water enough to cover and cook until the vegetables are soft. Cook the other vegetables separately and when soft add with the milk to the other mixture. Reheat and season.

The protein in the above dish is equal to that in about three-fourths pound of beef of average composition Any vegetables may be used in place of the beans

Farmers' Bulletin 871

CREAM OF VEGETABLE SOUPS

Cream vegetable soups are nutritious and are a palatable dish to serve for luncheon or supper. Great care should be used in combining acid vegetables, such as tomatoes with milk, as the milk may curdle and spoil the texture of the dish. A very small quantity of soda added to the puree (strained vegetable pulp) will neutralize the acid, and then it may be added to the milk
General Directions.

Cook vegetables until soft, strain the vegetables and keep the stock in which they are cooked. Make a thin white sauce, using 1 tablespoonful butter, 1 tablespoonful flour, ½ teaspoonful salt and ⅛ teaspoonful pepper to 1 cup liquid (milk or stock or part of each), add the strained vegetable (puree) to the white sauce, then reheat and serve at once. Onion or other seasoning vegetables may be used

TOMATO BISQUE

Equal quantities of thin white sauce and tomato puree.

FISH CHOWDER

A 3-lb. fish,
4 tbsp. drippings,
1 medium onion chopped fine,
1 qt sliced potatoes,
3 cups hot milk.

Skin and bone the fish, and cut into inch cubes. Cover the bone and trimmings with cold water and let simmer for one-half hour. Cook the onion in the fat for 5 minutes, then pour into a stew pan. Parboil the sliced potatoes for 5 minutes, then drain and add layers of fish and potatoes to the fat and onion in the stew pan Season each layer with salt and pepper. Strain the liquor in which the fish bones have been cooking over all and cook about 20 minutes until fish and potatoes are tender. Then add the scalded milk. If desired thicker, sprinkle a little corn meal between each layer of fish and potatoes.

U. S. Food Administration.

OYSTER SOUP

Heat the strained liquor from one quart of oysters. In another vessel heat one quart of milk, ¼ cup butter substitute, a dash of cayenne, salt and pepper to taste. Add two powdered crackers, and when scalding hot put milk and oyster liquor together. Add oysters and let them come to a boil

Helen Labagh Johnson.

Note: Celery leaves may be dried and used in soups. Use water in which vegetables have been cooked for soup and gravies, as it contains nutritive value Have a soup pot; add bones from steak, roast pork, fowls, etc , after bones have been scalded Bones are valuable as fertilizer, containing the elements Calcium and Phosphorus.

VEGETABLES

It may be said in general that no meat or vegetable should be cooked longer than is necessary to soften the connective tissue or the cellulose. Sometimes only a very short time is needed to develop flavor, while long cooking may wholly change this flavor Shredded cabbage, for instance, cooked a half hour, has become tender, and has a good color and flavor; if the cooking is continued for three hours, as is the custom in the German kitchen, its color darkens and its flavor has become at least to the American palate strong and disagreeable The importance of not over-cooking applies to all tender succulent young growths, as peas, beans, asparagus, spinach. If, when cooked, their serving is unavoidably delayed they should be closely covered and kept in a water bath; while starchy vegetables, as rice and potatoes, should be covered under the lid with a cloth which will absorb the steam that might otherwise fall back to make the vegetables sodden.

PLANNING VEGETABLES FOR A MEAL

In planning the main portion one rule is invalid. potatoes, rice and spaghetti should never appear in the same meal, because they are too similar. When two vegetables are to be served, one should be green, like asparagus or string beans, and one of more plebeian character, like onions or beets.

METHODS OF COOKING VEGETABLES
TO BOIL

Wash, pare, peel or scrape the vegetables, cut into pieces of convenient size, cover with boiling salted water, using 1 teaspoonful of salt to 1 pint of water. Cook until tender, drain and dry.

Great loss of food substance in the water in which vegetables are cooked, including starch, protein and mineral salts, all of which are valuable in the diet. The water in which vegetables have been boiled should be used for soups, sauces, etc.

2. Steaming—Better method than boiling because the loss of food material is much less.

3. Baking—Best method for vegetables suitable for baking, as there is no loss of food material.

4. Sauteing—Recommended for variety.

5. Scalloping—Recommended for variety.

6. Frying in deep fat—not recommended on account of scarcity of fat.

GENERAL PRINCIPLES UNDERLYING BOILING
VEGETABLES

1. Cook all vegetables uncovered after they reach the boiling point.

    a. To retain color..

    b. To lessen odor of cooking.

    c To allow undesirable compounds to escape in steam.

2. Cook all fresh vegetables in boiling salted water.

ROOTS, LEAVES, STALKS, ETC.

Carrots—Contain no true starch, 25 per cent of pectose gum, etc, 4.5 per cent sugar, 0.5 per cent albuminoids and 89 per cent water. When carrots are boiled they lose over 90 per cent of their nutrient material. This fact suggests that to retain any food value at all, carrots should be cooked in a soup or stew.

Parsnips—3.5 per cent of starch, 5 per cent of sugar, 3.7 per cent of gum pectose, 15 per cent fat, 1.2 per cent of albuminoids and only 82 per cent of water. It loses a large amount of nutrient material in boiling.

Turnips—Contain 92.8 per cent of water, 3 per cent of pectose and extractives. They contain more water than milk. They are of little value except for their flavor and to furnish variety to the bill of fare.

Beets—Are a more important food than any of those just mentioned, for the ordinary garden beet has been cultivated so that it contains from 10 to 15 per cent of cane sugar Beets also contain 2.4 per cent of pectose and more cellulose than the other roots. The addition of vinegar to boiled beets helps to soften the cellulose and it is said does not interfere with the digestion of the other carbohydrates. After beets are boiled they contain only 3 per cent sugar.

Leaves and Stalks—As celery, lettuce, etc., though they contain over 90 per cent water, yet their value should not be overlooked, for the gluten and starch which they contain are often in such a condition that they can be readily assimilated Prominent among foods of this class should be mentioned the cabbage, cauliflower and kale.

Cabbage—Contains 5.8 per cent of carbohydrates, 1 8 per cent of nitrogenous matter and 1.3 per cent of mineral matter, but when cooked the per cent of water is increased to 94.4 per cent and other constituents decrease in like proportion. (In general, it may be said that the effect of cooking is greatly diminished in the amount of nutrients in this class of foods)

CREAMED VEGETABLES

Use potatoes, turnips, celery, onion, cabbage, cauliflower, beets, parsnips, salsify, brussels, sprouts, carrots, etc.

Make a white sauce, using equal portions fat and flour or two tablespoonfuls to one cup hot milk, melt fat, stir flour into it until it makes a smooth paste, add hot milk and salt and pepper to taste, and stir constantly until it thickens.

One-half as much cornstarch may be used for thickening instead of flour.

Put a layer of vegetables and a layer of cream sauces until the baking of casserole is full. Cover top with buttered bread crumbs and brown in oven. Grated cheese may be added between the layers when vegetables which do not have strong flavors are used.

VEGETABLE SOUFFLES

These dishes are a good way to combine eggs and vegetables. If made with the green-shelled legumes (peas, beans, soy beans or cow-peas) they may be considered meat savers Corn starch or rice flour should be used for thickening sauces. Use half as much as you would of wheat flour.

1   A thick sauce made with ¼ cup fat, ¼ cup flour and 1 cup liquid, which may be milk (whole or skim), cream, meat stock or the water in which vegetables have been cooked

2.   One cup thick vegetable pulp made by draining cooked vegetables and then mashing them or putting them through a sieve

3   Three eggs, the whites and yolks beaten separately.

4.   Flavoring, salt, pepper, onion juice and any one of the following may be used: Very finely chopped parsley, chives, or one-eighth teaspoon curry powder. Mix the vegetables, pulp, seasoning sauce, and well-beaten egg yolks. Carefully fold in the well-beaten egg whites of the eggs, put into a buttered baking dish and bake in a slow oven until firm. Serve immediately.

The amount of vegetables in this dish may be increased by serving vegetables around the souffle.

VEGETABLE FRITTERS

Mash cooked vegetables, such as salsify, parsnips, carrots, etc., season with butter substitute, salt and pepper, shape into small flat, round cakes, roll in flour and saute in vegetable oil or substitute for butter.

SCALLOPED CORN

2	cups or 1 can corn,	2	tbsp. fat.
1	tsp. salt,	½	cup crumbs,
1	cup milk,	1	tbsp. fat,
⅛	tsp. pepper,		Speck salt.

Mix the corn, milk, seasonings and the melted fat.

Place in greased baking dish with buttered crumbs over top and bake in moderate oven until crumbs are brown.

To prepare crumbs, melt butter substitute, stir the crumbs into it and add salt.

SAUTED CORN

Cut boiled sweet corn from cob and saute in vegetable oil or fat.

SOY BEAN FRITTERS

Soy bean meal may be made into fritters and sauted.

POTATOES

Eat More Potatoes and Save Wheat

Our Government asks us to eat potatoes to save wheat. We have large crops this year. One small potato—3 oz.—contains as much starch as a slice of bread. (Farmers' Bulletin 871.)

The following tables give comparative food value of wheat and potato.

Potato
- Protein, 2.5%
- Carbohydrates, 18 to 20% (starch)
- Almost no fat
- Ash, 1%
- Water, 75 to 79%

¼ cup whole wheat=100 calories.
1¼ medium-sized potatoes=100 calories.

Wheat
- Protein, 13.8%
- Carbohydrates, 71.9%
- Ash, 1%
- Water, 11.4%
- Fats, 1 9%

1¼ medium-sized potatoes equal in food value to ¼ cup whole wheat (Lab. Manuel-Rose).

Potatoes in their simplest forms baked and boiled make a good dish for luncheon or dinner. But there are numerous ways in which they may be prepared which gives pleasing variety.

A potato is done when a fork will pierce easily.

POTATOES AU GRATIN (see Cheese)

POTATO BREAD (see Breads)

Potatoes diced may be used in all meat stews, such as chicken, pork, rabbit, mutton, etc

SAUTED POTATOES (Raw)

Peel and slice thin the raw potatoes, have in skillet hot 1½ tbsp. of fat Mazola or other vegetable oil. Put in potatoes, cover tighty, stir often with thin knife or spatula to keep from burning. Serve very hot. The left over cold potatoes may be treated in the same way, taking less time to prepare. Cold potatoes may also be diced and put into hot cream sauce with chopped parsley

SARATOGA POTATOES

Slice potatoes thin. A pretty effect is to slice around and round in form of shavings. Let stand in very cold water for ½ hour; a bit of alum added to water will make them firm. Let drain, wipe dry with soft towel. Fry a few at a time in deep kettle of fat, take up into hot dish with wire basket or perforated skimmer when light brown. Serve hot.

RICED POTATOES

Riced potatoes are very pleasing; simply press the mashed potatoes through potato ricer. Mashed potatoes put into pudding dish with cheese or Mazola smoothed over and browned in oven are very nice.

FRENCH FRIED

Wash, peel and cut potatoes into lengthwise sections about ½ in. thick, dry between soft towel, fry a few at a time in deep vegetable oil, drain on paper, sprinkle with salt. Serve very hot with meat sausage; especially nice for breakfast or luncheon

MASHED POTATOES

May be delicious or impalatable—"why not the former?"

Pare potatoes carefully, let stand for short time in cold water, drain and put in stew kettle with sufficient boiling water to cover. Cook till thoroughly done, drain, let stand a moment uncovered on fire to dry. Mash thoroughly, beat till creamy with a little hot cream or milk and salt and Mazola or other butter substitute. Serve hot.

SCALLOPED POTATOES

Peel and slice raw potatoes, cover baking dish with vegetable fat, put in layer of potatoes, salt, pepper, a little Mazola and minced onion if liked Sprinkle over a little rice flour or powdered arra-root. Another layer of potatoes, etc, until the dish is filled Pour over a good thin cream sauce and bake ¾ hour.

POTATOES SAUTED

Boil, skin, brown in fat, sprinkle with salt.

STUFFED POTATOES

6 potatoes,	⅓ cup milk,
½ tsp. salt,	¼ lb grated cheese,
¼ tsp. pepper,	1 egg, if desired.

Select medium-sized potatoes. Wash well, dry, bake in hot oven about ¾ hour or until soft. Remove from oven and at once slice off top or cut in half, but do not otherwise break skin. Scoop out inside with spoon, mash, add salt, pepper, hot milk, beat in grated cheese and egg Return to shell, bake 10 minutes.

Boiled potatoes may be mashed and prepared same way and piled as a cone on dish and baked 10 to 15 minutes.

Mary Sherzer.

SWEET POTATOES GEORGIAN STYLE

Season mashed boiled sweet potatoes with butter substitute, salt, pepper and sherry wine Moisten with cream or milk and beat 5 minutes, put in a greased baking dish, leaving a rough surface Pour over a syrup made of boiling two tablespoons of molasses and one teaspoonful fat 5 minutes. Bake until delicately browned.

Notes: Eat skins of Irish and sweet potatoes, as they contain "growth determiners" or vitamines.

Boil potatoes with skins on them—this saves waste.

Apply this note to above recipes Vary recipes by always seasoning with common sense.

Mashed potatoes may be used in place of biscuit crust in making meat pies.

Sweet potatoes may be used in much the same way as white potatoes

SPINACH

Use one-fourth peck of spinach, remove roots, carefully pick over (discarding wilted leaves) and wash under running water to free from all grains of sand Put in a stew pan, allow to heat gradually and boil 25 minutes or until tender in its own juice. Drain thoroughly, chop finely, reheat and season with 3 tablespoonfuls butter substitute, salt and pepper. Form in pleasing shape on serving dish and garnish with slices of hard cooked egg.

CORN FRITTERS

1	cup flour,	2	rounded tsp. baking powder,
½	cup milk.	1	tsp. salt,
2	eggs,	⅛	tsp pepper,
1	tbsp. Mazola,	1	cup grated or chopped corn.

Sift flour, baking powder, salt and pepper into bowl, add milk, well beaten eggs, Mazola and grated corn, or if canned corn is used put it through meat chopper, and mix well and fry in deep hot vegetable oil.

Milk

The world is desperately hard up for butter and milk. For small children nothing can take the place of milk and butter; they die if they don't get them. For grown folks they are next to meat.

Milk from the cow is almost a complete food Skim milk is nearly the same in food value as lean meat. One quart of milk has more fuel value than half a pound of good beefsteak, and more than eight eggs. Milk contains vitamines and much lime, which makes it a food for growing children.

Before the war we had a hard problem to get milk enough. Now we are sending ten times as much condensed milk to Europe as we did five years ago.

Our Allies have been killing their dairy cattle for food to an alarming extent. They had to because they needed the meat and were short of cattle feed.

Our own dairy herds are less than they were as some have been slaughtered because of the high cost of feed—and because farm hands are scarce to milk the cows.

Milk is too valuable to waste Give it to the children to drink, or if you give them skim milk, give plenty of butter to match it up. Drink SKIM MILK, use it in cooking.

If it sours it is still good for cooking or for making cottage cheese.

Don't let a drop of milk be wasted.

Until the school age, milk may well be the main part of the diet. Give children milk, which is good for them, instead of coffee and tea, which destroys their appetites, makes them nervous and does not nourish them. If a child refuses plain milk, serve the milk combined with bread or cereal, or as milk soups, junkets, custards, cocoa, etc. It is almost impossible to give any other food in place of milk to a baby without danger of harm.

Mr. Hoover has distinctly told us that children must have whole milk and butter; these together with fresh fruits and vegetables contain that newly discovered element necessary to bodily growth known as vitamines, and right here let me state that the form of fat most commonly used, lard, is entirely lacking in vitamines. It produces bodily heat, but not life.

¾ lb. of lean round of beef,
8   eggs,
2   lbs. of potatoes,
6   lbs. spinach,
7   lbs. lettuce,
4   lbs. cabbage,
2   lbs. salt codfish,

3   lbs. fresh codfish,
2   lbs. chicken,
4   lbs. beets,
5   lbs turnips,
⅙ lb. butter,
⅓ lb. wheat flour,
⅓ lb. cheese.

MILK AS A LIQUID

Milk coagulates and becomes a solid in the stomach and should not be regarded as a drink but as a food. It should not be swallowed down rapidly, but sipped slowly, as the faster the milk is swallowed the larger the curds in the stomach and the harder to digest. Procure the very best.

There are special methods of varying milk in the diet Taste may be altered by heating or adding seasoning, spices, coffee, cocoa, mineral water.

SOME KINDS OF MILK

Whole
*Koumiss
*Buttermilk

Modified
*Lactic acid

* These milks are good in digestive disturbances as the lactic acid bacteria (flavorable bacteria) destroy the putrifactive bacteria, which are harmful bacteria, which produce a disturbance called intestinal intoximia. This comes when the food remains in the intestines for a long time.

FOOD FOR YOUR CHILDREN

Help your child to grow big and strong

Uncle Sam is determined to save our babies America has been startled by the physical defects of the young manhood revealed by the selective draft and, therefore, the government has started a campaign to free the rising generation from like disability. It is a startling fact that according to records the soldier has seven times more chances for living than an American baby during the first year of its life.

The most desirable foods for children are milk, eggs, beefsteak, mutton chop, roast lamb and chicken, baked, boiled or steamed vegetables, fruits, custards, junket, rice pudding, tapioca, gelatine, milk, water, cocoa.

The following should not be given to children: Dried or salted fish or meat, fried or sauted foods, raw vegetables, fresh and rich preserves, tea, coffee, or alcoholic drinks.

Here's Good Food for a Real Youngster's Day

A good breakfast to start him off. Milk, corn meal mush, apple sauce. It makes him fit for school and fit for play.

MILK, and plenty of it, makes him grow—a quart each day if you can. Put it on his cereal and in his soup. Make it into puddings or custards for him. Try the recipes on the next page and watch him smile.

WHOLE milk is best, of course, but skim milk is good if there is a little butter in his meals. Cottage cheese is good, too.

NO COFFEE OR TEA—not even a taste. Leave them for the grown-ups. Milk, cocoa, not too strong, and fruit juices are the drinks for children, and plenty of water always.

FRUIT they enjoy, and they need it, too; baked apples, apple sauce, thoroughly ripe bananas, prunes, oranges, etc. Give them vegetables, fresh or canned. Plenty of fruits and vegetables tend to prevent constipation. Use proper food and do not depend upon laxatives.

OTHER FOODS a child needs: Whole wheat bread, not too fresh corn bread, well-cooked oatmeal, corn meal, rice. They help make strong boys and girls. Some fats, butter or margarine or meat fats on his bread or in gravies. An egg, perhaps, particularly if he doesn't get his full quart of milk, or he can have a little meat or fresh fish, but he does not need much

SWEETS are good for them—the right kinds at the right time Dates, raisins, stewed fruits, simple puddings, sugar cookies are better than candy Give them at meal times.

Betweeen meals let them have bread and butter, a cracker or fruit They won't spoil the appetite, and candy will.

PLAN MEALS LIKE THESE

Here are two sets of the right kind for your youngster. Grown people will like them, too. If sometimes these seem too much work, bread and milk alone will make a good meal.

BREAKFAST

No. 1
Apple sauce,
Oatmeal with milk,
Milk to drink.

No. 2
Stewed prunes,
Cocoa (weak),
Toast and butter.

DINNER

No. 1
Stew, with carrots, potatoes,
    and a little meat,
Whole wheat bread,
Creamy rice pudding,
Milk to drink

No. 2
Fish, with white sauce,
Spinach or any greens,
Corn bread,
Milk to drink.

SUPPER

No. 1
Cream of bean soup,
Crackers and jam,
Milk.

No. 2
Baked potato,
Apple Betty,
Milk.

Your Child Must Have the Best of Foods

GOOD DISHES FOR CHILDREN

These dishes are good for children and grown-ups, too. The recipes provide enough for a family of five.

MILK-VEGETABLE SOUPS

1   qt. milk,
2½ tbsp. flour,
2   tbsp. butter or margarine
    or other fat,
1   tsp salt,

2 cups thoroughly cooked vegetables, finely chopped, mashed or put through a sieve. Spinach, peas, beans, potatoes, or asparagus make good soups.

Stir flour into melted fat and mix with the cold milk. Add the cooked vegetables and stir over the fire until thickened. If soup is too thick, add a little water or milk.

RICE PUDDINGS

1   qt. milk,
⅓ cup rice,
⅓ cup sugar,
½ cup raisins or chopped
    dates,

½ tsp. salt,
⅛ tsp ground nutmeg or cinnamon.

Wash the rice, mix all together and bake three hours in a very slow oven, stirring now and then at first This may be made on top of the stove in a double boiler, or in a fireless cooker. Any coarse cereal may be used in place of rice

For more suggestions send to the U. S. Department of Agriculture for Farmers' Bulletin, "Food for Young Children " It tells more about feeding children and the reasons why right food is so important. It shows every mother how to give her children their chance in life

U. S. Food Leaflet No 7.

Reference, Holts' "The Care of Feeding Children."

Mrs. Rose, "Feeding the Family."

Sauces

To make good sauce is to be master of an art. It requires great care and attention to the smallest detail A sauce is intended as an accompaniment to meat, fish, vegetables or dessert with which it is served, and should be in perfect harmony with it. It should never be so prominent in flavoring as to overbalance the flavor of the food. Certain sauces are associated with certain particular foods. Mint sauce with lamb, caper sauce with mutton, cranberry sauce with turkey, and Hollandaise sauce with fish. Color adds to the attractiveness of a sauce and may be obtained by the addition of browned flour, caramel or fruit vegetable juices

GENERAL RULES FOR MIXING

The thickening material must be separated by mixing with either fat, cold liquid or sugar before heat is applied. Use an equal amount of fat, double amount of liquid, double amount or sugar. Either the thickening material is cold, the liquid is hot, or the thickening material is hot and the liquid is cold. When the two parts of the sauce are mixed the sauce must be stirred until it thickens. Mix the salt with the flour

METHODS OF MIXING

1. Hygienic—Mix the thickening material with the cold liquid, stir into the heated liquid. Stir until the starch is cooked 3-5 minutes over direct heat, 15-20 minutes in double boiler when milk is used. Add butter just before serving.

2. American—Mix thickening material with fat. Heat liquid and stir into it the thickening material. Cooked as the first method

3. French—Heat the fat and stir into the thickening material Add the cold liquid and cook 3-5 minutes over direct heat.

STARCHY SAUCES

Ingredients	Liquid	Thickening	Seasoning	Flavoring	Use
PROPORTIONS	1 cup milk	1 tbsp. flour	½ tsp. salt	1 tbsp. butter substitute	cream soups
	1 cup milk	2 tbsp. flour	½ tsp. salt	1½ tbsp. butter substitute	creamed or scalloped dishes or gravies
	1 cup milk	3 tbsp. flour	½ tsp. salt	2 tbsp. butter substitute	soufflés
	½ cup milk	4 tbsp. flour	½ tsp. salt	2½ tbsp. butter substitute	croquettes
KINDS	1 cup water 1 cup veg. sub. " 1 cup meats " 1 cup milk 1 cup cream 1 cup vinegar	1 tbsp. flour or 1½ tbsp. browned flour for light brown or 2 tbsp. browned flour for dark brown	salt pepper sugar bay leaf cloves mustard celery salt onion salt	butter or meat fat	with meat, vegetables or cheese
	1 cup water 1 cup fruit 1 cup milk 1 cup cream	1 tbsp. flour ¾ tbsp. corn-starch	cinnamon cloves nutmeg	butter sugar extracts	with puddings

CREAM SOUPS

Use equal portions of sauce and stock with pulp of cooked food This is obtained by pressing through a sieve. Combine and reheat.

CREAMED DISHES

Use equal portions of sauce and food to be creamed. Pour the sauces over the food and reheat, if necessary, in double boiler.

SCALLOPED DISHES

Use equal portions of sauce and food. Place alternate layers in a buttered dish Cover with buttered crumbs. Reheat and brown in the oven.

SOUFFLES

Use equal portions of sauce and food with 3 eggs to each cup of sauce Add the egg yolks to the sauce. Mix with the food Fold in the egg whites and bake in buttered baking dish set in a pan of hot water.

CROQUETTES

Use equal portions of sauce and food. Mix and cool. Shape roll in crumbs slightly and add 1 tablespoonful of water or milk

Eggs

The Nature of the Nutrients in eggs is of almost as much interest and importance as their amount. The fact that when an egg is kept at a proper temperature for about three weeks, without the addition of anything from without, it produces a chick so well developed as to begin to walk and eat the same food as the adult, suggests at once that the egg must contain substances which are very efficient as sources both of the energy and the materials for growth and development. Children from one year to twelve years should not be deprived of the growth-determining substances, namely, vitamines in eggs and milk and butter; eggs contain the iron for the anemic.

7-8 eggs=1 pound of meat of food value

See effect of heat on protein

Eggs are used as

1. A meat substitute.
2. A flavor.
3. A leavening agent.
4. A thickening agent.
5. A clarifying agent.

Cookery of Eggs.

1. As leavening agents.

The egg white of a beaten egg is full of air bubbles surrounded by the cell wall of protein. The air is a gas and expands with heat, thus making the substance (as in cake) light.

2. Thickening agent.

Heat coagulates the protein of the egg, thus forming a thickened mass (as in custards). Egg as a thickening agent is equal to 1 tablespoonful cornstarch

3. Eggs act both as a leavening and flavor in quick breads They can be omitted in these foods. The flavor may be omitted when eggs are high by using good brands of desiccated or powdered egg.

4. As a clarifying agent. The albumen surrounds and coagulates around the coffee grain, making coffee grain heavy, and it settles to the bottom of the pot in which it is cooking.

Note: Add a speck of salt to egg white; it toughens the protein (albumin) just a little and makes it beat up better.

Percentage Composition:

White:
- Water ____ ____76.2%
- Protein ____ ____12 3%
- Fat _____ .2%
- Ash _____ 6%

Yolk:
- Water _____ ____45.5%
- Protein ____ ____15.7%
- Fat _____33.3%
- Ash _____ ____ 1 1%

Mineral matter or ash: Sulphur, phosphorus, hydrogen, sulphide The blueish-green coating around the yolk of a hard cooked egg is due to the mineral matter. Because of the mineral matter (bone and nerve building materials) eggs are good for growing children They contain all the necessary elements in the right proportion for growth.

Testing Eggs:

A good fresh egg
1. Has a rough shell.
2. Is clear when held to a light.
3. Sinks in water.
4. Has no sound of movement when shaken

Methods of Preservation:

1. Coating shell (paraffine).
2. Putting eggs in lime water.
3. Putting eggs in brine.
4. Packing in bran or salt.
5 Water glass solution
6. Cold storage. 30-40° F.

Note: Eggs in water glass have been known to keep 3½ months and taste just as good as fresh eggs.

Methods of Cooking Eggs:

Soft Eggs.

1. Soft boiled: place egg in boiling water, cover and remove to place where water will keep hot, but not boil, 8-10 minutes. 180° F., 87° C.

2. Put in boiling water and boil vigorously from 2-3 minutes. (This toughens protein; is not a good method.)

3. Put egg on in cold water and bring to a boil and egg is done.

Hard Eggs.

1. Place egg in boiling water and remove to warm place for 40 minutes (double boiler).

2. Put eggs on in cold water and boil 30 minutes (not a good method).

Note: Place egg after cooking in cold water, this allows the egg to shrink from shell and lining.

Always wash eggs before breaking open or cooking. The shells are dirty and covered with bacteria

RECIPE FOR WATER GLASS

    ½ part syrup of Calcium Silicate,
10   parts water

BREAD OMELET

3 eggs,	¾ tsp. salt,
½ cup milk,	⅓ tsp pepper,
½ cup crumbs,	1 tbsp. oleo.

Soak bread in milk, add beaten egg yolks and seasonings. Fold in beaten whites, cook and serve as plain omelet

Anna Jensen,
St Joseph, Mo

DRIED EGGS

The method of using the dried egg is very simple. One slightly rounded tablespoonful is equivalent to one average-sized egg. This amount soaked for half an hour in 3 tablespoonfuls of water may be used in place of one egg The egg will soften up more easily and be ready more quickly if stirred with fork at intervals.

Substituting on this basis, one may use dried eggs in any recipe for cakes, cookies, muffins, custard, cooked salad dressings, etc., in which the whites and yolks are not separated. The following ways of using dried eggs are suggested.

SCRAMBLED EGGS

4 tbsp. dried eggs soaked in	¼ can milk,
¾ cup water,	Salt,
1 tbsp. butter sub.,	Pepper.

Soak egg and beat well, add milk, salt and pepper and cook in the hot fat. This amount serves four people. The food value will be increased if the egg is soaked in one cup of skim milk

CUSTARDS

Custards are combinations of milk and egg sweetened and flavored. Because of the protein present they should be cooked at a low temperature. This is accomplished by steaming or by baking in molds set in pans of water. Custards are classified according to the method of preparation. There are two kinds, steamed and baked.

To Combine a Steamed Custard scald the milk and pour it over the egg which has been beaten with the sugar and salt. Return the mixture to the double boiler and steam, stirring constantly until done Add the flavoring just before removing from the fire

To Combine a Baked Custard, beat the egg with the sugar and salt. Add the cold milk and flavoring. Pour into molds and set in pans of water and bake until done.

To Test a Steamed Custard, lift the spoon from the mixture. If the spoon is coated the custard is done.

To Test a Baked Custard, insert a knife. If it comes out clean the custard is done

SOFT CUSTARD

2   tbsp. dried eggs soaked in   1¼ cups milk,
⅓ cup water for 20-30 min.   ¼ cup (4 tbsp.) honey or syrup,
     or 1-2 eggs,   Flavoring.

Add the syrup to the milk; beat in double boiler, and when hot, add the egg well soaked and beaten. Stir while cooking, and when custard has thickened, strain it so that any particles of dried egg not soluble will be removed. It will be found that the amount of insoluble matter is very little greater than in a custard made with fresh eggs.

BAKED CUSTARD

2   tbsp. (slightly rounded) of   1   cup milk,
     dried eggs soaked with   ¼ cup honey or syrup,
⅓ cup water, or 2 eggs,   Flavoring.

Combine as in the soft custard, strain, add flavoring and bake in an earthenware or granite baking dish in a slow oven until "set." Attractive when baked in ramekins and served individually

COMPARISON FATS AND OILS

Kind	Price	Source	Physical Characteristics	Melting Point	Decomposition Point	Use
Butter	50c per lb.	cream	golden yellow	40°c	60°c	seasoning, shortening, table use
Renovated butter	45c to 50c per lb.	rancid butter	deep yellow	37°c	108°c	shortening, butter substitute
Oleomargarine	35c per lb.	veg. fat, lard, butter, milk or cream	more porous than butter	47°c	115°c	seasoning, butter substitute
Lard	28c per lb.	animal	grayish white creamy solid	36°c	170°c	shortening, frying, sauteing
Cottolene		beef fat, cottonseed oil	translucent solid	38°c	200°c	frying, sauteing, shortening
Snow drift		cottonseed oil, bf. fat, hog fat	white smooth creamy solid	50°c	160°c	frying, sauteing, shortening
Crisco	22c per lb.	vegetable fat hydrozen	white smooth solid	45°c		frying, sauteing, shortening
Olive oil		olive fat	straw colored liquid	18°c		salad dressing frying
Wesson oil		refined cottonseed oil	greenish yellow liquid	20°c		substitute for olive oil in salad dressing
Peanut oil		oil from c'shd peanuts	yellowish	Begins solid-ifying at 0°c		substitute for butter in cooking
Mazola	25c to 26c per lb. $1.10 per gal.	germ of corn grain	golden yellow			substitute for olive oil in salad dressing and frying
Troco	35c per lb.	cocoanut oil corn	white, solid			oleomargarine

Fats and Butter Substitutes

Note: Dairy butter has food value vital to children, therefore use it on the table as usual. Use vegetable oils, as olive, cotton seed and corn oil. Save daily one-third of an ounce of animal fat. Waste no soap, it contains fat and the glycerine necessary for explosives. You can make scrubbing soap at home, and in some localities you can sell your saved fats to the soap maker, who will thus save our needed glycerine.

U. S Food Administration.

HOW TO SAVE FATS

Bab Bell,

**Extension Assistant Professor of Home Economics,
Missouri University**

Fats are derived from two sources—animal and vegetable. Animal, such as lard, butter, cream, beef fat, mutton fat and poultry fat. Vegetables, such as corn, cotton seed, olive, peanut, cocoanut, soy bean and sesame oils.

Formerly more animal fats than vegetable fats have been used. Butter and lard were plentiful, accessible and in convenient form for household use. The average housekeeper depended upon them to the exclusion of all other forms of fat. Since there is a shortage in these particular fats, housekeepers must learn (1) to economize in the use of these by cutting down the amount of fat used; (2) to substitute wherever possible vegetable fats in place of animal fats.

Since the conservation of fats in the home is a very important means of increasing the supply needed for exportation and home use, it becomes imperative that housewives should have a thorough knowledge concerning their composition, food value, digestibility, uses in cookery and general rules for conservation.

COMPOSITION OF FATS

	Water	Protein	Fat	Carbohydrate	Ash	Fuel Value per pound in calories
Butter	11.	1.	85		3.	3605
Oleomargarine	9.5	1.2	83		6.3	3525
Beef Fat	13.7	4.7	84		.3	3540
Suet (Rendered)			100			4220
Lard			100			4220
Poultry fat (Rendered)			100			4220
Cottonseed Oil			100			4220
Corn Oil			100			4220
Peanut Oil			100			4220
Olive Oil			100			4220

Food Value: From this table the comparative food value of fats in general is seen It should be remembered that fat yields two and one-fourth times as much energy for the body as equal weights of carbohydrates or protein. More and more is the importance of fat in the diet being recognized Thirty per cent of the total number of calories needed in the diet should be furnished by fat. In the ordinary diet this is approximately four table-spoonfuls or one-fourth cup.

The digestibility of fat is of more importance, especially when making substitutions. Generally speaking, animal fats and vegetable fats are equally digestible Recent investigations have shown that there is very little difference in the digestibility of fats that have a melting point below body temperature. While the eating of large quantities of fat may retard the digestion of food, it is unlikely that any serious discomfort will be felt if it is prepared intelligently. Fats in general are completely digested, but require a longer time than most foods.

Butter: Butter is the most widely used of all fats It has been estimated that from 17 to 18 pounds per person are consumed yearly. There are many good and wholesome butter substitutes on the market which may be used both for cooking and table use. However, if these are used exclusively in the feeding of children, care should be used that the supply of whole milk should not be decreased Whole milk and butter contain certain substances essential to growth which are entirely lacking or present in small quantities in butter substitutes.

Oleomargarine: Oleomargarine is a name given to butter substitutes made by churning fats other than butter with milk or cream. The principal fats usually used in the manufacture of oleomargarine are oleo oil made of beef fat and neutral lard made of leaf and cotton seed oil Oleomargarine is a good, wholesome product, and there should be no objection to its use if it is properly labeled The best grades of oleomargarine contain nearly one-third as much of the growth-promoting substances (vitamines) as butter does.

Beef Fat: Beef fat is harder than lard and has a more pronounced flavor For these reasons it is not used extensively in cooking. However, in certain dishes, finely chopped unrendered suet is used, and in some countries drippings from the cooked beef or rendered beef suet are used in place of butter on bread

Suet alone is of a hard consistency, but a good and satisfactory compound may be had by mixing cotton seed oil, corn oil, etc., with suet   Mix one part of oil with two or three parts of rendered suet. If ½ cup of skim milk be added to 1 cup of suet before rendering, the flavoring is improved. In summer, suet may be added to lard in small amounts in order to have a harder fat.

Lard: Lard is one of the most commonly used animal fats. It is made from the fat of hogs and heretofore has been plentiful and comparatively cheap   Owing to the fact that most women are in the habit of using lard, it is somewhat difficult to accustom them to the use of vegetable oils and fats.

Cotton Seed Oil: Cotton seed oil is obtained from the seeds of the cotton plant. One ton of seeds yields 50 gallons of oil   Preparations made of cotton seed oil are sold in the liquid form, Wesson oil being a typical example. In addition, cotton seed oil is treated chemically to form hard fats, such as Snow Drift, White Cliff, Crisco, etc   All of these compounds have been found to be good and wholesome products. Combinations of cotton seed oil and animal fats are also on the market   The label on all packages gives the ingredients.

Corn Oil: This oil, which is made from corn, has only lately come into general use for food purposes   It is a wonderful substitute for olive oil   Has a good flavor. May be used in all kinds of cooking

Peanut Oil: The oil made from peanuts is comparatively new in this country, since peanuts have been disposed of in other ways Its use in cookery is very limited at the present time.

Olive Oil: Olive oil is prepared from the olive fruit, and is one of the oldest oils now in use. The flavor depends upon the variety of olive, ripeness when picked, manner of handling, length of time of storage, etc. The extensive use of olive oil is due to its flavor. Olive oil has no more food value than the other oils   Its high price is due to its flavor alone.

All fats have advanced in price, yet a great saving may be accomplished by investigating the available fats on the market, their composition and their prices. As a general rule fats are less expensive when purchased in large quantities   A decided saving may be made by purchasing both oils in gallon receptacles and harder fats in corresponding amounts.

Many commercial fats are sold with the statement that one-third less may be used than lard. This statement is somewhat misleading. One fat should be substituted for another according to its composition. All 100 per cent fats given in the table on the composition of fats may be used interchangeably. Approximately seven-eighths as much of these fats will substitute for butter and oleomargarine.

Savory Fats: Savory fats may be made when undesirable flavors are to be eliminated. Usually strong seasonings, such as thyme, sage, marjoram, summer savory, bay leaves or onions are added to unrendered fats, having pronounced odors or flavors like those of beef or mutton.

These seasonings mask the strong original flavors Render in a double boiler and strain carefully through a cloth so that all bits of herb are removed. Adding salt after rendering improves the flavor.

Savory fats may also be prepared from rendered fats by adding the seasonings, heating the mixture and straining.

Fats with strong flavors, such as suet and mutton fat, may be improved by heating with water, milk, or charcoal. If charcoal is used, all pieces may be removed by straining through a heavy cloth.

Care of Fats: All fats which are to be stored for some time should be protected from heat, light and air, in order to prevent them from becoming rancid. Keep in tightly covered receptacles and in a cool, dark place.

In summer time scraps of fat which are saved should be rendered promptly to prevent them from becoming rancid. It is also important in rendering or clarifying fats that all moisture be driven off, since molds are very apt to grow if fats contain moisture.

Keep butter, oleomargarine and other butter substitutes in a cool place away from food having strong odors, since odors are readily absorbed by these fats. Store the oils in closed cans or bottles wrapped in paper in a cool place—the refrigerator is preferable.

How to Render Fats: Chop in small pieces or put through a meat chopper, heat in a double boiler until all the fat has melted. The use of a double boiler prevents too high a temperature. If fat is over-heated it will become rancid. Strain through a cloth, heat again to sterilize and drive off moisture.

How to Clarify Fats: Method I: Melt the fat with an equal proportion of water in a double boiler Strain through a cloth When cold remove the layer of fat from the water.

Method II: Follow directions given in I, using sour milk Flavors and odors are modified.

Method III: Follow directions in I, adding several pieces of clean hardwood charcoal. If beef fat is being clarified, the yellow color is removed and a white odorless fat is secured.

In many homes the practice of making soap from drippings, trimmings, etc , has long been the custom. At the present time when fats are so scarce every effort should be made to utilize every particle for good If the scrap jar is watched carefully, no fats will be available for soap making.

Many people are eating more fat than their bodies require This extravagance means that our soldiers and the working people, who need generous amounts of fat, will be denied this necessity If everyone realizes the seriousness of the situation and will cut down on his daily allowance of butter, cream, oil and cooking fat, a large amount of fat will be saved.

SUGGESTIONS FOR FAT CONSERVATION

1. Eat just enough fat to supply body needs. Thirty per cent of the total number of calories in the ration is sufficient, or four level tablespoons.

2. Leave no fat on the plate This means fat from meat as well as butter.

3. Use pure butter on the table, especially for children, but sparingly for cooking.

4. Do not use it in cooking

5. Peanut butter, jellies, or nut and fig paste are excellent substitutes.

6. Use vegetable fats (made solid by treating commercially with hydrogen).

7. Use vegetable oils for frying and salad dressings

8. Make gravies to conserve the flavor of the extractives and the food value fats from meats

9. Keep all rinds of bacon and salt pork Use as seasonings when cooking cabbage, greens, vegetables, soups, etc.

10. Save all trimmings from beef, pork, mutton and fowl. Render and use in cooking.

11. Keep a small jar for bits of fats, drippings or gristles When a sufficient amount has been collected, render the contents.

WAR BUTTER

How to make 2¼ pounds of butter out of 1 pound. of ½ pound.

1 lb butter,	1 tbsp. gelatine.
1 pt. rich milk,	

Method No. 1. Cream butter Put small amount cold milk with gelatine Heat rest, pour over soaked gelatine. Add to butter, heat until it begins to thicken, place on platter by spoonful to thicken. 1 pound makes 2¼ pounds.

½ lb butter,	½ lb whole milk.
1 tsp. salt,	

Method No. 2. Churn 2 minutes. Can be done with mason jar and spoon beater, ice cream freezer, Daisy churn.

PASTRY

Use little pastry when you do make pies, use one crust instead of two.

Try the New England deep apple pie, with only one top crust

Use the vegetable fats instead of animal fats in making pastry

If vegetable oils are used the quantity of fat may be reduced by one-third; that is 2¾ tablespoonfuls of oil to 1 cup of flour is sufficient. The oil itself helps to moisten the flour so that very little water is necessary. The dough should be made as dry as possible to make a tender pastry.

U. S. Food Administration.

CONSERVATION OF PIE CRUST
CORN MEAL CRUST

Grease a pie plate well Cover with raw corn meal, giving the plate a rotating motion so that an even layer of the meal will

stick to the plate about 1/16 of an inch in thickness. Fill the
plate with pumpkin pie mixture Bake in hot oven.

OATMEAL CRUST

2 cups finely ground oatmeal,   1 tsp salt.
1 cup boiling water,

Scald the oatmeal with the water. Add fat and mix thoroughly
Roll very thin and line small pie or tart tins with the mixture
Bake in hot oven. Fill with apricot marmalade or other thick mixture. If desired spread a meringue on top and brown in the
oven.

MEATLESS MINCEMEAT

Another culinary triumph in the art of food conservation has
been brought to the attention of housewives of the country by the
National Emergency Garden Commission as a worthy companion
of pumpkinless pumpkin pies and gingerless ginger bread. The
new mincemeat, officially described as "camouflage," was tried on
500 troops on a transport, who pronounced it perfect and called
for more. Half a package of raisins, half a pound of prunes
stewed with lemon juice and peeled; ¼ cup of sweet cider, 4 tablespoonfuls or brown sugar Chop raisins and prunes together and
the result is said to be a meatless mincemeat pie in accord with
the Food Administration's meatless Tuesday

MOCK MINCEMEAT (No Meat)
To Be Baked in U. S. Food Administration Crust

11 cups chopped green to-   2 cups water,
      matoes,   5 cups brown sugar,
 7 cups chopped apples,   ½ cup suet,
1½ cups vinegar,   1 tsp salt.
 2 packages raisins,
 2 tbsp mixed spices (allspice, cloves, cinnamon and nutmeg),

Grind tomatoes, add salt, drawn over night through bag. Mix
all ingredients and cook slowly for 2½ hours

Note: Best results are obtained by using fireless cooker, and
cooking 6 or 7 hours   Mrs R J Winters.

BRER RABBIT OLE SOUTH MOLASSES PIE
A Southern Pie That Will Make Any Cook Proud

1 Boil 2 cups of Brer Rabbit Molasses and 1 tablespoonful of
butter.

2 Break 4 eggs in bowl or pan; add pinch salt; beat until well mixed.

3 Pour the molasses over the eggs, stirring briskly.

4. Have pie pans lined with crust. Pour in and bake. This makes two pies If you wish to make but one pie, equally divide the ingredients.

PREPARATION AND PROPERTIES OF SOAP AND EQUATIONS SHOWING THE REACTIONS

Natural fats and oils are essentially mixtures of stearin, palmitin and olein Beef and mutton fat are chiefly stearin, lard is mainly palmitin and olein, and while oils, such as olive, are chiefly olein, stearin and palmitin are solids at the ordinary temperature, but olein is a liquid.

Tallow is chiefly stearin, but human fat and palm oil are largely palmitin. The soft and liquid fats and oils contain considerable olein as a rule. The proportion of the olein determines the consistency of the fats and oils Thus olive oil contains 72 per cent of olein (and a similar fat) and about 28 per cent of stearin and palmitin.

Butter consists of fats corresponding to the following acids· palmitic, stearic, oleic, butyric, capric and caproic. The last three, together with traces of other substances, give butter its pleasant flavor. Oleomargarine and other substitutes for butter resemble real butter very closely in composition.

$C_3H_3(OH)_3$.

Glycerine is a thick, sweet liquid. It is used to make nitroglycerine. It is also used as a solvent, a lubricator, a preservation for certain foods as a sweetening substance in certain preserves and candy

Glycerine is a by-product in the manufacture of soap. Glycerine is an alcohol and for this reason is often called glycerol when treated with a mixture of concentrated nitric and sulphuric acids it forms nitroglycerine ($C_3H_5(ONO_2)_3$). This is a heavy oily liquid, a well-known explosive and an ingredient of other explosives

When mixed with infusional earth, fire and sand and even sawdust it is known as dynamite.

HARD SOAP

1. Stearin (beef or mutton fat)+Water=glycerine+stearic acid
   Stearic acid+sodium chloride=sodium stearate, or (hard soap)
   +Hydrochloric acid.
2. Stearic acid+sodium hydroxide=hard soap and water.

SOFT SOAP

Stearin (beef or mutton fat) potassium hydroxide=soap and glycerine

HOME METHOD OF MAKING SOAP

Empty the contents of a can of lye into a stone jar, pour over it 2½ pints of cold water and stir until lye dissolves Set aside until the temperature is not over 80° F. or 26 2/3° C Melt 5½ pounds of clean greasy tallow, or lard, and set aside until the temperature is 120° F. or 49° C., slowly pour dissolved lye into the grease, stir until lye and grease are thoroughly combined and mixture drops from stirrer like honey. Stir slowly but not too long, or you may separate the lye; from 5 to 15 minutes is enough, according to grease and weather Pour into a mold, set away for a day or two, empty out and cut up as desired.

SALADS

Vegetable Oils

Salads are divided into two groups, dinner salads and the more substantial salads served at supper and luncheon in the place of meats.

Fruit salads are much out of place in the dinner menu unless they figure as the last course, when they are served with crackers, cheese and coffee. This is an unusual custom that is rapidly growing in popularity Fruit salads are naturally sweet, and when followed by a dessert, the palate is not apt to become clogged with sweet. As a general rule sweets and savories do not mix, although occasionally they may be blended as currant or orange salad with game. These exceptions must, however, be introduced with sparing hands, as they often strike a discordant note.

The heavy salad, swathed with mayonnaise or boiled dressing, is entirely out of place at dinner, because it overloads the menu with fat. Only those salads of green vegetables should be selected, like lettuce, beets and cabbage, tomatoes and cress, asparagus, etc., French dressing with variations alone being suitable.

Heavy salads fit into light luncheon better than into any **other** meals, and may often form the main dish, while a fruit salad is always acceptable in place of dessert.

Salads are of exceeding importance in metabolism.

The green vegetables and fruits contain the so-called inorganic elements as mineral salts, which must exist in the body and take part in functions in at least three different ways: (1) as the constituents which give rigidity and comparative permanence to the skeleton; (2) as essential elements of the protoplasm of the active tissues; (3) as salts held in solution in the fluids of the body, giving these fluids their characteristic influence upon the elasticity and irritability of muscle and nerve supplying the material for the acidity or alkalinity of the digestive juices and other secretions and yet maintaining the neutrality of slight alkalesence of the internal fluids as well as their osmotic pressure and solvent power.

Left over greens, vegetables, string beans, peas, carrots, turnips, cauliflower, cooked spinach, beets and leeks may take their place in the dinner salad. Use them mixed, alone, or as a garnish for lettuce.

The oil used in the salad dressings has much food value. It is a heat and energy producing substance.

MAYONNAISE DRESSING

2 eggs (yolks),
2 cups Mazola oil,
2 tbsp. vinegar,
Juice of 1 lemon,

1 tsp. salt,
1 tsp. mustard,
Dash cayenne

Set the mixing bowl in a pan of chopped ice and have ingredients very cold.

Mix the seasonings and add to the beaten yolks of the eggs. Beat with a small wooden spoon or silver fork. At first add **the** oil drop by drop, beating vigorously. When too thick to beat, add 1 teaspoonful vinegar. Continue to add the oil slowly, alternating with the vinegar and the lemon juice until at least ½ cup of oil has been added. Onion juice may be added if desired.

If the oil is added too rapidly the dressing separates and has a curdled appearance. This should never happen if the oil is added very slowly at first; but in case it does, put the yolk of another egg into a clean bowl and beat in the curdled dressing slowly.

After a half cup of oil has been added the dressing may be beaten with a Dover egg beater and the oil added more rapidly.

NORWEGIAN MAYONNAISE

Add a tablespoonful of anchovy paste to a half pint of mayonnaise dressing, stir in a tablespoonful of tomato catsup, ten drops of Worcestershire sauce and 2 drops of Tabasco. Use with broiled or fried fish.

FRENCH DRESSING

½ tsp. salt,	1 tbsp. vinegar (malt or
⅛ tsp. white pepper,	Tarragon preferred),
Dash paprika,	3 tbsp. Mazola or other veg oil

Mix the seasonings and stir into the oil. Add the vinegar and beat vigorously till the mixture thickens slightly.

Green salads should be dressed at the time of serving. The flavor is improved if the bowl in which the salad is arranged is rubbed with a clove of garlic or slice of onion

A—1 SALAD DRESSING

Mix ⅛ teaspoonful of freshly ground pepper, ½ teaspoonful salt and one teaspoonful of prepared mustard. Then stir in 4 teaspoonfuls of Mazola, and when blended, add 1 tablespoonful of claret.

Serve it on any plain salad of lettuce, or a mixture of lettuce, chives and cucumbers. The lettuce should be washed several times, drained and wrapped in a napkin and laid on the ice until chilled and crisp. Do not slice the cucumbers nor chop the chives until just before serving.

Put the salad into a bowl in any preferred way, the lettuce arranged like an open head with a sprinkling of chives and a border of sliced cucumbers overlapping, or have the cucumbers diced and heaping in the center and the lettuce for a border. Add the dressing when serving, as the vegetables wilt quickly after the dressing is blended with them.

HOLLANDAISE SAUCE

Beat the yolks of 4 eggs and beat in gradually ½ cup Mazola or other vegetable oil. Add ¼ teaspoonful salt, dash of paprika and ½ cup boiling water. Cook over hot water, stirring constantly until thick, adding gradually the juice of ½ lemon. Chill before using Serve with fish. or a fish salad.

SAUCE TARTARE

Make a mayonnaise dressing, using Tarragon vinegar To each cup of dressing add 1 shallot, or small onion, chopped fine, 2 tablespoonfuls each of finely chopped capers, olives and cucumber pickles, 1 tablespoonful chopped parsley and ¼ teaspoonful powdered Tarragon.

GREEN MAYONNAISE

This is used frequently for apple salad, and is made by adding 2 or 3 drops of apple coloring to ordinary mayonnaise, or it may be colored by adding finely chopped parsley rubbed to a paste.

ITALIAN DRESSING

Rub the mixing bowl with a clove of garlic, add the salt, Tabasco sauce, a teaspoonful of tomato catsup and stir until well mixed Add 6 tablespoonfuls of Wessen oil or other vegetable oil, a teaspoonful of grape or Tarragon vinegar; beat thoroughly and pour at once over sliced tomatoes on lettuce leaves. Serve with fried or broiled fish or lobster cutlets.

WALDORF SALAD

2 cups hard tart apples (chopped),	1 cup celery (cut fine),
	1 cup English walnuts (chopped)

Mix with French dressing or mayonnaise dressing made of vegetable oils.

COMBINATION FRUIT SALAD

1 grape fruit,	1 banana,
2 oranges,	1 cup Malaga grapes

Pare the oranges and grape fruit and remove from pulp in sections, slice the banana and cut grapes in half and remove seeds. Mix with ½ cup sugar and set on ice for ½ hour. Arrange on lettuce leaves and put a tablesponful of mayonnaise on the top of each salad.

CHERRY SALAD

Stone carefully large red cherries, arrange them neatly on crisp lettuce leaves, pour over French dressing made of vegetable oil and serve

GRAPE FRUIT SALAD

Pare the grape fruit, remove the white skin, and with a sharp knife take out the carpels, keeping them whole. Dish on Romaine or lettuce leaves, baste with French dressing and serve.

CELERY AND GRAPE FRUIT SALAD

Cut the fruit in thirds lengthwise, remove the pulp and cup up with an equal amount of crisp celery. Refill the shells with this mixture and garnish with celery tips. Serve with mayonnaise dressing.

DATE SALAD

½ lb. dates,
2   slices pineapple,

¼ cup chopped walnuts or pecans.

ORANGE AND SMALL ONION SALAD

Slice oranges and place small slices of tiny onions on the orange. Serve with French dressing.

PINEAPPLE AND CHEESE SALAD

Place large-sized slices of canned pineapple on crisp lettuce leaves and cover pineapple with Star Brand White Cheese or Neufchatel cheese forced through the potato ricer, and serve with French dressing. Garnish with olives or Maraschino cherries.

WHITE SALAD

½ cup chopped celery,
½ cup shredded cabbage,
½ cup nut meats,
2   slices pimento,
2   cups water,

4 tsp. gelatine,
2 tsp. lemon juice,
2 tsp. sugar,
2 tsp. salt.

Make a liquid lemon jelly, add celery, cabbage, nuts and pimentos, mold, serve on white lettuce leaf with white salad dressing In absence of white lettuce, salad may be garnished with parsley, cabbage leaf or celery.

BANANA SALAD

3 bananas,   ½ cup chopped nuts

Peel bananas, cut in halves and fourths and place 2 pieces on crisp lettuce leaves, and sprinkle ground nuts over bananas and serve with mayonnaise dressing.

ASPARAGUS SALAD

Dish a bunch of well-boiled asparagus on a cold platter, pour over French dressing and serve.

STRING BEAN SALAD

Arrange carefully cooked string beans over lettuce leaves Pour over carefully prepared Italian salad dressing and use at once.

CABBAGE SALAD

Cut a hard head of cabbage into halves and then with a cabbage cutter or sharp knife shred fine the desired quantity. Cover with ice water and soak for two hours, changing the water once or twice. At serving time, shake and dry cabbage in a towel, toss it lightly in the salad bowl Pour over a well-made French dressing. Mix thoroughly and serve at once. This is one of the nicest of all the winter dinner salads Chopped celery or celery seed may be added as preferred.

CHIFFONADE SALAD

This salad is made by mixing all green vegetables in season, and is frequently called "The French Salad." Lettuce, dandelion, chicory, a little chopped beet, chopped celery, a bit of tomato are mixed and covered with French dressing. The dressing is usually flavored both with onion and garlic.

BOHEMIAN SALAD

Cover the bottom of the salad bowl with crisp Romaine or lettuce; arrange over the alternate slices of hard-boiled egg and boiled beets. Sprinkle with finely chopped onion, cover with Italian or French dressing, toss and serve

LETTUCE SALAD WITH CHEESE BALLS

2	pkgs. Neufchatel cheese,	2	tbsp. pecans, chopped,
½	tsp. onion juice,	¼	tsp. salt,
2	tbsp. lemon juice,	⅛	tsp paprika
1	tbsp. parsley,		

Mix all the seasonings with the cheese, make into small balls with butter paddles and serve with head lettuce covered with French dressing For variation do not put the parsley into the balls, but chop more of it very fine and roll the balls in it very lightly.

GREEN PEPPER AND PIMENTO CHEESE SALAD

Stuff green peppers with pimento cheese, slice and lay on lettuce leaves, serve with French dressing.

SWEETBREADS SALAD

Plunge a pair of sweetbreads into cold water as soon as they come from the market, and let stand 1 hour. Drain and put into salted boiling water to which has been added ½ tablespoonful of vinegar and cook slowly 20 minutes. Again drain and plunge into cold water, that they may be kept white and firm. Cut in ½-inch cubes and mix with an equal measure of cucumber cut in ½-inch cubes. Season with salt, pepper and paprika and moisten with dressing. Arrange in nests of lettuce leaves. For the dressing beat ½ cup of heavy cream until almost stiff, using an egg beater. Add 3 tablespoonfuls of vinegar very slowly, continuing the beating until mixture is stiff; season with salt, pepper and paprika.

CHICKEN SALAD

Use by measure twice as much chicken as celery. Cut the chicken in small cubes; do not chop it, and mix with French dressing. When ready to serve drain, add celery and mix with mayonnaise dressing. If boiled dressing be used, mix the chicken with part of that, adding more when ready to serve. Mayonnaise dressing can be used alone without French dressing if preferred

FISH SALAD

Remove skin and bone from 1 can salmon. Mix with ½ cup finely cut celery and hard cooked eggs and cooked salad dressing, or mayonnaise, and serve on a bed of lettuce

LOBSTER SALAD

Mix cold boiled lobster with nicely seasoned mayonnaise dressing, and serve on lettuce.

CRAB SALAD

Mix crab flake with mayonnaise dressing and serve on lettuce leaves.

POTATO SALAD

4 medium-sized cold boiled potatoes,	4 hard cooked eggs,
	1 red onion

Cut potatoes into small, thin slices, add chopped onion and egg cut in quarters and sliced, moisten well with cooked salad dressing, to which cream has been added Serve on lettuce and garnish with slices of egg.

TOMATOES EN SURPRISE

Peel small, solid tomatoes, cut off the stem and remove the core and seeds. Fill the tomato with crab flakes, put over a teaspoonful of lemon juice and turn them upside down on crisp lettuce leaves, cover with mayonnaise dressing and send to the table. Sardines may be substituted for crab flake

TOMATO ASPEC JELLY

Stew 1 quart can of tomatoes until soft, cutting and mashing the pulp to hasten the process. Flavor by stewing with them ½ teaspoonful of mixed whole spices, 2 level teaspoonfuls of celery salt and 1 small Bermuda onion. Strain the tomato through puree strainer, and, if needed, add boiling water to make 2 cups of juice. Have ready ½ box of gelatine soaked in ½ cup of cold water until soft. Heat the tomato juice to boiling and add the soaked gelatine, stir until dissolved and strain it through fine cheese cloth. Pour it into ring mold, or into small cups or fancy molds, which have been first wet in cold water Chill, and when firm and ready to serve, turn out on a nest of lettuce leaves and spread on top with mayonnaise dressing.

STUFFED TOMATO SALAD

Peel medium-sized tomatoes, remove thin slice from top of each, take out seeds and part of pulp, sprinkle inside with salt. Fill tomatoes with pineapple, cut in small cubes or shredded, and nut meats, using ⅔ pineapple and ⅓ nut meats Mix with mayonnaise dressing, garnish with mayonnaise, halves of nut meats and slices cut from tops, cut square. Serve on a bed of lettuce leaves.

Any of the following mixtures may be substituted for the pineapple and nuts:

Cubes of cucumber with tomato pulp mixed with boiled salad dressing or mayonnaise. Apple and celery mixed with any salad dressing. Shredded cabbage and green pepper mixed with boiled dressing or mayonnaise.

K. S. A. C.

FROZEN TOMATO

2½ cups tomato juice,   3 bay leaves,
8   pepper corns,   6 cloves.
1½ tsp salt,

Add spices to tomato, bring to a boil, and boil 1 minute. Press through a sieve and freeze as an ice. Serve with boiled salad dressing or mayonnaise.

K. S. A C Cook Book

SOY BEAN SALAD

One cup soy beans cooked and drained. Add one small onion chopped, 4 small sour pickles, paprika and celery seed, or ¼ cup chopped celery Serve with a boiled dressing.

Sugar Substitutes

Americans eat more sugar than other folks do; more than is really good for them. We have been using 4 ounces a piece daily, other people half as much, and now our allies are down to 1 ounce a day or less.

One ounce a day (2 tablespoonfuls or 6 teaspoonfuls), that is all it takes to make a stock of 1,185,000 tons this year for our army and our allies. Saving that ounce a day is part of your war service.

U. S. Food Administration.

Your principal way of substituting for sugar is the diet.

1. All the ripe fruits contain sugar. The amount varies from about 3 ounces or 6 tablespoonfuls per pound in fresh figs and plums to about ½ ounce per pound in watermelon

2. Dried fruits: If the water is driven off from fruits as in the drying process, the sugar becomes more condensed than it is in fresh fruits.

3 Syrup may replace sugar in most recipes; give the children syrup, honey, molasses, preserves. It is better for them than candy.

Sorghum molasses _____1½ cups is equiv 1 cup sugar.
Corn molasses _____1⅔ cups is equiv. 1 cup sugar
Honey _____ _____1⅕ cups is equiv. 1 cup sugar.
Maple syrup _____1½ cups is equiv. 1 cup sugar

4. Add more salt to cereals in cooking them. This saves the amount of sweetening necessary at time of serving.

Note: 1. When using honey in place of molasses in any recipe, use less soda, according to the acid in the honey. When in doubt use less. 2 Do not substitute vegetable syrups or preserves in the regular diet of the child These are lacking in vitamines or "growth determiners," which are absolutely vital to the physical development of the child. Butter, eggs and fresh fruits are rich in vitamines and are essential. 3. To replace 1 cup sugar by 1¼ cups molasses, subtract ¼ cup from the liquid called for in the recipe. See table of syrups composition and apply to other syrups.

To test the stages of syrups in candy cooking.

These tests are made by dropping a small portion of the syrup into cold water. Each stage or test corresponds to a definite temperature as indicated by the thermometer.

Soft Ball—When mixture will make up into soft ball, 236° F or 113° C.

Hard Ball—When mixture forms a firm, or rather hard, ball, 230° F. or 123° C

Soft Crack—When mixture becomes crisp and too hard to form a ball, 260° F. or 127° C.

Hard Crack—When mixture will crack or break when crushed between fingers, 290° F. or 143° C.

Caramel—A fifth stage is known as the caramel stage. This may be reached by boiling the syrup beyond the hard crack stage or by melting dry sugar over direct heat   The test for this stage is a golden color, 348° F. or 176° C.

EAT LESS SUGAR

Mary E. Robinson

Missouri University

The average American eats approximately 90 pounds of sugar a year. This includes not only the amount eaten at the regular meals, but also that taken between meals in the forms of candy, cakes, ice creams and soft drinks.

Sugar is used as a source of energy for the body. When eaten in excess, it tends to ferment and cause digestive disturbances. The average amount of sugar which may be eaten by an adult per day is four tablespoonfuls or four tablespoonfuls of honey, 3½ tablespoonfuls of syrup or four tablespoonfuls of molasses. However, soldiers on long marches, athletes or school children may use more sugar in the diet than less active persons of the same size and weight. In the case of children there is danger that in eating too much sugar, especially in the form of candy, the appetite will be dulled for more wholesome foods and a lack of mineral matter in the diet will result.

The following table gives the composition of the sugars and syrups in common use:

	Water Per cent.	Protein Per cent	Fat Per cent	Mineral Salts Per cent	Fuel value in calories per lb.	Total Carbohydrates Per cent
Sugar—Gran. (cane or beet)					1814	100
Sugar—brown					1723	95
Sugar—powdered					1814	100
Sugar—maple	5.				1685	93
Syrup—maple	34.2				1160	64
Molasses—cane	25.1	2.4		3.2	1300	69.3
Syrup—corn	19.0			0.5	1468	80.5
Sorghum	28.6			4.0	1154	63.3
Honey	18.2	.4		2.	1470	81.2

Sherman's Food Products

SUGGESTIVE METHODS FOR THE CONSERVATION OF SUGAR

1. No adult should eat more than 4 tablespoonfuls of sugar per day. A part of this amount may be in the form of honey, syrup or any other sweet.

2. Reduce to a minimum the amount of sugar used in beverages. Many beverages are served sweeter than they need to be, and sugar is often left in the cup or glass in which they are served.

3 If cereals are prepared carefully, salted and thoroughly cooked, they will be palatable without the addition of sugar. If the sweet taste is desired, sweeten the cereals with fruit, rather than sugar. (Ex. oatmeal and raisins or dates)

4. Use recipes calling for less sugar, especially for cakes and other desserts; substitutes, corn syrup, sorghum, honey, apple syrup, and other fruit syrups for the sugar.

5. Use more fresh, dried and canned fruits and less sugar will be desired.

6. Omit rich, heavy desserts requiring sugar, such as puddings with rich sauces, iced cakes, sugar pies, etc.

7. When sugar is craved, eat fruits instead of candy, ice cream and soft drinks. Fruits will be better for the body and the substitution will render a patriotic service.

8. Give children fruit, fruit juice, fruit breads and fruit cookies instead of candy and rich cake.

SUGARLESS CANDIES

It is almost impossible for American people to break themselves of the candy-eating habit Therefore, at this time, some form of confection should be substituted which requires little or no sugar

The following sugarless recipes are suggested:

STUFFED DATES

Remove seed by splitting the fruit lengthwise. Fill the center with chopped nut meats or cherries and wrap in oiled paper.

FRUIT SQUARES

Run equal parts of figs, raisins and dates through the food

chopper. Add ¼ the amount of cocoanut or nuts. Moisten with orange juice. Shape into balls or squares.

These may be dipped into melted chocolate or not, as desired. Dried peaches, apricots or prunes may be substituted for fruits given above.

DRIED PINEAPPLE

Peel fruit and slice crosswise in very thin slices. Place in oven, the door of which is left open, or in a drying rack over the stove. Dry as for apples.

SYRUP OR MOLASSES TAFFY

3 cups syrup or sorghum,   1 tsp. vinegar
1 tbsp. butter,

Cook syrup until it forms a hard ball when dropped in cold water   Add one tablespoonful strong vinegar for flavoring. Pour on cold buttered or oiled platter. Allow to cool until it can easily be handled and pull until light.

CARAMELS

2   cups sorghum or Karo   ½ cup cream or condensed
      syrup,   milk,
1½ squares chocolate,   2   tbsp. vinegar.

Cook until it forms a firm ball in cold water. Pour on buttered pan, and when cut in squares wrap in wax paper.

FRUIT PASTE

Put through the meat chopper enough cherry, peach or quince preserves to make ½ pint with the juice. Heat fruit and add 2 tablespoonfuls of gelatine previously softened in a very little cold water. Stir well and continue stirring until it begins to cool and thicken, then pour into oiled dish to make a layer 1 inch thick Let dry slowly, sprinkle with sugar and place in box with waxed paper between layers A mixture of dried apricots and soaked over night in enough water to cover may be used for this paste   Pour off water, bring it to a boil, pour over apricots, and let stand until cool. Put apricots and dates through meat chopper and proceed with the proportions above.

PASTE BONBONS

Soak 1 ounce of gelatine in ½ cup of water, add to hot syrup; makes 2 cups hot corn syrup. Take from fire, add 2 teaspoonfuls each of lemon and orange juice and 1 of rum or brandy, and if for mint bonbons, add also 2 teaspoonfuls of creme de menthe and 2 drops of spearmint and color green; if for fruit, color pink and add ½ cup each minced candied fruits, pecans or almonds Turn into a wet pan ¾ of an inch thick, put on ice and in 12 hours turn out on board dusted with powdered sugar. Cut in squares and roll in sugar.

BITTER SWEETS

An attractive variety of candies may be made by dipping sweet fruits in bitter chocolate Use for this purpose dates, citron, candied orange peel or crystallized fruit. Melt unsweetened chocolate in double boiler. Keep the chocolate just warm enough to prevent solidifying With a fork drop pieces of fruit in chocolate. See that each piece is completely coated, then remove to waxed paper to harden.

OLD-FASHIONED MOLASSES CANDY

2 cups molasses,	½ tsp. baking powder,
1 tbsp. vinegar,	1 tsp. vanilla or ginger extract.
2 tbsp (1 ounce) butter sub ,	

Put molasses, vinegar and butter into a sauce pan, bring to a boiling point and boil, stirring all the time until the mixture is brittle when dropped into cold water Stir in baking powder and extract and pour into buttered tin. When nearly cold, pull until glossy Cut into small pieces and lay on a buttered plate or wrap in waxed paper Sufficient for 1 pound of candy.

PEANUT BRITTLE

2 cups New Orleans molasses,   1 cup roasted peanuts.

Cook molasses until it cracks when dropped in cold water, caramel stage; have ready the peanuts rolled fine, stir in, pour on oiled marble slab, roll with flat blade of knife as it cools; this should harden in the thin sheets

POPCORN CANDY

1 cup syrup,   1 tbsp. vinegar.
2 qts. of popped corn,

Boil together the syrup and vinegar until it hardens when dropped in cold water. Pour over freshly popped corn and mold into balls or fancy shapes for the Christmas tree. Little popcorn men will please the children. Mark in the features and outlines with melted chocolate.

Either honey, maple syrup, molasses, white cane syrup or corn syrup may be used.

U. S. Food Administration.

PLAIN HONEY TAFFY

1 cup sugar,   ⅓ cup water,
1 cup honey,   1 tsp. vanilla

Boil the honey and sugar together until the mixture makes a hard ball in cold water (270° F.). Add vanilla or other flavor if desired. Put in a buttered dish to cool and pull until white. If the pan the honey is cooked in is buttered around the top the honey will not boil over on the stove. It is possible to vary these proportions widely and always get a delicious taffy.

HONEY CANDY WITH PEANUTS

2 cups honey,   1 cup boiling water,
1 cup butter,   Pinch salt

Boil to a hard ball, and pour over layer of rolled peanuts which have been scattered evenly over the bottom of a buttered pan. When nearly cold, mark off in long strips and roll up tight, then slice across with a sharp knife before it gets quite cold. This recipe may be varied by adding 1 or 2 cups of sugar when it has cooled slightly; stir in 1 or 2 teaspoonfuls peanut butter to suit taste, keep stirring until creamy, pour into buttered pan, mark in squares.

HONEY BUTTER SCOTCH

3 h. tsp. butter,   2 cups honey,
¼ tsp. soda,   2 tsp lemon extract,
2 tbsp. vinegar,   2 cups brown sugar.

Boil the honey, butter and vinegar until it hardens when dropped into water (270° F), stir in the soda and extract; pour in buttered tins to cool.

HONEY CHOCOLATE CARAMELS

½ lb. cocoa,   ¾ lb. pecan nuts,
2 cups honey,   2 lbs. sweet almonds.
1 tsp. vanilla,

Cut the nuts fine and boil them with other ingredients until thick (260° F), cool and roll out, cut in squares and dry in oven.

CHOCOLATE HONEY TAFFY

1 piece chocolate, inch square, ⅓ cup sugar,
1 cup honey,   1 tsp. vanilla

Boil until it makes a hard ball in cold water (270° F.). Add vanilla and put in a buttered dish to cool. Pull until light.

CAKES

Bake only those cakes in which syrup may be substituted for sugar. Vegetable fat or oil for butter. A part other cereal flours for wheat flour.

Do not use frostings unless you can make them without sugar.

The following table was worked out by Mary E. Robinson in Missouri University.

This standard recipe may be varied by adding 3 squares of chocolate to make a devil's food cake, or the flavor may be changed by adding spices, nuts, fruit, etc

Mary E. Robinson,
University of Missouri

Note: Remember that any cake or other food containing molasses is very apt to burn rapidly. A moderate oven is one that will brown a paper a cinnamon brown in 5 minutes.

SUBSTITUTES FOR GRANULATED SUGARS IN CAKE

Flour	Fat	Syrup	Eggs	Liquid	B. Powder
Standard Recipe 3 cups	½ cup	1½ cups Gran. Sugar	Whites 4 or 2 whole eggs	1 cup	2 tsp.
X Substituting Sorghum 3 cups	½ cup	1½ cups Sorghum	Whites 4 or 2 whole eggs	⅔ cup	2 tsp.
XXX Substituting Karo 3 cups	½ cup	1⅕ cups Karo	Whites 4 or 2 whole eggs	⅘ cup	2 tsp.
XX Honey 3 cups	½ cup	1½ cups Honey	Whites 4 or 2 whole eggs	⅘ cup	2 tsp.
Maple Syrup 3 cups	½ cup	1½ cups Maple	Whites 4 or 2 whole eggs	⅔ cup	2 tsp.

X add 1 teaspoonful soda for each cup Sorghum.

XX add ¼ teaspoonful soda for each cup Honey.

XXX when Karo syrup is substituted in cakes as given above the cake will not be as sweet as if granulated sugar is used, but the food value will be the same. If a sweeter cake is desired the amount of Karo used may be increased to two cups and the liquid decreased accordingly.

WAR CAKES

No 1—EGGLESS, BUTTERLESS, MILKLESS CAKES

A good cake from the standpoint of thrift when eggs are selling at 70c per dozen, butter 59c a pound, milk 13c per quart.

½ cup veg. fat or oil,
¼ of grated nutmeg,
1 tsp. cloves,
1 tsp. cinnamon.
1 cup sugar,
1 cup water,
1 cup raisins,
Pinch salt,

Put all in sauce pan and boil 3 minutes, then cool and stir in 1 level teaspoonful of soda dissolved in a little warm water; add 2 rounding cups of flour into which 1 teaspoonful baking powder has been sifted. Bake in slow oven.

Mrs Randel.

No. 2—EGGLESS, BUTTERLESS, MILKLESS AND SUGARLESS

1 cup good molasses,
½ tsp soda,
1 cup hot water,
(Mix with molasses),
1 tsp. cinnamon,
1 tsp. cloves,
Ginger and nutmeg (small quantity)

Mix thoroughly, add ½ package raisins, nuts and other fruits if desired. Now mix in enough flour to make a soft batter, add one teaspoonful baking powder and flour, bake in loaf in very slow oven until it will not stick to straw; should be eaten while fresh The above recipe is excellent.

No. 3—EGGLESS, SUGARLESS, BUTTERLESS CAKE

2 cups molasses (dark),
2 tbsp. veg. oil,
1 cup water,
1 tsp. cinnamon,
Pinch nutmeg and cloves,
Salt.

Boil 3 minutes. When cool stir in 1 teaspoonful of soda dissolved in a little water

1 box raisins,   3 cups flour.
Nuts may be added. Bake in slow oven.

Mrs. C. Bruno,
Wellston.

BARLEY AND OATMEAL CAKES

½ cup shortening,
¼ cup brown sugar,
½ cup corn syrup,
1 egg.
3 tbsp water,
2 level tsp. Rumford baking powder,
½ level tsp. salt,
1¼ level cup rolled oats,
⅓ cup chopped nuts.

METHOD: Cream the shortening and sugar together. Add

the well-beaten egg. Add the syrup and water alternately with the flour, in which the baking powder and salt have been sifted. Add the oats and nut meats. Drop by teaspoonful upon well-greased baking sheets. Bake in moderate oven 12 to 15 minutes. Always bake a test cookie first to be sure the mixture is the right consistency.

OATMEAL DROPS

¾ cup butter sub.,   1 cup chopped raisins,
2 cups rolled oats,   1 tsp. soda dissolved well in
1 cup flour,   ¼ cup boiling water,
1 cup corn syrup,   A pinch of salt.

Mix all together and drop on hot buttered tins.

SPECIAL OATMEAL CAKES

1½ cups flour.   ¼ tsp soda,
½ cup cooked oatmeal,   ½ tsp. baking powder,
¼ cup sugar,   3 tbsp veg. oil,
¼ cup raisins,   ½ tsp. cinnamon
¼ cup molasses,

Beat molasses and fat to boiling. Mix with all the other ingredients. Bake in muffin pans 30 minutes. This makes 12 cakes

U. S Food Administration.

OATMEAL COOKIES

1 tbsp. butter sub.,   1 cup flour,
1 egg,   3 tsp. baking powder,
½ cup milk,   ½ tsp. salt,
¼ cup sugar,   1 tsp. flavoring.
1½ cups oatmeal (fine),

Cream together lard, egg and sugar, add milk, oatmeal and the flour to which the salt and baking powder have been added, add flavor and raisins that have been powdered with flour. Drop on an oiled pan and bake in moderate oven

Elizabeth Mount Walker,
5165 Cabanne

DATE OATMEAL WAFERS

2 cups rolled oats,   ¼ cup shortening,
2 cups flour,   ¼ cup sugar,
1 tsp. salt,   ½ cup water.

Cream shortening, add sugar, water, and then add remaining ingredients. Roll out very thin, cut, and bake in a moderate oven.

CORN MEAL COOKIES

½ cup melted fat,	6 tbsp. sour milk,
½ cup molasses,	½ tsp. soda,
½ cup corn syrup,	2 cups corn meal,
1 egg,	1 cup wheat flour

Combine the melted molasses, fat, syrup, beaten egg and milk. Sift the dry ingredients and combine with the liquid Drop from a teaspoon onto a greased pan and bake in a moderate oven for 15 minutes. This makes 55 to 60 cookies about 2 inches in diameter.

U. S. Food Administration.

CORN MEAL GINGERBREAD

1 cup corn meal,	1 tsp. cinnamon,
1 cup wheat flour,	½ tsp. cloves,
1 tsp. soda,	1 cup sour milk,
¾ tsp. salt,	1 cup molasses,
2 tsp. ginger,	2 tbsp. shortening.
1 egg (omitted if desired),	

Sift together the dry ingredients. Combine the milk, molasses, melted shortening and beaten egg. Add the liquid ingredients to he dry, stir well. Bake in moderate oven. Two cups of buckwheat may be substituted for the corn meal in the above recipe This will have the characteristic flavor of buckwheat. If it is too strong use only 1 cup of buckwheat and 1⅛ cups of white flour; 2½ cups of rye flour may also be substituted In using rye and white flour a larger quantity is necessary because these flours absorb less liquid than do the corn meal and the buckwheat.

U. S. Food Administration.

MAPLE GINGERBREAD

¼ cup shortening,	¼ cup water,
1 egg,	2 cups flour,
1 cup maple syrup,	½ tsp. soda,
½ tsp. ginger,	½ tsp salt

Cream shortening, add beaten egg, mix syrup and water and add gradually to the first mixture. Sift dry ingredients and add gradually. Pour into shallow, greased pans and bake 25-30 minutes in a moderate hot oven.

Miss Ella D. Rode,
Domestic Science Instructor, Patrick Henry School.

COTTONSEED MEAL GINGERBREAD

1 cup molasses,
1 cup sour milk,
1 tsp. soda,
1¼ tsp. baking powder,
2 tsp. ginger,

1 tsp. cinnamon,
½ cup fat,
1 egg,
¾ cup cottonseed meal,
1¾ cups flour.

Mix and bake in slow oven.

U. S. Food Administration

BRAN COOKIES

3 cups bran,
½ cup sugar,
½ cup molasses,
½ cup milk,

½ cup veg. oil,
1 tsp. ginger,
½ tsp. cinnamon,
½ tsp. soda

Sift dry spices with bran and mix, add other ingredients and mix thoroughly Drop from spoon upon oiled pan Bake 15 minutes.

Oswego College War Recipes.

OATMEAL ROCKS

Put 2 cups of oatmeal,
1½ cups seeded raisins,
1 cup English walnut
meats through meat
grinder, add
1 cup black walnut meats,
½ cup whole pecans,
Small quantity flour, if needed,

½ cup sugar,
⅚ cup corn syrup,
1 cup veg. oil,
2 well-beaten eggs,
1 tsp. soda,
5 tbsp. sweet milk,
1 tbsp. vanilla

Drop from spoon on greased tin, bake in moderate oven; will keep for a long time in earthern jar covered.

Federated Clubs' Calendar

COFFEE CAKE

1 cup brown sugar,
1 cup molasses,
1 cup cold coffee,
1 cup raisins,

1 cup veg. oil or butter sub.,
1 tsp. soda,
1 tsp. baking powder,
Spices to taste.

And whole wheat flour to make a rather stiff batter.

BARLEY COFFEE CAKE

2 level cups sifted barley
flour,
1 level cup sifted white flour,
¾ cup sugar,
1 level tsp salt,
4½ level tsp. baking powder,

1 level tsp. round mace or cinnamon,
1 cup small raisins,
1½ cups milk or water,
3 tbsp. melted veg. fat or oil,
1 egg

METHOD· Sift the dry ingredients 3 times, add the raisins, milk, egg and shortening and mix thoroughly. Place in shallow pans, sprinkle with sugar and cinnamon and let stand undisturbed 5 minutes Bake in a moderate oven about 20 minutes. This will fill 3 twelve-inch pans.

CINNAMON CRUMB CAKE

2 cups flour,
8 level tsp. baking powder,
¼ cup water and ½ cup milk (enough to make a very stiff dough),
½ tsp. salt,
4 tbsp. veg. oil (Mazola),
2½ tbsp. sugar.

Mix dry ingredients thoroughly, then add oil and mix again. Finally add liquid and put in oven to bake 20 minutes. To make the crumb covering, 2 tablespoonfuls flour, 4 tablespoonfuls sugar, 1 teaspoonful cinnamon and enough Mazola to make it easy to spread

Mrs. R. E. Eggebrecht.

CORNFLAKE COOKIES

2¾ cups corn flakes,
1 cup ground peanuts,
1 cup sugar,
2 eggs, beaten separately.

Add 2 parts together, add peanuts, then cornflakes; work it slowly; make balls and drop on buttered pans. Bake in hot oven 10 minutes. Put under broiler flame a second to brown.

Mrs. O. K. Bovard.

INDIAN MEAL DOUGHNUTS

¾ cup milk,
1¼ cups very fine white corn meal,
1½ cups wheat flour,
¼ cup Crisco (veg. oil),
2 eggs, well beaten,
1 tsp. cinnamon,
2 tsp. baking powder,
1 level tsp. salt,
1 cup corn syrup.

Put milk and meal into a boiler and heat together for about 10 minutes, add the butter and syrup to the meal, sift together the wheat flour, baking powder, cinnamon and salt. Add these and the eggs to the meal Roll out on a well-floured board, cut into the desired shapes, fry in deep fat, drain and roll in powdered sugar. This makes 30 medium-sized doughnuts.

GRANDMOTHER'S DOUGHNUTS

3   tbsp. veg. oil,
1   cup molasses,
1½ cups sweet milk,
2   eggs,

3   cups flour,
¼ cup cornstarch,
3   tsp. baking powder.

Stir the Mazola into the molasses and the milk and the eggs well beaten, sift the flour, cornstarch and baking powder together, stir into the first mixture, beating well. Add enough more flour to make a soft dough. Roll out and fry in Mazola.

HONEY DROP COOKIES

¾ cup honey,
¼ cup fat,
1   egg,
2½ cups barley flour,
½ tsp. soda,

1   tsp. baking powder,
½ tsp. salt,
1   cup raisins,
1   tsp vanilla.

Heat honey and fat together to combine. Cool and add eggs. Sift dry ingredients. Mix well and add the raisins; a little water will probably be necessary to make a drop dough of this mixture (about 2 tbsp.) Drop by teaspoonfuls on a well-greased sheet and bake in a moderate oven.

PEANUT DROP COOKIES

The constituents are the same as for oatmeal drop cookies, with the substitution of 2⅓ cups of ground peanuts for the rolled oats and nuts called for   Combine and bake in same way.

GINGER SNAPS

1   cup sorghum,
½ cup fat,
1½ cups rye flour,
1½ cups barley flour,

½ tsp. soda,
1   tsp. baking powder,
1   tsp. salt,
1   tsp. ginger.

Combine the fat and the syrup. Sift the dry ingredients and add to the above mixture. When thoroughly chilled this should form a stiff dough   If it does not, add more flour. Roll thin and cut out with a small biscuit cutter. Bake in a moderate oven until a delicate brown

PUDDINGS

STEAMED BARLEY PUDDING

1 cup sour milk,
1 cup molasses,
1 egg,
1 tsp. soda,

¾ cup corn meal,
1   cup barley flour,
¼ tsp. salt,
1   cup chopped raisins.

Beat egg; add molasses, milk and soda dissolved in a little cold water. Sift corn meal and barley together and combine with first mixture Add chopped raisins and pour into well-greased baking powder tins. Steam two hours. Serve with a fruit sauce.

Try One When You Have a Light Dinner or Supper

OATMEAL BETTY OR BROWN PUDDING

2 cups cooked oatmeal,	½ cup sugar,
4 apples cut up small,	¼ tsp. cinnamon,
½ cup raisins,	½ cup molasses.

Mix and bake for one-half hour. Serve hot or cold. Any dried fresh fruits, dates, or ground peanuts may be used instead of apples Either will serve five people.

U. S. Food Administration.

Here is a Delicious Corn Meal and Milk Dessert

INDIAN PUDDING

4 cups milk (whole or skim),	¾ tsp. salt,
¼ cup corn meal,	1 tsp. ginger.

Cook milk and meal in a double boiler 20 minutes, add molasses, salt and ginger. Pour into buttered pudding dish and bake two hours in a slow oven or use your fireless cooker. Serve with milk. This makes a good and nourishing dessert. Serve six

U S Food Administration.

Eat Bananas.—Do you know that bananas are great producers of energy? Bananas are peculiar in combining the sweet quantities of the fruit with the nourishing quantities of the vegetable. On account of the presence of so much nutriment and because bananas grow so luxuriantly, it is stated that a given area of ground will support a greater population if planted to bananas than if planted to wheat. Do you know there is a banana flour?

BANANA PUDDING

1 cup flour,	3 bananas,
¼ tsp salt,	1 egg,
1 tbsp. sugar,	¼ cup milk.
1 tbsp. lemon juice,	

Mix and sift dry ingredients, add milk, egg beaten well, lemon juice and then the bananas put through a sieve Heat mixture well, put into a greased pan and bake in a moderate oven 30-45 minutes. Serve with lemon juice.   Miss Ella D. Rode,

Domestic Science Instructor, Patrick Henry School

1.—DATE PUDDING

1 cup sour milk,	1 tsp. soda,
2 cups graham flour,	⅓ cup molasses,
⅓ cup brown sugar,	⅛ tsp. salt,
1 tbsp. melted butter,	1 lb. dates

Mix the milk, molasses, sugar and dates, which have been stoned and cut fine, add the unsifted graham flour, mixed with soda, and lastly the melted butter. Steam for 2 hours in pound baking powder cans. This pudding can be resteamed and served with lemon sauce

Miss Leigh Harris,
Domestic Science Instructor, Yeatman High School

2.—DATE PUDDING

Remove the seeds from half pound of dates, after picking over and stemming them. Boil half hour in three or four pints of water. Thicken with graham meal and cook slowly until meal is done, preferably over night in fireless cooker, pour into cups to cool. Sugar may be added to taste, but it is good without. Serve with whipped cream.

1.—RICE PUDDING

½ cup rice,	¼ tsp. cinnamon,
2 cups water,	¼ tsp nutmeg,
½ tsp. salt,	¼ cup raisins,
⅓ cup molasses or honey,	¼ cup nuts (chopped).

Wash rice, boil 20 minutes in salted water, drain, mix rice and molasses or honey, add spices, nuts, raisins. If mixture is dry add ¼ cup water Bake 20-30 minutes in moderate oven. Water drained from rice may be used as foundations for white sauces or soup or is very good for starching fine clothes

2.—RICE PUDDING

Two quarts of fresh nice milk with half a teacupful of rice, one and one-half cups sugar, a little salt, with a sprinkling of nutmeg Bake in very slow oven for three hours, stirring often so as to avoid burning; 4 eggs may be added to this pudding

CORN MEAL FIG PUDDING

½ cup corn meal,   3   cups milk,
¼ tsp. salt,   ½ cup finely chopped figs,
½ cup molasses,   1   egg.

To rapidly boiling water add corn meal and salt and cook for 5 minutes Mix the molasses, figs and egg and add to corn meal when partially cooked. Place in a buttered baking dish and bake 1½ hours, set in hot water in a moderate oven. Dates may be used in place of figs.

Hilda Z. Rollman,
Domestic Science Instructor, Cote Brilliante School.

FIG PUDDINGS

One-fourth pound figs chopped fine, two cups bread crumbs, one cup brown sugar, one-fourth pound suet chopped fine, two eggs, the grated rind and juice of one lemon, one dessert spoonful of molasses, one-half grated nutmeg, one tablespoonful flour. Steam three hours and serve with boiled sauce, flavored with lemon.

PRUNE TAPIOCA

⅔ cup tapioca,   ½ tsp. salt,
15   large prunes,   ¼ tsp. almond extract,
1⅔ cups corn syrup or 1⅓   ¼ tbsp. orange extract,
    cups honey,   ½ cup pecan nuts

Soak prunes and tapioca in twice enough water to cover (soak prunes over night), stone and chop the prunes, add enough water to the drained-off liquid to make four and one-half cups Bring this to a boil, adding prunes, syrup, tapioca, salt. Cook in double boiler for forty minutes. Add flavoring and nuts Serve cold with sauce This is a very nutritious dish for children.

HONEY BLANC MANGE

Half a cup of honey, four heaping tablespoonfuls of cornstarch, a quarter of a cup of cold milk, two cups of scalded milk and a pinch of salt. Moisten the cornstarch with the cold milk, then add scalded milk and stir until it boils for 8 minutes, then add the salt and the honey. Divide into small wet molds to cool Turn out, sprinkle a few chopped nuts over the top and serve with cream. Maple syrup may be used instead of the honey.

JELLY APRICOTS

Heat four cups of cooked dried apricots and their juice to the boiling point, add 1⅔ cups of syrup, molasses, and stew for ten minutes. Then add 2 tablespoons of gelatine softened in a quarter of a cup of water and 2 tablespoons juice. Turn into wet mold, stiffen and serve with apricot whip.

To make apricot whip, mix half cup of sifted cooked apricot pulp, the white of three eggs, half tablespoon lemon juice and half cup of powdered sugar. Beat the mixture with a wire whisk until it will hold its shape, and serve immediately. If it is desired to keep it some time pile it into buttered ramekins, set in a pan of hot water and bake for twenty minutes in moderate oven. In this case it becomes an apricot souffle, and may be served either hot or cold with plain stewed apricots.

STEAMED PLUM PUDDING

2 cups graham flour,	1 tsp. soda,
1 cup molasses,	1 tsp. salt, scant,
1 cup sweet milk,	1 tsp cinnamon,
1 cup seeded raisins (ground),	½ tsp. cloves.

Steam 3 hours. Serve with lemon juice.

Mrs. J. B. Suddath.

PUDDING SAUCES

QUEEN SAUCE

2 eggs,	1⅔ cups Karo or maple syrup,
1 tbsp. butter sub. (veg. oil),	Juice of 2 lemons and rind,
	1 cup water

Stir together over fire (double boiler) until mixture thickens

STRAWBERRY SAUCE

Juice and pulp (crushed) of strawberries, add ½ cup sugar and eggs beaten separately, add to juice and sugar. Set over boiling water. Whip with egg beater until the sauce is foamy and thick as custard; serve with sponge cake.

LEMON SAUCE

Boil together 1 cupful hot water and 1½ cups clear corn syrup for 5 minutes. Mix 3 heaping teaspoonfuls cornstarch mixed with a little cold water, add to mixture. Cook until clear like honey, add 1 tablespoonful Troco   Stir until Troco melts

FOAMY EGGS

1   egg,   ½ cup maple sugar,
½ tsp vanilla,   ½ cup whipped cream.

Beat egg white until stiff, beat in gradually the maple sugar powdered, when smooth and light, add vanilla and well-beaten yolks   Stir in whipped cream, serve at once.

WHIPPED CREAM

1 cup double cream,   Flavoring
1 tbsp. sugar,

Bowl and beater, as well as cream, must be thoroughly chilled Cream to whip well should be 36 hours old.

Hard sauce should not be used during war period.

BRER RABBIT CREOLE SAUCE

A delicious Southern sauce, used down South to give added zest to pudding of all kinds. Especially delicious with plum pudding.

Boil 1 cup Brer Rabbit Molasses and 2 tablespoonfuls of vegetable oil for about 5 minutes   Take from fire and add juice of two lemons.

SOFT CUSTARD SAUCE

See soft custard.

ICE CREAMS AND FANCY DESSERTS

HONEY MOUSSE

2 cups whipped cream,   1 cup honey.
4 eggs,

Beat the yolks of the eggs well, and then beat the honey in gradually. Heat slowly until thick, stirring constantly; remove and cool, and then add the whites of the eggs that have been whipped to a stiff froth. Then add the whipped cream and blend all together. Pack in large quantities of ice and salt and freeze without stirring.

SORGHUM GINGER MOUSSE

1 cup whipped cream,   ¼ preserved ginger, minced,
3 tbsp. sorghum,   Few drops vanilla.

Whip cream, fold in syrup, ginger and flavoring. Pack in ice and salt to freeze. The strong flavor of the sorghum is objectionable to some, but it seems to blend very well with ginger. A small amount of dried ginger may be used, but the preserved ginger gives it a more desirable product

HONEY CUSTARD CREAM

2 cups milk,   ⅓ cup honey,
2 tbsp. flour,   2   well-beaten whites,
2 egg yolks,   Few drops vanilla

Bring milk and flour to boil, pour over the yolk and honey; cook over hot water until it thickens This amount will serve six.

MAPLE NUT PARFAIT

½ cup maple syrup,   1   cup whipping cream,
2   egg whites,   ¼ cup nuts.
Vanilla,

Cook syrup to firm ball. Pour over the well-beaten whites Beating well, when cool fold in the whipped cream, add nuts and flavoring. Pack in ice and salt to freeze without stirring. This amount will serve six.

HONEY PARFAIT

½ cup honey,   1 tsp. gelatine,
2   eggs,   1 cup cream, whipped.

Soften the gelatine in the cold water and dissolve in hot water. Beat the yolks of the eggs and then heat the honey in gradually. Heat slowly with the gelatine until thick, cool. Add the well-beaten whites of the eggs and the whipped cream and freeze.

SHERBETS

1 pt fruit juice,   ¼ cup cold water,
1 tsp. gelatine,   ¼ cup lemon juice,
1 cup honey,   1   qt. water

Dissolve the gelatine in the usual manner, softening in cold water and dissolving in boiling water Stir in the honey rapidly, strain, cool and add the fruit juices. Boiling should cease as soon as the honey is added. Freeze as usual.

DATE ICE CREAM

2 cups milk,   2 beaten whites,
2 egg yolks,   Few drops vanilla,
3 tbsp syrup,   1 cup dates

Scald the dates and remove seed. Cook in milk to soften and rub through strainer; mix the yolks and syrup and pour the hot milk date mixture over it.

FIG AU FAIT

2 cups black cooking figs,   ⅓ cup nuts,
1 cup whipping cream,   Few drops vanilla.
3 tbsp. honey,

Wash figs well. Soak over night and cook until tender in water in which soaked. Cook down syrup and drain Whip cream and sweeten with the honey and the syrup from the figs Add vanilla. Pack cream to freeze without stirring. When frozen, open and repack in square mold, alternating layer of figs cut in halves with nuts and the frozen cream Surround with ice and salt until needed.

ORANGE MOUSSE

2 oranges,   1 tsp. powdered gelatine,
1 cup honey,   2 cups thick cream.

Peel and cut up the oranges, rejecting the white inner skin Heat the honey over boiling water. Soak the powdered gelatine in a tablespoonful of water. Add the orange and the gelatine to the honey and stir for 5 minutes Then remove it from the fire, and when cold add the cream, whipped stiff. Pack in ice and coarse salt (equal quantities) and let stand 3 or 4 hours. Pineapple or other fruit may be used instead of orange.

AIRLINE ICE CREAM

4 cups thin cream,   ¾ cup honey
Mix and freeze.

SAUCE FOR ICE CREAM

2 tbsp. butter,   ½ cup honey.
2 tsp. cornstarch,

Cook together the cornstarch and butter thoroughly, being careful not to brown them Add the honey and cook the mixture until it becomes hard when dropped into cold water, and until all taste of raw cornstarch has been removed

Farmers' Bulletin 653.

MENU FOR CONSERVATION LUNCHEON

Served at State Meeting Woman's Committee Council National Defense, by

Miss Louise Stanley, Missouri University

Wheatless, Meatless, Sugarless

Peanut Croquettes

Soy Bean Croquettes

Mashed Potatoes   Spinach

Corn Muffins

Date and Cheese Salad   Corn Flour Cheese Straws

Sorghum Ginger Parfait

Corn Flour Cookies   Oatmeal Cookies

Coffee Served With Honey

Peanut and Rice Croquettes

1 cup peanuts (ground),	1 cup rice (cooked),
⅓ cup cream sauce,	¼ tsp. onion juice,
Salt,	Pepper.

Soy Bean Croquettes

1 cup beans (cooked and ground),	Pepper,
¼ tsp. onion juice,	⅓ cup thick cream sauce,
	Salt.

Corn Muffins

1⅓ cup corn meal,	½ tsp. salt,
1 tbsp. oil,	1 egg,
1 cup milk,	1½ tsp. baking powder.

Corn Flour Cheese Straws

2 cups corn flour,	2 tsp. baking powder,
1 tsp. salt,	5 tbsp oil,
1 egg,	½ cup sweet milk
½ cup grated cheese,	

Roll thin, brush with melted butter and sprinkle with grated cheese.

Date and Cheese Salad

Pour boiling water over the dates to sterilize Remove stones and stuff with a mixture of cottage cheese, nuts and pimento. Cured cheese may be substituted for the cottage cheese.

Sorghum Ginger Parfait

1 pt. cream, whipped,
2 eggs, whites,
½ cup syrup,
½ cup candied or preserved ginger.

If preserved ginger is used, count the syrup as part of that used. Heat syrup and boil to thread, pour over well-beaten whites, beating well Cool and fold in the cream Pour in milk and pack to freeze

Oatmeal Cookies

3 cups oatmeal,
1 egg,
2 tsp. baking powder,
½ tsp. salt,
Flavoring,
1 cup honey,
⅓ to ½ cup fat,
Raisins or dates,
Nuts.

Corn Flour Cookies

2¾ cups corn flour,
1 cup honey (or ⅔ cup molasses and ½ cup syrup),
1 egg,
Flavoring or spices, (¼ tsp. cinnamon,
(¼ tsp. allspice,
(½ tsp. nutmeg.
¾ cup of the flour made into mush with ⅔ cup of water,
½ tsp. salt,
2 tsp. baking powder.

One-third to ½ cup fat (depending on amount of liquid sweetening).

Sterilization and Home Canning

In the preservation of foods by heat, it is necessary that a temperature be selected such that all organism capable of producing undesirable changes shall be destroyed, and yet no undesirable changes take place in the food itself. This means practically that the temperature selected should be just as low as is consistent with certain sterilizations.

Many articles of food are quite efficiently sterilized by being brought to the boiling temperature Such are those that contain considerable quantities of acid, as do the fruits. In this case, the antiseptic and disinfectant action of the acid is so increased by the temperature of boiling water that it quite certainly sterilizes the food material. Foods containing a large proportion of sugars are also easily sterilized by boiling, in as much as the boiling temperature of a saccharine solution is much higher than 100° C. A concentrated solution of sugar, by its high osmotic pressure, also acts as a preservative. Vegetables such as corn and peas are much more difficult to preserve, in as much as they contain neither acid nor sugar in considerable quantities and are ordinarily infected with certain of the anaerobic spore-producing bacteria, which are capable of withstanding high temperatures. Care must be used not to heat such foods to too high a temperature, or the flavor and appearance will be materially impaired. If the temperature is not high enough, however, the spores will not be killed and butyric acid bacteria and certain gas formers will begin to develop. The entire season's output of canneries has been destroyed in this way This difficulty may be obviated in several ways.

Temperatures considerably higher than those of boiling water may be used. The cans are filled with the vegetables, sealed, and placed in a steam cooker much resembling in action the autoclave used in the laboratory. Steam is admitted under pressure and the desired temperature can be reached by controlling the steam pressure. Experimentation is sometimes necessary to determine the temperature in particular instances which will certainly destroy all of the bacteria present, and at the same time not injure the material being canned.

Intermittent sterilization may be resorted to. This is the most common method used in the household in canning certain vegetables. The cans containing the material to be preserved are placed in water, the water brought to a boil and kept at a boiling temperature for a period of an hour or more. They are then allowed to cool, and the process repeated on three or more successive days. This is the principle of intermittent sterilization such as is used in the laboratory for sugar media easily destroyed by heat. The spores present begin to germinate in the first twenty-four hours. The second heating will kill all the vegetative forms which have developed. Repeating the heating in this manner several times will certainly destroy all the bacteria which may be present.

Some canners have made a practice of adding small quantities of chemicals as preservatives. This enables them to sterilize at a lower temperature and insure them from loss from decomposition. In canning factories, temperatures from 110° to 120° C. for twenty to thirty minutes are used for sterilization in small packages and longer periods for larger packages. The heat used in the preservation of food by sterilization produces few changes other than those which would be accomplished by ordinary cooking. Proteins are generally coagulated and sugar is usually inverted to some extent, i. e., changed to simpler sugars.

MICRO-ORGANISMS IN FOODS PRESERVED BY HEAT

Micro-organisms may gain entrance to foods by improper sealing or they may persist through a process of attempted sterilization.

Certain types of food materials, particularly the fruits, are most apt to be attacked by molds, such as Penicillium and Aspergillus. These molds do not develop unless there is oxygen present They fail to develop in hermetically sealed jars. They bring about changes which render the material undesirable as food, although there is no evidence that they produce poisonous substances in appreciable quantities. Usually the mold is confined to the surface, but the decomposition products of its growth frequently penetrate the flavor of the whole mass.

Vegetables and meats are commonly destroyed by bacteria. The most abundant types are those which have withstood heating because of the resistant character of the spores formed The organisms belonging to the butyric acid group of bacteria are relatively abundant in the soil and are present on the surfaces of most vegetables. They bring about decomposition with the evolution of considerable amounts of gas This gas may accumulate in quantities sufficient to bulge and even to break the tin in which it is sealed. The development of such organisms renders the food wholly unfit for use. Some bacteria have been described which bring about decomposition in vegetables and meats without the evolution of gas. They give evidence of their presence by the development of peculiar odors and flavors. In many cases these gain entrance to the food after it has been sealed, and are due to defective sealing.

STEPS IN PREPARATION

1. Preparation and cleaning of containers.

2. Preparation of products to be canned, washing, paring, cutting, etc.

3. Clean hands, clean utensils, clean, sound, fresh products and pure, clean, soft water.

4. If possible, the fruits and vegetables should be picked the day of canning.

5. The containers washed should be placed in a vessel of cold water over a fire to heat. They will then be hot and ready for use when the products have been prepared for packing.

I. (a) Scalding or blanching is done by placing the products to be canned in cheese cloth bag, or dipping basket into boiling water, and allowed to remain there from 1 to 15 minutes, depending on the kind of product.

(b) In the case of green vegetables, however, the scalding is accomplished most satisfactorily in steam, as volatile oils and other substances remain in the food under this treatment.

II. As soon as the product is removed from the boiling water or steam, it should be dipped into cold, clean water, and immediately removed and drained for a few moments. The temperature of the water used for cold dipping should be as low as possible.

III.   Packing. The product should be packed carefully into hot jars as soon as removed In this case fruits; boiling hot syrup or hot water is then added. In the case of vegetables, hot water is usually used and salt for seasoning. The scalded rubbers and tops of jars are put into place, the tops of cans sealed and the containers placed in a hot water bath preserve cooker or other similar device for processing.

IV.   Processing is the final application of heat to sterilize the product and is continued for a period determined by the character of the product and the kind of apparatus used. The containers should be placed in the processing vessel as soon as they are filled

V   Sealing: Immediately after the termination of the processing period, while the products are still hot, glass and similar containers must be sealed.

Jars should then be placed in a tray upside down to cool and closely examined for leaks If leakage occurs the covers should be tightened until they are completely closed.

A FEW SUGGESTIONS

Tin cans may be cooled by plunging them in cold water. Store them in a cool, dry place not exposed to freezing temperature.

Most products packed in glass jars will blanch or darken if exposed to light; it is well, therefore, to wrap the jars in paper. From time to time, especially during very hot weather, both glass jars and tin cans should be examined to make certain that there are no leaks, swelling or other signs of fermentation

TIME TABLE

PRODUCTS BY GROUPS.	Scald or Blanch	Hot water bath outfits at 212°.	Steam pressure 5 to 10 lbs
	Min	Min.	Min.
Tomatoes	1½	22	15
Pumpkin	3	120	60
Squash	3	120	60
Hominy	3	120	60
Corn, sweet	5	180	90
Corn, field	10	180	60
Mushrooms	5	90	50
Sweet peppers	5	90	60
POD VEGETABLES AND OTHER GREEN PRODUCTS.			
Beans, wax	5-10	120	60
Beans, stringless	5-10	120	60
Okra	5-10	120	60
Peppers, green or ripe	5-10	120	60
Cabbage	5-10	120	60
Brussels sprouts	5-10	120	60
Cauliflower	3	260	60
ROOT AND TUBER VEGETABLES			
Carrots	5	90	60
Beets	5	90	60
Turnips	5	90	60
Sweet potatoes	5	90	60
Other roots and tubers	5	90	60
COMBINATIONS AND SOUP VEGETABLES.			
Lima beans	5-10	180	60
Peas	5-10	180	60
Vegetable combinations	5-10	180	60

PRODUCTS BY GROUPS	Scald or Blanch	Hot water bath outfits at 212°	Steam pressure 5 to 10 lbs.
	Min.	Min.	Min
GREEN DOMESTIC OR WILD.			
Swiss Chard	15	120	60
Kale	15	120	60
Turnip tops (young, tender)	15	120	60
Spinach, New Zealand	15	120	60
Asparagus	15	120	60
Beets, tops	15	120	60
Spinach	15	120	60
SOFT FRUITS AND BERRIES.			
Apricots	1-2	16	10
Blackberries		16	10
Cherries		16	10
Currants		16	10
Gooseberries	1-2	16	10
Grapes		16	10
Huckleberries		16	10
Peaches	1-2	16	10
Plums		16	10
Raspberries		16	10
Strawberries		16	10
Fruits without sugar syrup		30	12

HARD FRUITS

Apples	1½	20	8
Pears . .	1½	20	8
Quinces	1½	20	8
Windfall apples (pie-filling) .		20	8
Quartered apples (salad)..		12	8
Whole apples and pared		12	8
Apple syrup ..		16	8
Fruit juices		15	8
Preserves after prep. and filling		15	8
		20	10

Notes: 1. Do not begin to count time when the jars are placed in the canner, but wait until the water begins to "boil hard".

2. Count time only while water is "boiling hard". If it stops for only a few minutes, make up for it with longer boiling.

3. Use only NEW RUBBERS. If they are so poor that they are destroyed in the boiling or if they slip from under the lid or are cut by the lid when it is screwed down, remove the rubber, replace it with a new one which has been placed in BOILING water for 10 minutes. Then place the jar back in the canner and sterilize 30 minutes longer.

4. Fit lids carefully before placing the product in the can.

5. DO NOT be alarmed if the water does not cover the product in the can. It will keep just as well. Some water will escape in the form of steam if the lid is not fairly tight and some will be absorbed by the product, especially if it is corn or mature peas and beans.

RELISHES

GREEN TOMATO CATSUP

Boil the tomatoes until soft, then put through a colander. To 1½ gallons of tomatoes, add 1 pound of sugar, 1 pint of vinegar, 1 tablespoonful of whole black pepper, a double handful of salt, a small onion chopped and 1 teaspoonful of ground cloves. Boil all together until the watery particles disappear and it becomes somewhat like marmalade, then bottle and seal.

UNCOOKED TOMATO RELISH

Cut one-half peck of peeled tomatoes, 1 cup each of celery, onion and green peppers, add 1 cup of salt and chop all together. Drain in a bag over night, and then add half cup of white mustard seed, 2 tablespoonfuls of celery seed and 1 tablespoonful of ground cinnamon. Pack in a jar, add 3 cups of good cider vinegar, cover and set away. It will be ready for use in 5 days and keeps indefinitely in a cool place.

CORN RELISH

Cut corn from cob of 18 ears, force 1 small cabbage through meat grinder. Separate 1 bunch of celery, remove leaves and chop stalks. Peel 4 onions and cut in thin slices crosswise. Wipe 2 green peppers and chop. Put prepared vegetables in preserving kettle and pour over 1 quart of vinegar. Mix thoroughly 2 cups of sugar, ¼ teaspoonful cayenne, 1 cup of flour, one-half cup of salt, 1 teaspoonful of mustard and one-half teaspoonful of turmeric and add 1 quart of vinegar slowly. Combining mixtures, bring to the boiling point and let boil 40 minutes. Fill glass jars and seal.

APPLE CHUTNEY

5 lbs. apples when peeled and cored,
1 pt. vinegar,
1 lb. Sultana raisins,
1 lb onions,
2 ounces of mustard seed,
2 ounces salt,
1 ounce of curry powder,
¼ ounce of cayenne pepper,
¾ lb. yellow sugar.

Stew the apples and onions in the vinegar until well cooked and tender, then chop the Sultana raisins and add them, then all the other ingredients. Mix well and boil for half hour. When cold it is ready for use and makes a pleasant change with cold meats instead of pickle.

APPLE RELISH

7 lbs. apples,
2 lbs. seeded raisins,
1 pt. vinegar,
2 oranges,
1 tsp. powdered cloves,
2 tsp. powdered cinnamon,
3½ lbs. of sugar.

Chop the raisins and put them into a porcelain-lined kettle, add the apples chopped and unpeeled, the juice and the chopped peel of the oranges, the sugar, vinegar and spices. Boil steadily for half hour. This relish will keep in unsealed cans all winter.

CUCUMBER CATSUP

Twelve large cucumbers laid in cold water for 1 hour. Pare and grate fine into a deep earthern dish. Grate 2 small onions and add the cucumbers. Season the mixture with salt, pepper and vinegar, making it as thick as marmalade. Mix thoroughly and seal in glass jars. Be sure to use pure cider vinegar and see that the jars are air tight. This is fine with cold meats.

E. C. H.,
Wisconsin.

PICKLED LIME RELISH

1   doz. thin skinned pickled   1   cup of vinegar,
 limes,   ½ cup water
1½ cups sugar,

Wash the limes and soak them in cold water for 24 hours. Change the water several times In the morning put them over the fire in a saucepan of cold water, and boil until a straw can penetrate easily. Let cool, cut in eighths and remove the seeds. Put the sugar, vinegar and water into a saucepan, boil it for fifteen minutes, and pour over the limes This is very good served with scalloped oysters and cold meats It may be prepared at any time and kept all the year round.

MINT CHUTNEY

1 handful mint,   2   tbsp. tomato catsup,
1 cup seeded raisins,   ½ tsp. salt.
2 tbsp. sugar,

Chop the mint fine, then mix it with the other ingredients until it becomes juicy. Serve in a little sauce boat.

CARROTS AND PINEAPPLE

1 cup ground carrots,   1 cup pineapple.

Cook until tender, add 1 cup sugar and 1 lemon quartered and sliced very thin. Boil slowly until thick, do not stir Pack into hot jars and sterilize.

GRAPE SAUCE

1   pk. wild grapes,   1 ounce cinnamon,
1   pk. apples,   2 nutmegs,
 ¾ lb. sugar to   1 ounce of ground allspice.
1   lb of fruit,

Pick off a peck of wild grapes from the stems and put on to boil When tender strain through a jelly bag. Cook 1 peck of apples that have been quartered. When done run through the colander Put the juice of the grapes and the apples in a porcelain kettle and to each pound of this add ¾ of a pound of white sugar, 1 ounce of ground cinnamon, 2 nutmegs grated, and 1 ounce of ground allspice. Cook until thick and put into glasses This is fine for cold meat

CONSERVES

GRAPE CONSERVE

5 lbs grapes,
5 lbs. of sugar,
1 lb. of raisins,

1 lb. shelled walnuts,
2 juicy oranges

Remove the stems and skins from the grapes and boil the pulp until tender, then press it through a sieve Boil the skin of the oranges until tender, then chop fine Put the grape skins and the pulp into a saucepan and add the orange juice, the boiled skins, the sugar and add the raisins and the walnuts and boil until quite thick.

BLUE PLUM CONSERVE

5 lbs. large blue plums,
5 oranges,
1 package raisins,

1 lb of English walnuts,
3 lbs. sugar.

Stone the plums and cut them into quarters, wash the oranges and take out seeds, then grind them through a food chopper. Chop the raisins, mix all together with the sugar and let stand over night. Cook slowly until the plum skins are soft, then add the nuts chopped and put into jars.

STRAWBERRY AND CRANBERRY CONSERVE

1 qt. cranberries,
1 pt of sugar,

½ pt water.

As a change from the regulation cranberry jelly or sauce, this combination of cranberry with strawberry will be found appetizing. Cover and cook for 10 minutes, then skin and add to the cranberry 1 cup of strawberry jam Mix well, then pour into molds and let stand until cool and set.

PICKLED FRUIT

WATERMELON RIND PICKLE

8 lbs of watermelon rind
    cut in little cubes,
4 lbs. sugar,
1 qt. of vinegar,

2 tbsp. ground cinnamon,
1 tbsp. of allspice,
2 tbsp. whole cloves.

Pare the rinds and cut off the pink inside, then weigh 8 pounds and put it into a porcelain-lined preserving pan and cover with boiling water; then set on the back of the stove and simmer until quite tender, having it closely covered all the time. It will re-

quire about 3 hours. When done have ready the syrup made of
the vinegar, sugar and spices. Tie the ground spices in a muslin
bag and put the whole cloves in loose. These ingredients will make
4 quarts of excellent pickle that is inexpensive and fine to serve
with meats.

PICKLED PEACHES

½ pk. peaches,	3 pts. sugar,
½ pt. vinegar,	A few cloves
½ pt. water,	

Do not pare the peaches, but wipe them carefully with a clean
cloth until smooth. Divide them into 3 equal parts Bring the
water, sugar and vinegar to the boiling point, then put in ⅓ of
the peaches and boil for 20 minutes; remove them to a platter,
then put in another third and in 20 minutes the remaining third,
until each part has been cooked for 20 minutes, thus making 1
hour for the syrup. Stick 1 clove into each peach, put the peaches
into jars, cover with the boiling syrup and seal at once in glass
jars The peaches should not be too ripe.

CHERRY PICKLE

7 lbs. of red berries,	1½ ounces of whole cloves,
3½ lbs sugar,	¾ pt. vinegar.
2½ ounces stick cinnamon,	

Wipe the cherries, then pit and drain them Tie the spices in
a cheese cloth bag and heat them with the vinegar. Pour the hot
vinegar over the cold cherries and let the mixture stand over
night. Keep draining off and reheating each day for 3 or 4 days,
then heat all together to the boiling point and seal.

GINGER PEARS

10 lbs. pears,	6 oranges,
7 lbs sugar,	1 box crystallized ginger
4 lemons,	

Peel the pears, cut them into small pieces, put them into a preserving pan with the sugar and cook slowly for 1 hour. Add the
lemons, oranges and crystallized ginger, cut into small pieces and
allow to simmer for 3 hours, divide into glasses and cover.

MARMALADES

A marmalade quite out of the ordinary is made with the following ingredients:

5   lbs. rhubarb,
3   large lemons,
1½ lbs. sugar,

6   medium sized oranges,
    (navels are the best),
1½ lbs. almonds.

Wash and trim the rhubarb stalks and cut them into very thin slices. Peel the yellow rind very thinly from the oranges and lemons; remove the thick white pith, slice the pulp and add to rhubarb. Cut the yellow rind of 3 of the oranges and 1 lemon into tiny strips, add to the other ingredients with sugar in measure to total quantity. Tie the remainder of the peel in a bit of cheese cloth and remove it after the marmalade is cooked. Stir the mixture thoroughly and set aside over night. Boil until thick, about ¾ of an hour will suffice, then add the almonds which have been shelled, blanched and sliced, boil for 10 minutes longer, pour into glasses and when cold cover with paraffin.

AMBER OR GRAPE FRUIT MARMALADE

1 orange,
1 lemon,
1 grape fruit,

Water,
Sugar.

Shave the orange, the lemon and the grape fruit very thin, rejecting nothing but the seeds and cores. Measure the fruit and add to it 3 times the quantity of water. Let it stand in an earthenware dish over night and on the second morning boil for 10 minutes only. Stand another night, and on the second morning add pint for pint of sugar, and boil steadily until it jellies. The product should have a lumpy appearance, quite different from most marmalades, the strips of fruit being well defined in a clear, pale jelly. To bring this about, stir as little as possible during the 2 hours or more of cooking which is required.

GOOSEBERRIES

Gooseberries and oranges make an excellent marmalade. Stem the gooseberries, wash, drain and place in a jar with an equal measure of white sugar. To 3 pints of berries use 4 oranges and 2 lemons. Peel off the rind very thinly and shred into threads Cover with cup of water and let stand over night. Add the thinly sliced pulp of the oranges and the lemons to the berries, with an equal measure of sugar Let stand until following day. Add altogether and cook until thick, pour into glasses and serve.

Another extremely good marmalade calls for 4 pounds of pears, 4 lemons and a can of grated pineapple. Peel and core the pears; cook in enough water to prevent them from burning Rub through a colander. Peel the lemons, shred the yellow rind and cut the pulp small, add all with the pineapple to the pears with an equal measure of sugar. Cook for 1 hour. This is improved by adding blanched shredded almonds. Let the mixture cook for 10 minutes longer.

Eleanor M Lucas.

RHUBARB AND ORANGE MARMALADE

Equal parts of sugar and
    rhubarb,
1 orange,

½ lb raisins to each pound of rhubarb.

Use equal parts of sugar and rhubarb unpeeled, but cut very fine; add 1 whole orange and ½ pound of raisins chopped fine to each pound of rhubarb Mix thoroughly and allow to stand several hours in a stone or agate kettle Then cook down until very thick Pour into glass or paper jelly cups.

CHERRY BUTTER

3 cups of pulp,   2 cups sugar, boil until thick

Select fine ripe cherries, testing them by pressure for bad ones as you leave the pits in. Cook the cherries with just a little water to start them. When cooked, run through a sieve, add the sugar and cook until thick.

APPLE MARMALADE

To make apple marmalade pare, quarter, core and slice apples to make 4 pounds, wash 3 lemons and slice them very fine; add them to the apples with 1 quart of water. Cook until the apples are soft, press through a colander, and measure; add an equal amount of sugar and 1 cup and a half of blanched almonds cut into pieces. Stir and cook until thick like jelly. Pour into glasses and when cold seal.

Apricots, pineapples and lemon make a marmalade which the college girl aptly defined as "delectable conglomerate of good things." Pare apricots, place in a large bowl and add an equal bulk of white sugar. To 5 pounds of apricots allow 1 large can of grated pineapple, 1 dozen apricots blanched and cut into fine strips and 3 lemons. Peel the lemons, cut the thin yellow rind of 2 lemons into very small pieces and slice the pulp thinly. Boil all together until thick, or about ¾ of an hour. Pour into glasses and treat like jelly when cold.

MOCK ORANGE MARMALADE

2   cups carrots through meat   1 cup sugar,
    grinder,   1 whole lemon through grinder.
½   cup water,
  Boil until it jellies

Mrs. Winters.

Note: Paraffin is used in dipping candles made by rolling six thicknesses newspaper, inserting a string in the center, cutting and dipping in paraffin. These may be used by the soldiers. Save paraffin from jelly glasses

JELLY

The process of jelly making seems simple, and yet it is frequently attended with uncertain results because the underlying principles are not understood. There are several factors.

Fruit juice contains vegetable acids and a substance called pectin, both of which are essential to the jelly making process. The amount of each varies in the different fruits, which accounts for the fact that some fruits make better jelly than others. The ideal fruit for jelly making should be rich in pectin and should be fairly acid; another important consideration is the proportion of sugar to the juice; a given volume of juice contains a certain quantity of pectin in solution and this quantity of pectin must bear a definite relation to the proportion of sugar. Up to this definite amount the texture of the jelly produced more nearly approaches the ideal, but beyond the definite proportion the jelly is increasing syrup, until it finally fails to hold together at all, and a gummy mass is the result. Experience and exercise of judgment are necessary to determine the correct amount of sugar to be used. If fruits are gathered after a rain, or if much water is added, the amount of pectin will be proportionately less and the proportion of sugar must also be diminished Experiments seem to indicate that the correct proportion of sugar to juice varies from three-fourths of a volume to one volume of sugar, to one volume of fruit juice.

The time during the process when the sugar should be added to the juice is also important. Experiments seem to indicate that to add it near either the beginning or to the end of the process is likely to result in crystallization of the sugar If added at the beginning of the process the sugar is changed by the action of the acid into two simple sugars, one of which is apt to crystallize. If added near the end of the process the original sugar may crystallize. If added midway in the process the sugar is only partially changed and is less likely to crystallize.

Experiments show that there is no difference in the texture, taste or appearance of jelly made from cane or beet sugar if these are equally pure. There is a slight difference in the volume of jelly made from a given amount of juice, the amount being slightly less when beet sugar is used. However, the difference is so small as to be almost negligible

TO STERILIZE GLASSES

The process is the same as for sterilizing jars

TO FILL AND TO SEAL

Fill the glasses, pour a layer of melted paraffin over the top, adjust the covers, label, and set away in a dry place.

APPLE JELLY

Wipe, quarter and core the apples, cover with cold water. Heat slowly and simmer until the apples are reduced to a pulp Drain through a double thickness of cheese cloth or jelly bag Measure and allow ¾ amount of sugar. Boil juice 15 minutes, add the sugar, heated in the warming oven, and continue boiling 10 minutes, skim, fill glasses, seal.

SMALL FRUIT JELLY

Green or ripe grapes, currants, cranberries, raspberries, blackberries, etc., may be used. Pick, wash and drain fruit, cook until juice is extracted from fruit. Follow directions for Apple Jelly.

CRAB APPLE AND PINEAPPLE JELLY

1 pk. crab apples,   Equal parts of sugar.
2 pineapples,

A delicately flavored jelly is made by adding one or two cut and peeled pineapples to every peck of crab apples, and equal parts of sugar to the cooked and strained juice of the fruit. Make the same as other jelly.

NOTES

DO YOU KNOW OATMEAL?

Do you know that oatmeal makes delicious puddings and other good things?

Of course you know it is a good breakfast food, but it is even better fixed up for dinner or supper. It makes

Excellent puddings,

Wholesome bread and cookies,

An appetizing soup for a cold day,

A baked dish for dinner in place of meat.

1. Food is Ammunition.
2. Every bit of food saved is a shot across No-Man's Land at the Huns.
3. Soldiers strenuously engaged must have sustaining food.
4. There is world shortage of 115,000 animals of the meat productive type (1918). The shortage in this country of 17,000,000 heads in comparison of 17 years ago.
5. In the Italian drive the Italians had to eat fish because of shortage of meat.   Dean Mumford.
6. Corn saved our pioneers. Do you know corn meal? Its use means service to your country, nourishing food for you.
7. Use common sense in making War Food and at this crisis it is the duty for each housewife to make her kitchen a laboratory for experiments in conservation of food subs.
8. The men of England, Scotland, Ireland, France, Italy and Belgium—our allies—are fighting; they are not on the farms The production of food by these countries has therefore been greatly reduced. Even before the war it was much less than the amount consumed. The difference came more largely from other countries than from America. Now this difference is greater than ever, at the same time supplies can no longer come from most of the other countries. They must now come from America. Therefore our allies depend on us

for food as they have never depended before, and they ask us for it with a right which they have never had before. For today they are doing the fighting and suffering and dying in our war. We must send them the food they have to have. We will send it. But we can only do it by a wise and loyal economy of food on the part of every one of us We must stimulate our food production, organize our food-handling, eliminate all the waste possible, substitute as largely as possible other foods for wheat, beef, pork, dairy products and sugar, and reduce consumption where it is excessive.

9.   Let us at this time utterly repeat the old saying that the waste in the kitchen of a prosperous American household would feed a French family.

10.   Wastefulness. The elimination of waste will save literally billions of dollars for the American people, and at the same time not disrupt in any degree the industrial progress of the nation.

TO SAVE GAS OR FUEL

Save Gas—Never leave burner lighted while preparing material —better to use an extra match.

When oven is used plan to bake at same time a roast, apples, potatoes and a pudding or cake

The boiling point is 212° F. No amount of heat will make it higher. Notice this and turn flame accordingly

There are three-cornered sauce pans—3 vegetables or sauces may be cooked at one time.

Rules for Red Cross Knitting

This circular is prepared primarily for the use of hand knitters. Knitting machines may be used if desired, provided the articles can be as well made and made of the same yarn.

The color of the yarn has been carefully considered with the authorities of the War Department, and with the American Red Cross Commissioner for Europe, in Paris. It has been learned from both of these sources that articles made in either gray or khaki yarn will be acceptable. Owing to the difficulty in securing khaki-colored yarn in large quantities, the American Red Cross Supply Bureau will carry the gray yarn (oxford mixture, 4-ply 10's construction).

Yarn and knitting needles may be procured either from Red Cross Chapters or from stores, provided the yarn is of the same grade and needles of the same size as those described here.

The needles referred to in these directions are standardized Red Cross needles which can be purchased from Red Cross Chapters. Their diameter is given opposite their respective number

Red Cross Needles No. 1—125/1000 inches
Red Cross Needles No. 2—175/1000 inches.
Red Cross Needles No. 3—200/1000 inches.

Stitches should not be cast on too tightly. Knitting should be done evenly and firmly, and all holes should be avoided.

Joining should be done by splicing or by leaving two or three inches at each end of the yarn to be darned in carefully.

All knots, ridges or lumps should be most carefully avoided, especially in socks, as they are apt to blister the feet.

SLEEVELESS SWEATERS

Two and one-half hanks yarn (⅝ lb.). 1 pair Red Cross Needles No. 3.

Cast on 80 stitches. Knit 2, purl 2 stitches for 4 inches. Knit plain until sweater measures 24 inches. Knit 28 stitches, bind off 24 stitches for neck loose. Knit 28 stitches, knit 7 ridges on each shoulder, cast on 24 stitches. Knit plain 21 inches. Purl 2, knit 2, stitches, for 4 inches Sew up sides, leaving 9 inches for armhole, 2 rows of single crochet around the neck, and 1 row single crochet around the armhole

KNITTED HELMET

One hank yarn (¼ lb.)   4 Red Cross Needles No. 2

Cast on 56 stitches loosely. Knit plain for 8 inches for front piece, and leave on extra needle. Knit another piece to correspond for back. These pieces must be at least 9 inches wide. Slip the stitches of both on to 3 needles, arranging for last 2 stitches of back piece to be on beginning of 1st needle, with 38 stitches of front piece added (making 40 on 1st needle). Divide rest of stitches on other 2 needles, 36-36. Beginning with 1st needle, knit 2, purl 2, for 18 stitches. Bind off 22 stitches for face opening. Try to keep same arrangement of stitches on needles for further directions.) Knit 2, purl 2 forward and back on remaining 90 stitches for 1½ inches, always slipping first stitch. Cast on 22 stitches loosely to complete face opening, knit 2, purl 2, for 2½ inches (adjust stitches by slipping 2 from end of 3rd needle to 1st needle, making 42 on 1st needle). Knit 1 round plain, knit 2 stitches together, knit 11, knit 2 stitches together, knit 1. Repeat to end of round. Knit 4 rows plain. Then knit 2 stitches together, knit 9, knit 2 together, knit 1. Repeat to end of round. Knit 4 rows plain Continue in this way, narrowing on every fifth round and reducing number of stitches between narrowed stitches by 2 (as 7, 5, 3, etc.) until you have 28 stitches left on needles. Divide on 2 needles, having 14 on 1st needle and 14 on the other and finish same as toe of sock.

WRISTLETS NO. 1

One-half hank yarn (⅛ lb). 1 pair Red Cross Needles No. 2.

Cast on 48 stitches, knit 2, purl 2, for 12 inches, and sew up, leaving 2 inches open space for thumb 2 inches from the edge.

WRISTLETS NO. 2

One-half hank yarn (⅛ lb.). 4 Red Cross needles No. 1.

Cast on 52 stitches on 3 needles, 16-16-20. Knit 2, purl 2 for 8 inches. To make opening for thumb, knit 2, purl 2, to end of 3rd needle, turn; knit and purl back to end of 1st needle, always slipping first stitch; turn, continue knitting back and forth for 2 inches. From this point continue as at first for 3 inches for the hand. Bind off loosely and button-hole thumb opening.

MUFFLER

Two hanks of yarn (½ lb.). 1 pair Red Cross Needles No. 3. Cast on 50 stitches, or 11 inches. Plain knitting for 68 inches.

WASH-CLOTH

White knitting cotton (medium weight), 1 pair Red Cross Needles No. 1.

Cast on 70 stitches, knit back and forth plain until cloth is about 10 inches square, and bind off. Sew a loop of tape to one corner.

HOT WATER BOTTLE COVER

White knitting cotton (medium weight), 1 pair Red Cross Needles No. 1.

Cast on 56 stitches, knit 2, purl 2, and repeat until the work is 4 inches deep. Then knit back and forth plain for 9½ inches more or until entire work measures 13½ inches. Next decrease 2 stitches at beginning and 2 stitches at end of each needle until there are sixteen stitches left and bind off. Make another piece in same manner and sew together. Attach a 20-inch piece of tape to seam at one side of ribbing to tie around neck of bottle

SOCKS

One hank knitting yarn. No 12 Steel Needles—four, or No. 1 Red Cross Amber Needles—four.

LEG

Cast on loosely 60 stitches (20 on each 3 needles).

Knit 2, purl 2, making a ribbed calf for 4 inches.

Knit plain for 6½ inches.

HEEL

Take 30 (or half of leg) stitches on one needle, knit across and purl back, always slipping the first stitch for 24 rows, or until there are 12 slipped stitches on edge of heel piece.

To turn heel, hold right side towards you and 1-inch row, knit 17 stitches (or two more than half of total number), slip 1, knit 1, bind off the one slipped and knit 1, turn

Second row, slip 1, purl 5, purl 2 together, purl 1 and turn.

Third row, slip 1, knit 6, slip 1, knit 1, bind off the one slipped and knit 1, turn.

Fourth row, purl across until you come to stitch before space, purl stitches either side of space together and purl 1, turn.

Fifth row, knit until you come to stitch before space, slip the stitch, knit 1, bind the one slipped and knit 1.

Repeat these two rows, always slipping the first stitch until all heel stitches have been knitted on 1 needle There should be 18 stitches

GUSSETS

First needle Begin with right side towards you Knit across heel Knit up the gusset or slipped stitches on side of heel piece and knit 2 stitches from the front on this needle.

Second needle. Knit the stitches from the two front needles on one needle leaving the 2 last stitches to go on third needle.

Third needle Take the 2 stitches left from front or second needle—pick up gusset stitches on second side of heel and take nine, or half, the heel stitches on this needle, making the center of the heel the beginning of the row.

Knit first round plain.

Second round, first needle, knit to within 4 of end of needle.

Knit 2 together, knit 2.

Second needle, knit plain

Third needle, knit 2. slip 1, bind it over the next stitch knitted, and knit plain.

Repeat these two rounds until the gussets are narrowed down to 16 stitches on both side needles.

FOOT

Knit plain until within 2 inches of desired length (10½ and 11 inches are usual sizes)

TOE

Knit 5 stitches plain, knit 2 together and repeat to end of row.

Knit 5 rows plain.

Knit 4 stitches plain, knit 2 together and repeat.

Knit 4 rows plain.

Knit 3 stitches plain, knit 2 together and repeat

Knit 3 rows plain

Knit 2 stitches plain, knit 2 together and repeat.

Knit 2 rows plain

Knit 1 stitch plain, knit 2 together and repeat.

Knit 1 row plain.

Knit 2 together—all the way around.

Break off wool and draw through stitches and fasten smoothly on wrong side.

SHIPPING DIRECTIONS

Completed articles should be sent, if possible, to the nearest Red Cross Chapter. When this cannot be done, they should be sent directly to the Red Cross Division Supply Depot in the nearest of the following cities:

Boston	Atlanta	Minneapolis
New York	New Orleans	Denver
Philadelphia	St. Louis	San Francisco
Washington	Cleveland	Seattle
	Chicago	

WHEN DAY IS DONE

I have eaten a bale
Of spinach and kale,
   And I've never raised a row
I have swallowed a can
Of moistened bran,
   And feel like a brindle cow
I am taking a snack
From the old haystack,
   In the evening shadows gray,
And I'm glad, you bet,
At last to get
   To the end of a meatless day.
                —Washington Star.

Index

Index

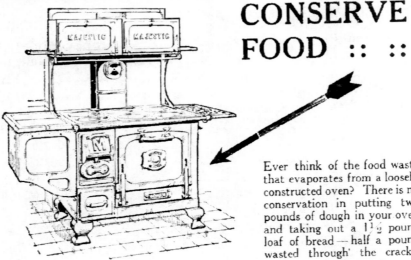

In The Hour of Economy

CPSIA information can be obtained at www.ICGtesting.com
Printed in the USA
BVOW07s1705240214

345850BV00008B/580/P

9 781177 707398

Prospects for

AFRICA

A special report by Save the Children Fund and the Overseas Development Institute for The Africa Review Group

——————— **Introduction by** ———————

HRH The Princess Royal

HODDER AND STOUGHTON

LONDON SYDNEY AUCKLAND TORONTO

Acknowledgements

Prospects for Africa was prepared under the editorial supervision of John Howell (Director, ODI), Andrew Hutchinson (Education Officer, SCF) and John Montagu. They would like to acknowledge the contributions of the following: Richard Turner, Tony Killick, Camilla Toulmin, Peter Gee, John Seaman, Mark Bowden, Matthew Bullard, Peter Poore, Alex de Waal, Barbara Tilbury, Nazneen Khanje and Mark Robinson. They also wish to thank staff of the Organisation of Economic Co-operation and Development (OECD) in Paris for their guidance.

Note: All figures used in this book are quoted in US dollars, since this is the international currency most widely used in Africa

Save the Children Fund
Mary Datchelor House
17 Grove Lane
London SE5

Overseas Development Institute
Regent's College
Regent's Park
London NW1

The publishers would like to thank the following for permission to reproduce copyright photographs:

Christian Aid pp 1, 89, 90; Maggie Murray cover, pp 3, 11, 25 top and bottom, 49, 71, 75, 85, 86; Mike Goldwater pp 5, 9, 21, 35, 55; Jenny Matthews pp 8, 58; the Overseas Development Institute (photo Peter Charlesworth) p 26 and (photos Liba Taylor) pp 30, 59, 61, 74; the Central Office of Information pp 33, 36, 39, 52; Penny Tweedie pp 43, 67; UAC Limited pp 46, 63; the Commonwealth Development Corporation (photos PGS Hall) pp 47, 57; Mike Wells p 78.

First published 1988

British Library Cataloguing in Publication Data

Prospects for Africa: a special report for the Save the Children Fund and the Overseas Development Institute.
  1. Africa. Economic development
  I. Save the Children Fund   II. Overseas Development Institute
  330.96′0328

  ISBN 0-340-42909-7

Typeset by Colset Private Limited, Singapore
Illustrations by Taurus Graphics

Printed by Richard Clay plc
for Hodder & Stoughton Educational, a division
of Hodder & Stoughton Ltd, Mill Road, Dunton Green,
Sevenoaks, Kent

Contents

Introduction

Africa occupies a unique place in our heritage and in our outlook on the modern world. Yet we understand little of this diverse continent. It is not, as sometimes appears, an area in despair. Like everywhere else, it is in the process of change with many achievements behind it and many problems still to be faced. It is these problems, economic, environmental and social, which give so many cause for concern. This concern is sometimes, but not always, translated into action, and it is rarely accompanied by enough knowledge or understanding.

A voluntary agency like the Save the Children Fund can only glimpse the effects of the giant economic forces sweeping Africa today and only in specific areas is it able to cope with them through small-scale support. Its chief concern, on behalf of tens of thousands of supporters around the world is for the well-being of families and especially children who are in need. It aims to help them through preventive action and development as well as, inevitably, emergency relief.

But it also has a responsibility to explain to a generous public what is happening in Africa, using the most up-to-date evidence. This is not easy, because the opinions of experts are not often in a form which the ordinary reader can or may wish to absorb. But in publishing this review the Save the Children Fund has determined to make the attempt, in the hope that Africa's successes and problems can be shared much more widely.

As a group, we support the broad findings and conclusions of this review and we commend it to the general reader as well as those who are more familiar with Africa. It is our hope that in understanding the issues facing Africans that more people will appreciate what is being attempted by governments and voluntary agencies not just on their behalf but in partnership with them.

If you would like a single message to give to your own family and friends; Africa today needs constructive assistance, encouragement and understanding. Together we must strive to provide it.

HRH The Princess Royal
(President, Save the Children Fund)

Chief Emeka Anyaoku
Deputy General Secretary of the Commonwealth

The Rt Revd Simon Barrington Ward
Bishop of Coventry

Mr Jonathan Dimbleby
Broadcaster and journalist

Mr Derk Pelly
Former Deputy Chairman, Barclays Bank

Baroness Young
Former Minister of State at the Foreign Office

Africa
in Perspective

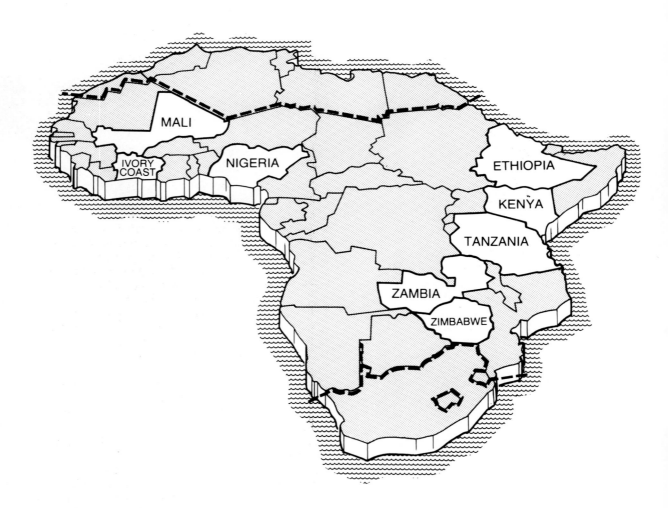

In this report we have chosen eight countries to represent sub-Saharan Africa (the independent countries south of the Sahara excluding South Africa). All statistics refer to sub-Saharan Africa, unless the whole of Africa or selected countries are referred to specifically.

It took the 1983–85 drought and its appalling consequences to focus widespread international public attention on Africa. Many people – whose consciences had already been stirred by the famine in Africa of the early 1970s – asked: Why were African countries seemingly so helpless in the face of drought? Did the massive reliance on help from overseas mean that Africa would again and again be turning to the international community? Would Africa on its own be able to feed and protect its citizens in the foreseeable future?

These were inevitable questions for outsiders to ask, but they were also inevitable questions for Africans themselves, and they were – and are – hurtful questions for people rightly proud of their traditions of self-reliance and resilience. They are questions which are being posed all over again in 1988 over Ethiopia – one of the countries with which this report is concerned.

In this report, we examine the nature of Africa's development challenge. We look at the background to what is now widely seen as a long-term crisis and investigate attempts since the worst drought for years to put Africa back on its feet. Naturally we are particularly concerned with what is happening in Africa itself, where governments are asking for major sacrifices in arresting and reversing the process of decline in many countries. But we are also concerned with the role of the outside world: the large official donors, the voluntary agencies and the world of trade and investment.

△ Africa and Other Developing Regions

Let us start in an even wider context and ask why 'Africa' has become so closely associated in the public mind with the crisis of development – a crisis of governments and people seemingly trapped in poverty and debt and in danger of being left behind as other nations become richer and stronger. In part, of course, the stark images of famine have coloured public attitudes; although the severest consequences of the recent drought were felt only in a relatively under-populated part of the continent and many African countries were well able to cope with climatic difficulties. But at the same time, Africa as a whole continues to experience declining or stagnant living standards and its long-term economic prospects continue to cause concern to its governments and external donors which is much deeper than the concern for other areas of the developing world. Why is this?

When we talk of 'Africa' we are talking of the independent countries south of the Sahara: in particular we refer in this report to eight countries: Nigeria, Ivory Coast, Mali, Ethiopia, Kenya, Tanzania, Zambia and Zimbabwe (see the map opposite). The countries of north Africa have long been part of a richer Mediterranean basin economy. Several have important natural resources such as oil; most have substantial industries and trade continuously and successfully in European markets. The relative prosperity of North

INCOME PER HEAD, SELECTED COUNTRIES, 1985

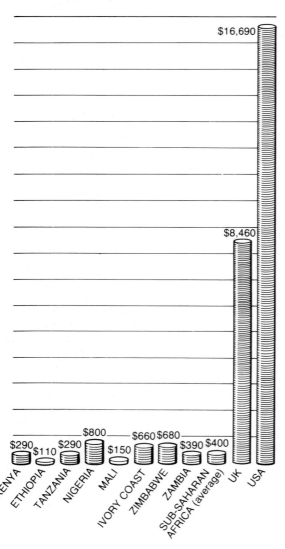

$16,690

$8,460

$290 $110 $290 $800 $150 $660 $680 $390 $400

KENYA ETHIOPIA TANZANIA NIGERIA MALI IVORY COAST ZIMBABWE ZAMBIA SUB-SAHARAN AFRICA (average) UK USA

Source: World Bank, 1987

Fig 1.1   Africa is poor by most international comparisons. This figure shows that its national income per head – gross national product divided by the population – is only one-twentieth of that of the UK and one-fortieth of that of the USA.

Africa makes it a rich and optimistic region among the less developed countries. A similar situation prevails in most of South-East Asia, which is also conventionally viewed as part of the less developed or 'third' world, although its economic successes have given millions of its citizens living standards comparable to those in many parts of Europe.

Even in South Asia, there is now much less talk of 'crisis' and 'challenge' than there was 20 years ago. There are many more people living in poverty in South Asian countries than in Africa, and some of their poorest people live in sub-human conditions. But the general progress in countries such as India, Sri Lanka and even Bangladesh – despite its natural and civil disturbances – has generated hope for the future. The poorest countries of South Asia appear to justify the term *developing*: even in areas of great poverty and inequality there is skilled and committed manpower working on new technologies, collaborating with local groups and voluntary agencies, using external aid with some effect, and often having a major impact. In Africa, there are also encouraging signs, as we show in this report; but these are few and isolated, and when they are set against the general picture of economic decline and the adversity of international conditions, it has to be said that the continent is not visibly 'developing'. In many respects, as we show later, it is getting poorer, and a major effort is needed to reverse this trend.

Thus Africa is seen by the public as the major current development challenge – for African governments and the international community in particular. And the public is correct. The problem is that the challenge is not being taken seriously enough by those governments which have the resources to respond effectively.

The UN's Food and Agriculture Organisation (FAO) in its major study of *African Agriculture – The Next 25 Years* (1986), wrote that mass starvation would be a 'chronic, widespread phenomenon' if current trends in food production per head continued. These are trends which since 1960 show a 20% fall in food production per head: a fall which has not been compensated by the production of other, internationally-traded, crops. This means that, even at a time of declining world grain prices, Africa is not in a position to buy in the food it requires. Food aid is thus an inevitable part of Africa's future – and future recovery, as Chapter 3 explains.

Africa's food crisis: most rice farmers need expensive imports and irrigation, which poorer farmers cannot afford without aid.

It is evident from reports such as FAO's that the African challenge has been identified for some time, certainly well before the 1983–85 drought. Although, compared with some other less developed countries, great strides have been made in health care and primary education, Africa is still in a special category among the less developed countries. Taking the region as a whole (with notable exceptions):

▲ it has only modest exploitable natural resources
▲ it consists of a large number of small economies barely trading with each other and trading on disadvantageous terms with the industrialised world
▲ it has much less technical and scientific expertise than other continents
▲ it is often handicapped by frequent changes of governments, which as a result are unable to follow consistent policies or provide conditions for productive long-term investment.

△Background to the 1986 Special Session

The unprecedented international concern over Africa, in 1985 especially, led to the convening of a UN General Assembly Special Session on Africa in the spring of 1986. The Special Session represented a major watershed in international agreement on development, because it brought together two politically divergent views on what should be done in Africa to reverse the process of economic decline. Back in 1981 many of the concerns of international institutions and bilateral donors had been voiced in the influential World Bank publication, *Accelerated Development in Sub-Saharan Africa*. The main thrust of that report was to encourage African governments to provide greater incentives to production and exporting, but it was generally seen as placing most of the blame for Africa's disappointments on its own leaders and their policies. In the following year the Organisation of African Unity (OAU) Lagos Plan of Action accepted that much economic policy needed re-thinking, but it also pointed the finger at the international trading system (which devalued Africa's commodities), and at inadequate financial support from the industrialised countries.

A new consensus emerged in 1986 in New York, where the UN Special Session formally adopted a *Programme of Action for African Economic Recovery and Development 1986–90*. The programme has two parts. The first part is an analysis of economic problems; it represents a closing of the difference in view between the Lagos Plan and the World Bank report. The second part is a series of relatively specific commitments by governments and donors for *Africa's Priority Programme for Economic Recovery* (APPER).

For their part, African governments' commitments on increased public investment in productive sectors, particularly agriculture, have necessarily implied a shift away from spending both on welfare and on various forms of subsidies to the town-dwellers and publicly-run industries. These changes have meant major sacrifices for African people: the real incomes of many are declining as costs of

The UN Special Session on Africa, 1986

△ **Extracts from Programme of Action for African Economic Recovery and Development**

Africa's Priority Programme for Economic Recovery stipulates the following priorities:

Agricultural Development: The main objective will be to give a new impetus to agricultural development in order to achieve increasing levels of productivity and production through:

▲ raising substantially the level of investment in agriculture

▲ establishing remunerative produce pricing policies, establishing and strengthening incentive schemes, eliminating pricing policies that discourage production and providing effective agriculture credit programmes.

Trade and Finance: In the field of trade the aim is to improve distribution channels for domestic trade, by improving market arrangements and reversing the present consumption pattern in favour of domestically produced goods.

Drought and Desertification: Although drought and desertification require a long-term approach, there is need for immediate action by the African countries to implement a comprehensive programme.

Population Policy: Special importance will need to be given by each African country to a population policy that will, *inter alia*, address issues of high fertility and mortality.

The full implementation of Africa's Priority Programme for Economic Recovery would require $128.1 billion during the period 1986–90. In spite of severe constraints, the African countries commit themselves to provide $82.5 billion, or 64.4% of the total cost of financing the Programme. There is a gap of approximately $46 billion between the total financial requirements for the implementation of the Programme and the resources to be made available through domestic efforts.

Accordingly, effective implementation of the Programme will require $9 billion annually, on average, through external resources.

Extensive international support is needed for the priorities and policies that Africa has identified as necessary. The international community agree on the importance of increasing official development assistance to Africa, its improved quality and effectiveness. They also agree to:

▲ place greater emphasis on non-project aid including balance of payments support

▲ in the case of countries concerned, work towards the rapid implementation of the International Monetary Fund Structural Adjustment Facility which provides longer term concessional resources in support of adjustment efforts.

---

living continue to rise sharply, and unemployment is rising, especially in the public sector on which so many rely. Services and public utilities are being cut back or made more expensive. Such sacrifices by individuals represent unpopularity for governments and in a continent beset by political instability it has taken considerable courage to introduce such changes.

Yet in the face of this preoccupation with trade and production performance it has been left to voluntary organisations and agencies· such as UNICEF to keep in the forefront the importance of developing the welfare of African citizens, not simply as a 'benefit' of increased wealth but also as a condition for creating that wealth.

△ The Human Resource of Africa

African governments are sometimes criticised by visiting economists for having 'overspent' on health, education and public utilities such as drinking water and electricity. They have created, say their critics, 'premature welfare states': that is, there is insufficient wealth in their economies to pay for services demanded as a right from citizens who are unable to provide sufficient tax income to cover their cost. This used to be called the 'crisis of rising expectations'. Governments and donors have now accepted the need to dampen expectations, to cut public spending and to claw back more of the costs of providing services from consumers, parents and patients.

To anyone from the developed world visiting Africa and seeing schools in Ghana without exercise books or pencils, or rural clinics in the Sudan without bandages or antiseptic, it is understandable why governments are unwilling to reduce spending. Also, it must be remembered that African governments have rightly seen their people as their main resource. Only a few countries have

exceptionally valuable natural resources such as precious metals, and Africa, in the 1950s and 1960s, seemed to its leaders to be trapped at the bottom of the ladder of international trade. It was natural that African leaders decided to invest in getting their people healthier, better housed and better educated, and great gains have been made, as we show in the following chapters. These are not only improvements in school enrolment, infant and child health, and access to clean water. There are also advances in enterprise, in management and in technology. They are, at

Africa's Recovery – One Year Later

The UN Secretary General's 1987 Report on Africa demonstrated that the economic crisis had deepened in intensity since the UN Special Session, despite concerted efforts on the part of African governments to confront the crisis and revive economic growth. These efforts included:

Policy Reforms: Twenty-eight African countries embarked on economic policy reforms during the course of 1986. These entailed sharp reductions in social expenditure and government payrolls, and the rationalisation of unprofitable state corporations in an attempt to restore financial stability.

Agriculture: Food production was given highest priority with two-thirds of the countries allocating 25% of total investment to agriculture in line with the recommendations of the UN Special Session. This resulted in the introduction of price incentives, improved distribution and subsidies on inputs, bringing about a shift in the terms of trade in favour of the rural sector. Stimulated by favourable weather conditions across much of the continent, food production increased by three per cent in 1986.

Trade and Debt: Despite widespread international concern and the launching of a number of initiatives to alleviate the debt crisis, developments in the international economic sphere have negated the impact of many African efforts. The most important of these have been:

Export Losses: Almost $20 billion was lost in 1986 by African countries as a result of commodity prices falling to their lowest level in fifty years. According to the UN Economic Commission for

Africa, income from the sale of commodities – virtually the sole source of hard currency – plunged from $64 billion to $45 billion, the sharpest fall in export revenues for Africa since 1950. At the same time, prices of manufactured imports grew by 20 per cent, thereby exacerbating balance of payments difficulties.

Debt Servicing: Despite some rescheduling of official debt, the fall in export income increased debt service ratios to an average of over 50% in 1986. Total debt grew in excess of $150 billion, representing at least 300% of annual export earnings. Seventeen low-income and highly-indebted countries face scheduled debt-service payments in 1988–90 triple those of 1985 (from $2.3 billion to $6.9 billion annually).

External Resources: The African Development Bank increased its resources by 200 per cent for 1987 to 1991, enabling it to plan a lending target of at least $6–8 billion for the period. Against this encouraging trend, official development assistance stagnated in real terms in 1986. World Bank commitments rose from $1.1 billion to $1.7 billion, but few bilateral donors managed to enlarge their programmes. On the other hand, grants made available to sub-Saharan Africa by non-governmental organisations in 1986 came close to $1 billion.

In view of these trends, the Secretary General's Report concluded:

'It will have become very clear that unless deficiencies in resource flows are dealt with in a comprehensive manner, the continent's economic recovery will be aborted.'

A primary school in Mozambique.

present, small advances; and Africa continues to need external assistance in developing its capabilities. But such visible progress, we argue, helps to justify past investment in developing 'human resources' and gives cause for optimism about Africa's future if investment in education and material well-being can be maintained.

In this report we investigate how Africa is reacting to the new challenges of the 1986 Special Session, how donors, voluntary agencies and investors are responding, and how, as a result, the prospects for Africa now appear. In the next chapter, on Africa in the 1980s, we look at current evidence on economic development, particularly in agriculture and industry, and try to build a picture of what this economic performance means for living standards and welfare generally.

In the subsequent chapters we look first at the ways in which the outside world is responding to Africa's development crisis and we examine, in turn, the official aid institutions, the private sector and the voluntary agencies. We then look at what African governments are doing. In particular we dissect 'structural adjustment', a term used to describe the policy measures which most African governments are taking to meet the challenge of development.

In this report, we see development as a series of economic and environmental challenges, and in Chapter 5 we investigate three of Africa's main challenges. The challenge of debt, we explain, is not a challenge to avoid repaying loans but a challenge to build Africa's economy and particularly its trading performance. The debt problem, we claim, is chiefly a balance of payments problem. We also discuss the population challenge: and here we are writing of the unprecedented rate of population increase in Africa, the strains this is imposing on the natural environment, and of the ability of governments to generate jobs and provide services. Finally, we address specifically the challenge of a particular environment: the drylands of Africa, now more than ever prone to severe drought and erosion and seemingly requiring permanent support from outside.

△ War, Conflict and Development

Yet these challenges – long-term, formidable and endlessly discussed in international fora – are only one side of the contemporary story of Africa's development. Equally urgent a challenge is the scourge of war and conflict. In large areas of southern Africa, particularly in Mozambique and Angola, but also throughout the region, the normal conduct of trade and production and the most rudimentary functions of government are at a standstill. Until peace and stability can be achieved in South Africa and Namibia, the entire region will remain contaminated by the strains of conflict (see Box on p. 10).

Elsewhere in Africa, there are areas that have suffered from long-sustained insurrection and prolonged conflicts over borders and the allegiance of border peoples. In some cases this has spread like a cancer into debilitating civil war, as in Ethiopia, the Sudan and Chad. In other cases, entire areas, such as Acholi in Uganda, are in virtually permanent states of lawlessness and consequent poverty.

This challenge – the challenge of establishing peace and security – is not a subject of this report.

To advocate the conditions for peace in the several different conflicts of Africa is inappropriate for a group such as ours and would not be helpful. But we feel compelled to emphasise the importance of national and

The front line in Eritrea, one of Africa's battlegrounds, but also where survival techniques are highly developed.

international action, particularly in southern and north-east Africa where the staff of voluntary organisations and development agencies are caught up in national conflicts and are often forced to take sides. It makes little sense if such organisations with an entirely humanitarian purpose see their work destroyed again and again because of the lack of any genuine attempt at negotiation or political settlement, which foreign governments have some power to influence.

The Impact of War on Health Care in Mozambique

After Mozambique became independent in 1975, the health system was nationalised. A new policy based on primary health care was formulated, which sought to extend services to rural areas, giving priority to preventive rather than curative medicine. The number of peripheral health units rose from 446 in 1975 to 1039 in 1981. Thousands of para-medical staff were trained and mass vaccination campaigns carried out. The percentage of the state budget allocated to health rose from 3.3% in 1974 to a high of 11.2% in 1982, which represented a per capita increase from US$ 1.5 to $4.7.

Since 1982 the war waged by the Mozambique National Resistance (MNR) with support from South Africa, combined with the effects of drought and world economic recession, has had a devastating effect on the health of the people. An estimated 4.6 million people are in need of food aid due to the combined effects of war, displacement and natural disasters. The MNR has destroyed 25% of the primary health care network. By the end of 1986, an estimated two million people had lost access to health care because of the closure of facilities or displacement. This loss of access is almost entirely in rural areas where people are most in need of health care.

Not just health facilities but health workers too have been targets of the MNR. Not all cases are recorded, but by 1988 at least 21 health workers had been murdered, over 30 kidnapped and 243 had had all their belongings looted.

Malnutrition has increased owing to the combined effects of low food production, displacement and infectious diseases. Both acute and chronic malnutrition in children is worse in war-affected areas. Mortality rates have risen rapidly, in particular for children, the most vulnerable section of the population. Many thousands of children have been orphaned or separated from their families and are particularly physically and mentally vulnerable. War and destabilisation are estimated to have caused 84,000 child deaths in 1986 alone and 320,000 between 1981 and 1986.

Most of these deaths are due to diseases that are preventable or can be cured by simple treatment. Successful vaccination requires a good logistics system and a high level of community participation. In the capital, Maputo, where these conditions exist, immunisation levels reached 90% in 1987 but in war-affected provinces coverage has fallen.

War and displacement have created ideal conditions for the spread of infectious diseases. Crowded living conditions with limited access to water have resulted in an increase in all the common infections such as pneumonia, diarrhoea, measles and skin diseases. There are serious drug shortages at all levels. Shortages of foreign exchange have led to a reduction in imports.

Blocking of normal transport routes has led to an accumulation of drugs at ports and airports. At the local level, lack of transport and fuel and attacks on the roads have made distribution increasingly difficult.

Although the picture is grim, people continue to work under the most difficult conditions and to rebuild after destruction. Health workers make dangerous and difficult journeys to get medicines and to vaccinate people. All over the country, health posts have been rebuilt. By the end of 1985 a total of 158 closed health posts had been reopened. In Inhambane province, the improvement of security conditions in 1985 enabled the health authorities to carry out a successful accelerated immunisation programme followed in 1986 by a mobile mother and child clinic programme.

Africa
in the 1980s

△ Economic Crises

Africa has been in serious economic decline
throughout the 1980s and for much of the
1970s. This decline was accelerated by severe
drought between 1982 and 1985. Although
conditions have improved since then, with
good harvests in much of Africa (but see Box),
the economies of the region remain fragile.
Income per person has fallen by 12% since
1980 and on average most people are worse
off than they were in 1970. Declining real
wages have become the norm, despite
considerable variation between countries. The

contrast between the optimism of the 1960s
and early 1970s and the reality of the 1980s
could not be more stark.

This decline in average incomes in Africa
over the last two decades has had particularly
serious effects on the poor and it has been
estimated that over half the people of Africa
are living near or below the poverty line. This
means an income per person of less than $100
a year, chronic malnutrition, women having to
walk five miles to fetch drinking water, houses
with no doors or windows, too little fuel to
heat and light homes, and no money to pay for
schoolbooks or clothes. For the very poor a
12% reduction in income a year does not

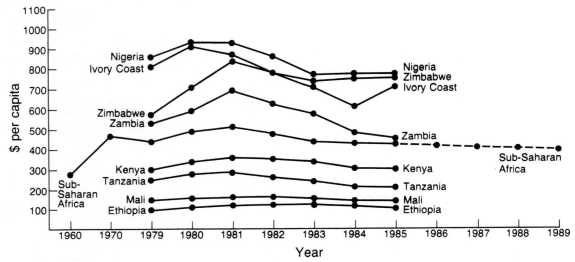

Source: World Bank

Fig 2.1 Most people in Africa are now worse off than they were in 1970. Income per head rose during the 1960s and
again in 1979, but since 1981 it has declined, especially in higher-income countries.

Famine in Ethiopia

Since the autumn of 1987 it has become clear that Ethiopia and other parts of East Africa are suffering from an emergency which may turn out to be as serious as that of 1984–85. Once again, the world has watched a terrible famine develop even while attempts were being made by the aid agencies to prevent it happening, through long-term projects such as soil and water conservation as well as immediate relief.

There are a number of reasons for this situation occurring again so soon. The immediate cause of the crisis in Ethiopia is crop failure (almost total in some areas) caused by drought and locust swarms across large areas of the north. Crop failures do not necessarily mean famine, but in much of Ethiopia farmers have been unable to store enough food, even in good years, for use when crops fail. This is partly because of the previous drought, but highland Ethiopia also has to cope with the long-term problems of high population density, inefficient agricultural techniques, deforestation and soil erosion.

Long-term development is a gradual process. It takes time to get results from new farming techniques, and the two years since the last famine have simply not been long enough. There are other obstacles which make it particularly difficult to bring about rapid improvements:

▲ lack of infrastructure: there are very few good roads, fewer railways, limited water and power supplies.

▲ war: large areas of northern Ethiopia are affected by the conflict between the Ethiopian government and its opponents in Eritrea and Tigray, diverting scarce resources.

▲ opposition to government policies: many peasant farmers are suspicious of the government's reform policies for rural areas such as resettlement and villagisation.

▲ lack of investment: comparatively little foreign aid has been made available for long-term development, largely because western donors disagree with the government's social and economic policies.

If famine is to be prevented and future development to succeed, three factors must be taken into account. First, it will take many years to make Ethiopia self-sufficient in food, and it is important to build up a buffer stock for use in times of shortage and to provide adequate transport and access roads. Secondly, any development programme must take account of the needs and desires of Ethiopian peasant farmers, or it will not work. Finally, the political and military obstacles to aid and development in particular regions will have to be overcome.

mean cutting down on the amount of meat or other protein they eat, but more likely eating no meat at all.

This fall in income has had long-term consequences. Investment, crucial for future growth prospects, has fallen to a low level as governments have not been able to maintain expenditure on roads and other public programmes. Total investment in Africa has fallen from an average of 20% of income in 1980 to just over 14% in 1986. Again, the picture for individual countries is quite varied. In Kenya, investment as a proportion of income has fallen only slightly, while in Zambia investment has fallen from 28% of total income to 18% over a similar period.

Governments have also been forced to cut back on social expenditure, such as schools, hospitals and housing, by reducing the growth of these facilities, with the result that they do not keep pace with population growth. This has long-term consequences for Africa because well-housed, educated, healthy people are essential if Africa is to achieve continuing economic and social development. In Kenya total expenditure in real terms on education fell from $348 million in 1980 to $272 million in 1983. In expenditure per pupil the fall was even greater; from $79 in 1980 to $60 in 1983. Even in Zimbabwe, where expenditure on education went up in 1980–83, it fell, on a per pupil basis, from $249 to $166, although this was because of the sudden increase in enrolment after the fall of the Smith government.

The economic decline in Africa must be placed in perspective. In Britain an economic growth rate of 3% is considered satisfactory and with a population growth rate close to zero this means that real incomes per person have been rising. In Africa, which has had a population growth rate of 3% per annum over the last decade, the total wealth of the continent has to increase by 3%

INVESTMENT AND SAVINGS

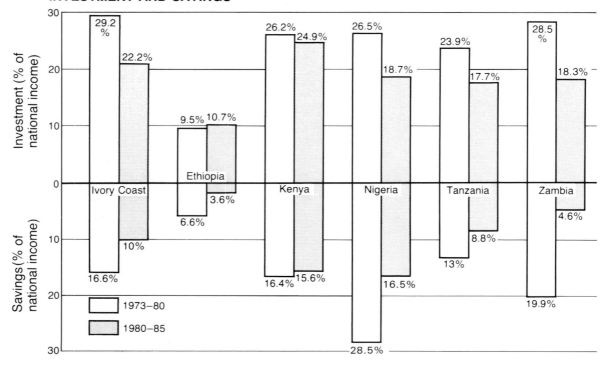

Source: World Bank

Fig 2.2   Investment and savings in Africa have fallen to a low level. Of the countries shown only Kenya has been able to maintain almost the same level as in the 1970s.

What is Wealth in Rural Africa?

Whether measured in the conventional terms of gross domestic product or in terms of the material quality of life, most of Africa is poor. Yet in another sense, and in contrast to poverty in Asia and other regions of the world, much of Africa is still relatively wealthy.

For much of rural Africa the type of poverty seen in countries such as Bangladesh, where many people live hand-to-mouth, is still a rarity. The extended African family, which may sometimes be as large as one hundred people, forms an economic unit of great strength. Working as a group allows for a diversity of sources of income, economies of consumption and the accumulation of wealth. It is not unknown for the total capital worth of a rural family, particularly in the Sahelian zone, to amount to the equivalent of thousands of pounds per person.

Capital is generally kept in the form of cattle, as well as cash, gold and other saleable items. In some areas agricultural populations may have larger numbers of stock than people. These savings provide security for the group, the effectiveness of which has been demonstrated by the extraordinary ability of some populations to withstand repeated failures of production as a result of drought.

In a sense, therefore, the poverty of much of Africa is a poverty of opportunity, not of resources. Material poverty often arises from the lack of opportunity for safe productive investment, not from the lack of resources as such (cattle and gold may produce an uncertain and small return) and from the lack of reliable health and education services. The paradox of many areas of Africa, even where wealth has been eroded by years of drought, is of a population with considerable means and wealth from which they cannot directly benefit.

per annum for incomes per person just to stand still. This means that since 1978 the total economy of Africa would have to have expanded by 29% for average incomes per person to be the same as they were in that year.

Rapid population growth is only part of the story. Africa has felt the brunt of the shocks to the world economy since 1973. The oil price rises of 1973 and 1979 hit the economies of Africa harder than most other developing regions. Most African countries depend on oil imports and could not increase their exports rapidly enough to pay these increased prices. They also suffered from declining prices for their major exports and commodities, and from increased prices for other imports, mainly manufactured goods from the developed world. Africa now has to export over 25%

more goods than it did 10 years ago to buy the same quantity of imports. A shortage of foreign exchange, and of the imports it can buy, is at the heart of many of Africa's economic problems.

The External Economy – The Squeeze on Resources

The crises in Africa's external economic relations began with the first oil crisis. The quadrupling in oil prices that took place in 1973 and the further doubling in 1979 created enormous problems for most countries in Africa. The price rise affected Africa in two ways: first, it meant that foreign exchange had to be used to meet the higher cost of oil; second, the price rise triggered a recession in the developed world which substantially

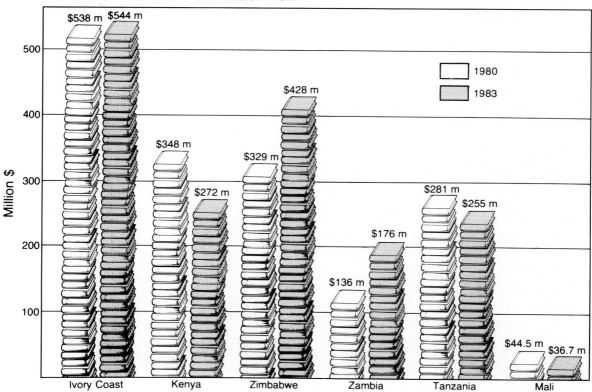

PUBLIC EXPENDITURE ON EDUCATION

Source: World Bank

(At constant 1983 prices)

Fig 2.3 Social service spending in Africa has been cut back sharply during the 1980s. Countries like Zimbabwe were able to spend more on education, but not enough to meet the needs of the growing number of pupils.

WORLD OIL AND COMMODITY PRICES: 1970–86 (1970=100)

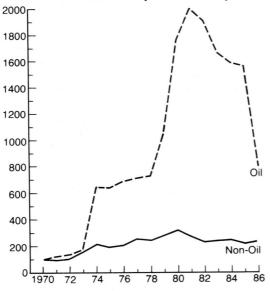

Source: IMF

Fig 2.4   Africa's oil and other imports have cost more, while the demand for its exports has fallen. The result has been a shortage of imports and of foreign exchange to pay for them.

THE VALUE OF AFRICA'S EXPORTS IN RELATION TO IMPORTS

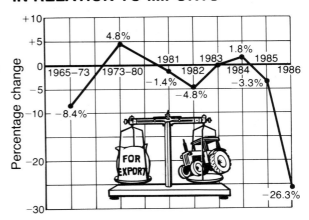

Source: IMF

Fig 2.5   A falling line means that countries have to pay more for their imports relative to the price they receive from their exports. Africa has to export over 25% more goods today than it did ten years ago to pay for the same imports.

reduced the demand for primary commodities. Between 1973 and 1980 exports by volume from Africa fell sharply, by about 5% a year.

Africa's export performance was also weak in comparison with other developing countries. As a result, Africa suffered a loss in its share of world exports. Africa's share of the world commodity markets fell from 7.9% in 1971 to 4.9% in 1983. During the last decade there have been major losses in markets for copper, zinc, coffee, cocoa, beef, palm oil, maize, timber, cotton and rubber. Only in aluminium ore, tea and tobacco has Africa's share increased.

The effect of this squeeze on resources created substantial balance of payments problems for Africa. Most developing countries can expect to have a deficit on the current account and the gap is usually financed by grants and loans from the richer countries. These capital transfers, as they are called, allow countries to import more goods and services which, if they make a permanent contribution, are essential to the process of

economic development. For Africa, however, the deficits got out of hand. By 1981 the current account deficit reached over $16 billion, or just under 40% of total export earnings.

The deficits that occurred throughout the 1970s and early 1980s were financed by borrowing at a level that was unsustainable.

MALI: IMPORTS AND EXPORTS

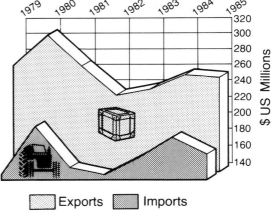

Source: World Bank

Fig 2.6   Mali has recovered from drastic falls in both exports and imports, but it has had further setbacks.

ZAMBIA: IMPORTS AND EXPORTS

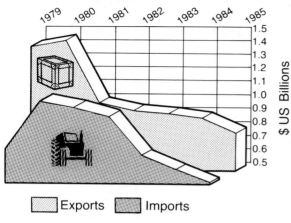

Exports   Imports

Source: World Bank

Fig 2.7 Zambia has suffered a steady economic decline in the 1980s and is not yet on the road to recovery.

Most of this borrowing was from government sources, though concessional lending by the World Bank has become increasingly important in recent years. In 1975 the total debt outstanding to the rest of the world was $16 billion. By 1982 this had grown to $54 billion. Since then the situation has deteriorated even further.

In 1986 the total debt reached $82 billion. In the 1980s there has been a further deterioration in export earnings. Between 1980 and 1986, export earnings from trade fell by about 34%. Interest and loan repayments rose from 12.6% of total export earnings in 1980 to 41.6% of export earnings in 1986. About 9% of the total annual income of Africa is now used in repayments to banks, overseas governments and international institutions.

The increased need for foreign exchange in Africa over the 1980s has not been covered by a sufficiently rapid rise in the flow of capital into Africa. In fact the contrary has occurred. Even ignoring the effects of inflation, total capital flows to Africa fell by 23% between 1981 and 1984 and only in 1986 did capital flows exceed those of 1981. The main source of the decline has been in private transfers, which fell from $4.6 billion in 1981 to $0.3 billion in 1985. This reflected the general loss of confidence by investors. Official aid to Africa rose only slowly in nominal terms during the early 1980s and actually fell

slightly in real terms. The levels achieved in 1980 were not met again until 1984.

The resulting shortage of foreign exchange is one of the major causes of the decline in the economies of Africa. Many countries have not had enough money to buy essential imports. It is now estimated that, for low-income African countries, imports per person are now at only 60% of their level at the end of the 1960s. The effect of this has been to reduce the availability of essential agricultural inputs such as fertiliser and pesticides, thus adversely affecting production. A shortage of

Fig 2.8 In 1985 Africa was paying out in debt almost as much as it received in aid. Aid has risen only slowly and has actually fallen in real terms. Meanwhile debt has continued to rise.

DEBT HAS CAUGHT UP WITH AID

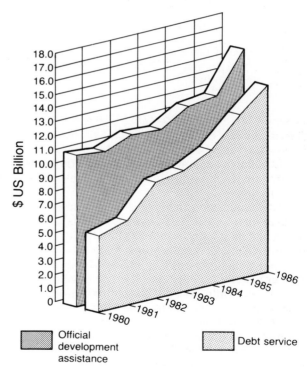

Official development assistance   Debt service

Notes

Debt service includes all interest and loan repayments. Official development assistance, or aid, includes all loans and grants from governments but not private investment or voluntary aid.

Source: OECD

The Exchange Rate

The exchange rate is simply the price of one currency in terms of another – e.g. the number of pounds that must be paid for one dollar – and a country will have as many exchange rates as there are different currencies. Those exchange rates can be set by market forces, by governments, or by a combination of both – as, for example, where the Bank of England buys or sells pounds to influence the market exchange rate. In Africa most governments fix the levels of their most important exchange rates, although some, as part of their agreements with the IMF, now allow markets a greater role in determining the value of their currencies.

The prices of most of the goods that Africa imports are set on world markets, and usually in one of the major western currencies. To take an example, Tanzania could import oil which sells at one dollar per gallon in the international market. Suppose that Tanzania's exchange rate is ten shillings to one dollar: then the oil will sell for ten shillings in Tanzania. If the exchange rate were set at five shillings to the dollar then the oil would be cheaper in Tanzania to the benefit of consumers (who will be mostly urban). Industrialists will also want to pay five – instead of ten – shillings for each dollar's worth of oil they import for their factories.

For these reasons many African governments have often fixed the value of their currencies at levels which provide cheap imports for urban consumers and industrialists. But let us look at the issue from the point of view of exporters, again taking Tanzania as an example. The Tanzanian government buys coffee from the farmer and sells it on the world market for, say, one dollar per bag. Now if the government sets the exchange rate at TSh5 = $1 in order to benefit urban consumers and importers, it can only pay its coffee farmers five shillings for each bag of coffee exported. If the exchange rate were TSh10 = $1 it could pay farmers ten shillings, which could encourage them to produce more.

Exchange rates can also affect food production. For example, Tanzanian farmers may sell their maize at seven shillings per bag, but consumers will prefer imported rice if the exchange rate prices a bag of rice at only five shillings. When the rate is set at a level which undermines exports, and discourages the domestic production of goods which are also imported, economists say that the currency is overvalued. 'Overvalued' currencies result in countries losing their share of export markets and in foreign imports taking larger shares of domestic markets. In such circumstances the IMF and the World Bank recommend devaluation. In our Tanzanian example the government would thus be encouraged to set the exchange rate at TSh10 = $1, rather than TSh5 = $1.

spare parts and raw materials for many factories has further reduced production and contributed to the decline of the industrial sector.

This squeeze on resources is alternatively known as a balance of payments crisis. The pressure on governments to alter their exchange rate regimes stems from this. The burden of adjustment to a changed world has fallen heavily on Africa and other developing countries, while Europe, the United States and Japan have done little to assist the process. The EEC continues to produce excess food and dump the surplus on the world market.

For example, the EEC surplus production of sugar (an important export crop from Africa) is roughly equivalent to the total world stocks. The world price of sugar has dropped dramatically, impoverishing many small producers. The United States subsidises cotton producers and no longer imports cotton, so contributing to the decline in world cotton prices. Tariffs are imposed by industrialised countries on many exports from Africa. This discourages local manufacturing by developing countries. For instance, the average tariff on cocoa beans imposed by the industrialised countries is only 2.6%, but on processed beans it is 4.3% and on chocolate 11.8%.

Recent developments indicate some improvement in Africa's overall trade position. Total imports rose in 1986 and this trend continued in 1987. Even so, imports are still below the level they were in 1982 and some 16% below 1980 levels. Exports also grew slowly in 1987 but still remain at a very low level.

Capital flows have also increased and by 1986 were at their highest ever level of almost $19 billion, although official aid accounted for over 85% of this as opposed to 67% in 1980. Private capital is still wary of Africa, with direct investment at a very low level.

The Internal Economy – Getting Policies Right

By no means all of Africa's problems are due to external factors such as world prices. Some stem from the mismanagement of domestic economies, particularly the neglect of agriculture, the creation of unviable public enterprises, the protection of inefficient industries, and uncontrolled public spending. African governments are now more self-critical of policy weaknesses.

Since 1980 many African countries have tried to change some of the basic characteristics of their economies in order to overcome these problems. Changes have included:

▲ making exchange rates responsive to demand and supply
▲ promoting export industries that are economically viable
▲ closing down, privatising, or establishing better controls on public enterprises
▲ allowing market forces to set internal prices, particularly for food
▲ using more private enterprise to provide goods and services.

This process is known as 'structural adjustment' (described fully in Chapter 4) and has largely been carried out at the instigation and with the help of the World Bank and the IMF.

Currently most countries in Africa are undergoing structural adjustment programmes and almost without exception the process of change has been very painful. Incomes have fallen; prices, particularly of food, have risen, and governments have been forced to cut back on expenditure. The changes have caused severe political problems in many countries: for example, in Zambia and Sudan they have led to riots over food price rises. It is too early to say whether the results have justified the pain of adjustment. Current indications are that many of the African countries that have undertaken structural adjustment programmes have not reaped the expected benefits in the short run.

△ The Crisis in Farm and Factory

Agriculture – Africa's Backbone

Africa is a diverse continent, and this is particularly true of agriculture. Some countries, including Zimbabwe and the Ivory Coast, have had considerable success in increasing agricultural output and improving the availability of food for the poor. But for most of Africa, agricultural production since the early 1970s has either declined absolutely

Balance of Payments and Aid

No country can expect to produce everything it needs. All countries, therefore, need to trade. Africa trades mainly with Europe and, typically, the relationship is based on Africa providing agricultural produce and raw materials while Europe, and increasingly Japan and the United States, provides in exchange manufactured goods and services such as banking and insurance.

Goods imported must be paid for by exporting goods or receiving financial inflows. The total exports of goods and services from a country less the total imports of goods and services is called the *current* account surplus or deficit. The total import of financial capital (including aid flows, loans, direct investment and remittances from nationals working overseas) less the total export of financial capital (including loan repayments and

repatriated profits) is called the *capital* account surplus or deficit. The current account and capital account together are known as the overall balance of payments account.

A country can run a current account deficit indefinitely if there is enough surplus on the capital account to pay for the deficit. If at the end of a year a country has imported more goods and services than there are funds available in the capital account, then it has an overall deficit on its balance of payments. To pay for this deficit it must either draw down on its reserves, borrow from other countries or institutions, or, in the case of developing countries in Africa, obtain additional official development assistance, usually known as aid.

SHARE OF PRODUCTION: AGRICULTURE AND INDUSTRY (1965–1986)

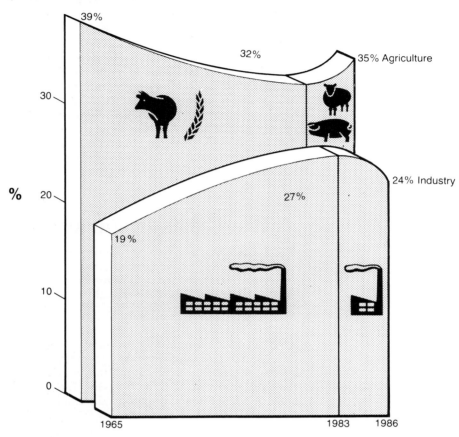

Source: World Bank

Fig 2.9   The proportion of Africa's income earned on the land fell during the 1960s and 1970s, but it has since gone up again. Meanwhile, industry's share has declined. In countries like Tanzania, agriculture still accounts for over half of national income, compared with 2% in the UK.

or grown too slowly to keep up with population growth.

Between 1973 and 1984 only 10 countries in Africa increased food production per head. The combination of economic recession, accelerated land erosion and overgrazing, and a general bias against agriculture in government policy is potentially fatal to rural development.

Agriculture is important to Africa both for food supply and because in many countries it is usually the dominant economic sector. Three-quarters of the working population derive their income from the land. Agriculture contributes about one-third of the total income

generated and about two-thirds of total export earnings. But this varies between countries; in Nigeria, agriculture produces slightly under one-quarter of national income and under 10% of exports, while in Tanzania it is over half of national income and 80% of exports. By comparison, Britain's agriculture produces about 2% of national income and about 6% of exports. The poor performance of agriculture overall is a key factor in the economic crisis that faces the continent.

This economic crisis has a human face – the face of hunger. In the past, food imports (including food aid) have kept large numbers of people from starvation or acute malnutrition.

Malnutrition has long been common in much of Africa, but it has been worsened by food shortages, the lack of money to purchase food, and high food prices.

Food availability, according to FAO estimates, has stagnated at 2150 calories per person per day for the region as a whole, but there are wide variations both between and within countries. For example, in the Ivory Coast more food is available than is required, whereas in Ethiopia only 75% of nutritional requirements can be met in a good year. In Mali in 1986 there were food surpluses, yet many poor farming families had to go hungry. Food may be available but people cannot always afford to buy it. In 1987, only six countries in Africa had consumption levels higher than the minimum recommended by the FAO (Burundi, Congo, the Ivory Coast, Madagascar, Mauritius and Swaziland).

Perhaps the most important reason for agriculture's failure to meet demand is the bias against it in government policy. This bias has its origins in strategies of development that give agriculture a role secondary to the manufacturing sector. This strategy has led to governments spending less than 10% of their budgets on agriculture. Governments also tried to keep food prices down for town dwellers, so reducing pressure on wages. The effect of these policies has been to starve farmers of the money they need to develop agriculture and reduce the incentive to produce surpluses.

One unforeseen effect of these policies has been on the rate of uptake of new ideas and technology. Governments have been reluctant to invest heavily in research and advisory services and many of the technical changes put to farmers have been inappropriate to their circumstances. These factors, combined with the lack of incentives to adopt new, potentially risky, farming techniques and the scarcity of credit to buy the new equipment and inputs, have meant that productivity has risen only slowly.

The slow rise in productivity has not been balanced by an increase in the amount of land under cultivation. The erosion of existing land has further reduced any potential expansion. New land has not come to the rescue, for a

Sudan – bales of cotton ready for export, essential if the country is to pay for vital imports such as machinery.

What is Famine?

The popular notion of famine is of people starving to death. But this generalisation needs to be refined if aid is to be more effective. The people of Darfur, Western Sudan, see regular famines ('maja'a') quite differently from 'famines that kill' ('maja'a al qatala') – a distinction which should also concern all those seeking to alleviate the effects of famine. This is the conclusion of a Save the Children Fund study of the famine which struck Darfur in 1984–85.

The famine of 1984–85 was caused not by drought alone, but by a combination of ecological decline and economic crisis. The people of Darfur had faced such a combination for several years before 1984, and even in 1984–85 their responses were, in some ways, successful. Although some 95,000 people are estimated to have died due to the famine, these deaths were primarily related not to economic poverty or even lack of food, but to factors such as poor water supply and health services.

The evidence of the Darfur famine gives several important messages to governments and relief agencies seeking to alleviate the effects of famine in Sudan and elsewhere. Above all, they must decide whether their primary aim is to prevent destitution or to prevent excess deaths, and therefore whether they should intervene at all in 'famines that do not kill'.

The Darfur report says that, having made the decision to intervene, agencies should recognise that the main effect of general food distribution is the prevention of destitution. This is an economic effect, so the distribution policy of the agencies should be guided by an understanding of local economic forces. If, however, the main concern is to prevent excess deaths, agencies should aim to tackle the major causes of famine mortality by targeting 1–5 year olds and focusing specifically on the provision of health services, clean water supplies and supplementary foods.

Decisions concerning the appropriate form of intervention rely on accurate information about the nature of the famine, so there are equally important lessons for those involved in developing early warning systems. They need, above all, to identify the phenomenon they are trying to predict; is it 'famine that kills' or 'famine' in the sense of economic slump or shortage?

number of reasons. First, it is a myth that Africa has surplus land: according to the FAO (1986) about one-quarter of the land area available is too dry to support crops without expensive irrigation, and about half of the remainder is of marginal quality and vulnerable to degradation. When grazing land and forest reserves are taken into account, the picture in much of Africa is one of land shortage for arable purposes. Second, poor producer prices have discouraged farmers from expanding areas under cultivation. Third, even in relatively well populated areas, there are insufficient people available at critical times in the farming calendar for ploughing and harvesting, due to migration to the towns or other countries (such as from Mali to the Ivory Coast).

The fourth reason for the slow-down in the increase of land under cultivation is the general reduction of rainfall on the continent and the length of the recent droughts (1968–72 and 1983–85). The weather risk in some areas has become so great that farmers are not prepared to make the investment required to increase food production. This climatic factor has been accentuated by poor land management in much of Africa, allowing soil erosion and the encroachment of scrubland and even desert. This has reduced the amount of land available for pasture and crop cultivation.

Production trends established over the last 15 years or so cannot continue. If they do, food deficits in the next 25 years will become so great that no plausible combination of commercial imports and food aid could feed Africa. In 1982–84 food imports to Africa amounted to $5.2 billion, the equivalent of two-thirds of all agricultural export earnings from the continent. The FAO estimates that on current trends food imports will cost $25 billion by the year 2010, twice the estimate for Africa's entire agriculture export earnings.

There are solutions to Africa's food shortage. But if production is to rise it will require more policy changes and more investment in roads, railways and ports to enable food and other agricultural products to reach markets, and inputs such as fertiliser to reach farmers.

The need for improved farm incentives has been accepted by all concerned. In 1985 African leaders at the OAU General Assembly pledged to increase total public investment in agriculture to 20–25% of the total. But if agriculture is going to get a bigger share this requires a major shift in spending priorities. Such a shift is likely to be at the expense of health, education and housing, and this poses difficult decisions for governments. In addition, many governments are concerned that industrial development is not neglected.

Industrialisation – The Need for Reform

Industrialisation has traditionally been seen as the pathway to economic development. In post-independence Africa the governments of the newly emergent countries eagerly embarked on this process. During the 1960s and early 1970s industrial growth played an important part in economic progress, with production growing at 14% a year. The climate changed

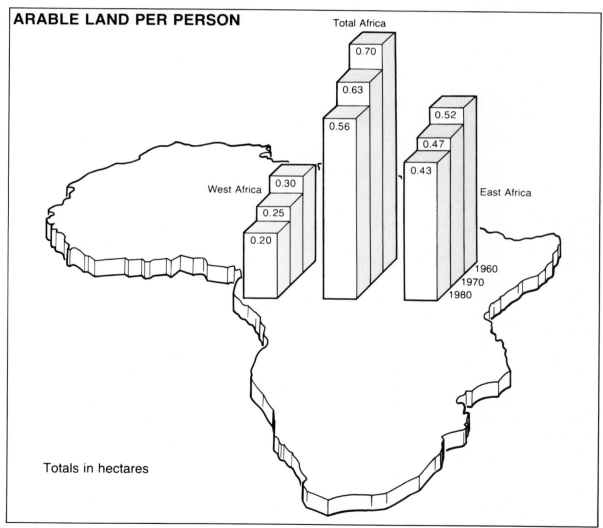

ARABLE LAND PER PERSON

Total Africa

0.70
0.63
0.56

West Africa   0.30
0.25
0.20

East Africa
0.52
0.47
0.43

1960
1970
1980

Totals in hectares

Source: FAO

Fig 2.10 Agricultural land is becoming scarce in Africa. In 1980, arable land in West Africa was down to 0.2 hectares or half an acre per person, compared to 0.3 hectares twenty years earlier. This is partly because much of the land is of poor quality and because farmers need more investment and incentives to irrigate and improve it.

Corned Beef from Ethiopia

Most of Britain's large food retailers such as Sainsbury, Tesco and Marks and Spencer now import fruit, vegetables, processed meat and fish etc. from developing countries. Corned beef is one such product; much of it comes from developing countries, particularly in South America.

In 1985, a major UK food importer suddenly found itself confronted with a shortfall in its supply of corned beef, as its regular source was unable to meet its requirements. An alternative supplier was Ethiopia's government-run corned beef industry, which had been struggling along for a number of years with a limited export market.

At the time, Ethiopia's food crisis was in the forefront of the public mind in the UK. Money was being collected to pay for food imports and schoolchildren were collecting tins of food and packet soups to send to Ethiopia. Would not tins of corned beef 'Made in Ethiopia' seem absurd – even offensive – to British shoppers? More to the point, would there be consumer resistance?

The food importers were unsure, and decided to investigate the circumstances of corned beef production in a country suffering from famine. Four important points quickly became evident. First, the animals being sold to the abattoirs and processing factories were *not* being fed on grain: they had been grazed largely on the open range. Second, the animals were often being sold by pastoral people dependent on the occasional sales of animals to buy food and other essential commodities. Third, because of the drought, it was proving very difficult to sustain animals on the rangelands and the subsequent increase in sales was having the effect of reducing cattle prices overall, especially in relation to grain prices. Fourth, there was no evidence that the corned beef industry was based on the acquisition of traditional pasture areas for modern commercial beef-ranching under the control of the state.

It was clear that the one measure which would do most to improve the livelihoods of many poorer Ethiopian stock-keepers was an increase in the price paid for the animals they were prepared to dispose of (their 'commercial off-take'). Going beyond this, it was also clear that in some of the poorer parts of Ethiopia, where crop cultivation is difficult and hazardous, the long-term prospects for improving incomes are more likely to be based on developing industries such as corned beef than on attempting to promote widespread cereal production.

The link between alleviating poverty and increasing exports could not be clearer in this case, and it showed the limitations of invariably applying the maxim that poor societies suffering from hunger should give priority to food production over all else. Buying corned beef 'Made in Ethiopia' suddenly becomes not only sensible but also a small contribution to development.

dramatically, however, in the early 1970s following the first oil shock. Industrial growth slowed to 5% per year between 1973 and 1980 and has been negative ever since. In 1980 industry in Africa produced 35% of income and employed about 8% of the workforce, but since then the figures have declined. By 1986 the industrial sector in Africa employed 6% of the workforce (though this varied from 2% in Niger to 24% in Mauritius) producing 24% of total income for the continent.

After independence governments commonly acted as entrepreneurs, with trade policy focusing on production for the domestic market. This approach meant that governments set up businesses or state-owned public enterprises directly or in partnership with privately owned companies, often protected from domestic and overseas competition. Protection at home was often achieved by legislation outlawing competition. Protection from abroad was maintained by restricting the quantity of goods that could be imported and by placing tariffs on imports.

The foundations of these policies were a combination of practical necessity and following the ideas of the day. It was not feasible to expect new industries to be started by local business when there was, and still is, a great shortage of capital and a lack of trained and experienced people. Governments were often compelled to invest in infrastructure and basic industries in order to lay the foundations for economic development. There was also a strong climate of opinion in Europe and among many of the international aid agencies in support of direct government intervention.

State-owned public enterprises came to dominate many of the economies of Africa, employing over half of all those people working in the formal economy (compared with only one-third in Asia), and taking a large share of funds available for investment. Directly or indirectly, government involvement has had a profound effect on the climate for investment in the industrial sector and on the viability of export-based enterprises (see also Chapter 4).

However, many of the newly created public enterprises and nationalised private companies soon became unprofitable under government management. Protection was frequently the only way in which industries could be established and maintain viability, even when private enterprise was given the job of producing the goods. Governments not only created industries; they also controlled their operations and pricing policies. Investment decisions were often made for political reasons and were inherently unprofitable. Prices were controlled to keep down inflation, but this led to subsidies and an inevitable drain on public finances. Any surpluses were frequently taxed away, reducing any incentive by managers to make profits.

Nonetheless, the picture of performance is not uniformly gloomy: many African public enterprises are efficiently managed and

A meat factory in Tanzania. Corned beef could be one of east Africa's strongest exports.

produce significant benefits for the state. For example, in Ethiopia the state-controlled manufacturing sector has performed reasonably well, showing sustained net profits, while some enterprises that have been restructured, such as the Investment Bank in Tanzania and the Palm Industry Corporation in the Ivory Coast, have improved their performance.

The need to shift from excessive reliance on the public sector towards a more balanced 'mixed economy' approach has now been accepted by most African countries. The challenge now is to attract and generate the new investment needed to get industry moving and to expand the domestic market. To do this, governments and aid agencies need to encourage private investment from overseas, which has been negligible throughout the 1980s. They also need to tackle the problem of internal finance for commercial development in Africa. It may be possible, by changing the structure of prices, to stimulate the small-scale informal sector, but larger-scale enterprises are seriously handicapped by the lack of capital markets, limited access to credit, a dearth of market information and perhaps a critical shortage of skilled manpower.

A tungsten carbide battery plant in Kenya. Industrialisation in Africa now needs major new investment.

△ Economic Crises and People

Africa's economic decline has so far been expressed largely in economic terms. But how have these economic crises affected people? What has been their effect on government services in health and education? Perhaps most important, are they causing African governments to revise their basic approach to social services?

Health – The Toll of Poverty

The state of Africa's health, measured by the health of new-born infants and young children, improved considerably between 1960 and 1980, though by most standards it was still bottom of the world's league table, with an average life expectancy at birth of only 49 years. The World Health Organisation (WHO) estimates that only about one-third of children in Africa are immunised against childhood diseases such as polio and measles: an immunisation rate of about 80% is considered necessary for effective control. Immunisation levels have dropped over recent years in Zambia and Tanzania and services have been interrupted by civil war in parts of countries such as Mozambique, as seen in Chapter 1. Sudan's rate, on the other hand, has crept up from a mere 0.5% to 2%.

The health of a nation is not determined by formal programmes of health care or by access to a doctor. The most important factors are access to enough food of sufficient variety to meet basic nutritional requirements, access to an adequate supply of clear drinking water and water for washing, and access to adequate shelter. These basic needs have not been met for the majority of Africans, and in some areas the position is deteriorating as the economy declines. In Zambia the incidence of

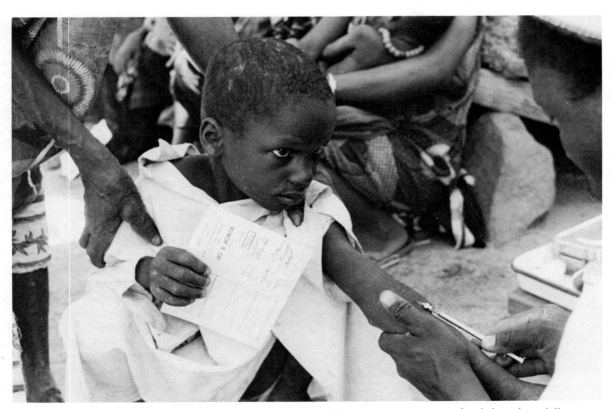

Mali – a village immunisation campaign, essential to primary health care. But immunisation levels have been falling.

The Khartoum Comprehensive Child Care Project

Health services in Sudan have suffered severely from the effects of national economic decline. Because of inflation and a shortage of foreign exchange, health workers are now paid at a very low rate and the services do not have basic equipment or a regular and reliable drug supply. As a result, people who need health care must pay for this privately and buy drugs at inflated prices from private pharmacies. For the poorest people and those in rural areas where there are no private services, this means no access to health care at all.

Preventive services have also suffered. Without a regular supply of drugs few patients attend health centres and it is therefore impossible to use these as a base from which to provide immunisation and other extension services.

The Sudan Ministry of Health and the Save the Children Fund are planning to reinstate the services in the Khartoum region, which has a population of about three million. The objective is to make these services effective and financially self-sufficient. The programme has three main elements: the repair and re-equipment of 61 health centres; the development of a revolving drug fund; and the organisation of services to provide basic preventive and curative care for mothers and children.

The key to the programme would be the revolving drug fund, as without a regular drug supply there are no patients; and without patients other aspects of the service cannot be developed. The idea, which SCF has used elsewhere in Africa, is to provide a stock of drugs which are then sold to the patients at cost plus a small margin. This covers the cost of replacing the drugs and the administration costs of the programme. The drugs provided through this system are essential non-branded preparations. Bought in large quantities, these drugs are very cheap and the prices paid by patients for them may in some cases be as little as one-tenth of the market price of the same drug. With drugs widely available, and patients brought back in contact with the services, reorganisation will allow for the more systematic development of referral and outreach services.

malnutrition as a reported contributory factor to the death of children under 14 years old rose from 27% in 1978 to 43% in 1982. Formal health programmes can only hope to mitigate some of the worst effects of economic decline.

Health services can make an important contribution, however, and in many areas these have become less available. There are a number of reasons for this decline, linked to the economic crisis in Africa and the squeeze on resources. Health budgets tend to be vulnerable to cuts during periods of financial hardship and since the early 1970s most low-income countries in Africa (see Box) have been forced to reduce health expenditure within the total budget. Health spending in these countries fell from 5.2% of the budget in 1972 to 4.5% in 1983, while public expenditure on health care in Africa overall has tended to remain static at about 6%. In most of the low-income countries, the annual government expenditure on health care is around $3 per head. Total government budgets have fallen in real terms in the 1980s and hence the real value of health expenditure has fallen. (However, there have been some countries which have increased their health spending, such as Kenya and Zimbabwe.) World Bank lending for the health sector, meanwhile, rose sharply from $23 million in 1982 to $80 million in 1986.

Low-income Countries

Ethiopia, Burkina Faso, Mali, Mozambique, Malawi, Zaire, Burundi, Togo, Madagascar, Niger, Benin, Central African Republic, Rwanda, Somalia, Kenya, Tanzania, Sudan, Sierra Leone, Senegal, Ghana, Zambia, Chad and Uganda – defined by the World Bank as having incomes less than $400 per head in 1985.

While more resources are necessary to improve health care, there is also scope for more efficient and equitable allocation of health expenditure. Hospitals are often located in the urban areas where only a small fraction (15%) of Africa's population live, and may consume a high proportion of the budget. This is particularly true of Uganda, Zimbabwe, Zambia and the Ivory Coast. But there are exceptions. Tanzania, for example, has achieved considerable success in providing basic services. Almost half its rural population now has access to safe water, compared with under 20% for rural Africa as a whole, and 'barefoot doctors' and health workers have enabled many more people to benefit from primary health care.

African governments have often provided a wide range of individually organised free services, but the most cost-effective approach is to achieve fuller coverage with basic services (including immunisation and treatment of widespread diseases such as malaria) through locally financed primary health care (see also Chapter 5).

Education – The Foundation of the Future

An educated workforce is essential to economic and social development. The rapid transition of countries in Africa from colonial rule to self-government to participation in the international arena was possible only because African educational systems produced people to fill the gaps left by the colonial departure and to replace expatriates at all levels. Today, it is the level of education that will determine whether Africa can harness scientific and technical knowledge for the region's benefit or whether it will fall further and further behind the rest of the world.

Education yields benefits in almost every sphere of human activity. A purely economic analysis shows that the rates of return from

Coping with Recession: Health Services in Gambia

In 1978 Gambia established a primary health care system to extend the outreach and effectiveness of the health service. By West African standards existing health services were good. Two hospitals and a network of health centres, health posts and village level 'dressers' provided a reasonable coverage. The health budget, running at approximately £3 per person per year, was relatively high, while the small size and good communications of the country allowed this to be spent efficiently.

From the outset, the plan allowed for any additional costs to be met by the village, by contributions to the worker and the sale of drugs in a 'revolving drug fund'. Only capital costs were to be sought from external donors.

The Save the Children Fund (SCF) assisted in the development of preventive health care in the Eastern region, covering approximately 260,000 people. The health services of Gambia had the potential to become entirely self-sufficient and it was expected that these services would have a large impact on the health of mothers and children.

However, this expectation has not been entirely realised. Economic recession, largely resulting from the drought, has hit the Gambia hard, entailing devaluation of the national currency. This created severe difficulties for the health services. With the flotation of the currency in 1986, the value of salaries fell sharply, the price of rice trebled and there were shortages of soap, disinfectant and other materials. Fuel and kerosene were not available at all for some periods and were otherwise in short supply.

Primary health care has survived because of international donations of fuel and other commodities, and through additional economies. In the Eastern region, SCF organised a system whereby each health post with motor transport was issued with only enough fuel for a single referral per patient: on arrival they were given enough fuel for the return journey and one further referral. The aim of self-sufficiency and the creation of an effective health system with complete coverage cannot be realised until there is economic recovery at the national level. This will partly depend on changes in the international economic situation and, in particular, on the price paid by industrialised countries for groundnut oil, one of Gambia's principal exports.

Mopeds — The Key to Primary Health Care in Burkina Faso

At first sight, it is perhaps curious that the participants of a two-day national seminar in Burkina Faso on primary health care should spend over half their time talking about the use and management of mobilettes (mopeds).

Establishing and maintaining primary health care is a long and fragile process of philosophy, management, incentive and economic analysis that weaves its way from the Cabinet in Ouagadougou to the furthest encampment of nomadic herders. The weakest link in this highly complex and relatively sophisticated chain is the moped.

Mopeds are essential to a health programme because they are the cheapest and most practical way of getting nurse to patient. So why, given this obvious importance, are mopeds a problem? The answer lies in a complicated mix of government red tape and human frailty.

One problem is that nurses are under considerable pressure to lend their mopeds to anyone to whom they have a social or financial obligation. This type of use inevitably leads to damage and abuse, so shortening the life of the bike. As well as

this pressure on even the best intentioned nurse, some nurses are simply irresponsible. Mopeds may be used for joy riding; others are not maintained, and eventually they cease to work. The upshot is that nurses cannot reach patients and the primary health care programme breaks down.

The government response to these problems is to forbid the use of mopeds except on business: a solution that is wholly unworkable in the rural area. Transport is at a premium and such arbitrary rules will inevitably be broken. One answer may be a system of charging so that misuse is penalised while normal use is not. Another problem is the necessity to import fuel and spare parts for the proper working and repair of mopeds. If the government has foreign exchange or payments difficulties, moped parts and fuel may be the last items on its shopping list, and as a result the whole chain of primary health care may break down. Meanwhile, a programme that could save many people's lives staggers from crisis to crisis – all for a few mopeds and a change in the rules.

THE EDUCATION PYRAMID
AFRICA'S LABOUR FORCE, 1985

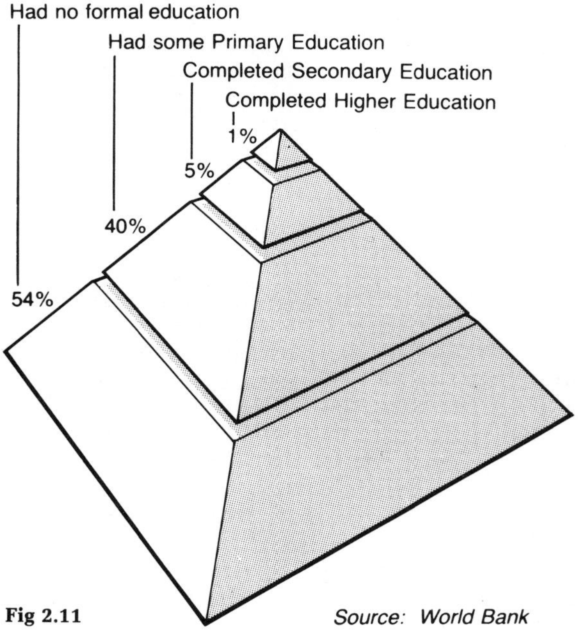

Had no formal education
Had some Primary Education
Completed Secondary Education
Completed Higher Education

1%
5%
40%
54%

Fig 2.11   *Source: World Bank*

education can be very high, between 10% and 20%. These rates compare well with other investment opportunities in Africa which show an average return of 7%. Benefits also come from the change in social attitudes that education brings.

Since independence African countries have invested heavily in education, with some impressive results. Primary school enrolment rose from 12 million in 1960 to over 50 million in 1983 and the proportion of literate adults rose from under 10% of the population to over 40% in the same period. These achievements are now under threat. This threat stems from the current economic decline in Africa combined with a projected growth in the number of school age children of 3.3% per annum between now and the end of the century. To keep up with this growth rate African countries will have to allocate a disproportionate amount of national wealth from a declining real base. Spending on education declined from $10 billion in 1980 to $8.9 billion in 1983, though as a proportion of total government expenditure it rose from 14% to 16%.

Education in Zimbabwe

If the general picture of educational achievement in the 1980s has been bleak in most of Africa, Zimbabwe stands out as a success story. Between independence (in 1979) and 1985 the number of primary school children increased by 160% and the number of secondary school pupils by an extraordinary 650%. Zimbabwe has almost achieved universal primary education and has managed to bring nearly half of all its secondary school age children into secondary schools.

The reform of the racially based, pre-independence education was seen by the government as a vehicle for promoting a new national identity and assisting in economic reconstruction.

Local communities have supported the government's objectives and provided fees and labour for rebuilding many of the schools destroyed during the struggle for independence.

Yet this undoubted success poses problems for Zimbabwe. Its educational achievements have been at considerable cost in terms of the government budget and a slower rate of modernisation elsewhere in the economy. The consequent lack of employment opportunities may prove to be the greatest problem Zimbabwe has to face, as an increasing number of educated citizens come on to the labour market.

Education in Africa faces two specific problems: stagnation in enrolment and a decline in the quality of education. In the 1960s total enrolment grew by 6.6% a year, increasing to 8.9% in the 1970s but in the 1980s falling to 4.2%. This decline can be traced to two main causes; lack of available places and increasing cost to families of educating children. As government budgets have come under increasing pressure and external funds have dried up, the governments of Africa have been unable to increase school places at the same rate, often resorting to imposing or increasing school fees to reduce the burden on central government.

It is very difficult to measure quality in education, but a recent African study by the World Bank concluded that 'Levels of cognitive achievement . . . are low by world standards, and the evidence points to a decline in recent years'. The major causes of this decline again come down to money – unpaid or poorly paid teachers, working in sub-standard accommodation with inadequate materials. These problems are compounded by the cost of using foreign-language text books. But there are also inefficiencies in the education systems of most countries. It is estimated, for example, that on average it costs about $3000 a year to educate a college student in Africa – eight times the cost in Asia and not much lower than in the UK.

Population – The Moving Targets

Africa's population is growing faster than that of any other continent. Between 1970 and 1980 Africa's population grew at 2.9% per annum, compared with 1.9% per annum for the world as a whole, 1.8% in Asia and 0.3% in the UK. Between 1980 and 2000 Africa's population will grow even faster, at over 3% per annum. This very high growth rate affects virtually every aspect of African society. Food production needs to rise at a very rapid rate and the provision of social services,

Mozambique – a young refugee catches up with homework. Perhaps she is one of the lucky ones.

SCHOOL ENROLMENT, SELECTED COUNTRIES, 1984

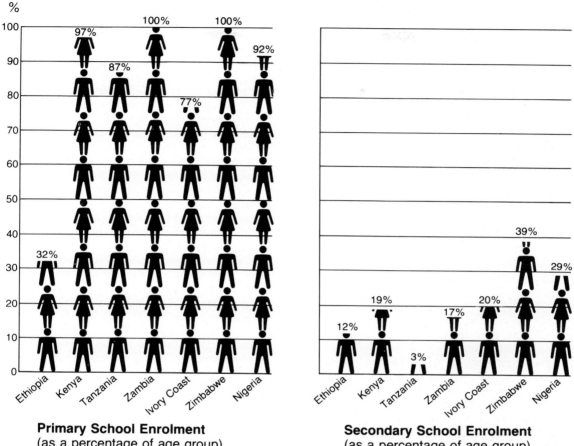

Primary School Enrolment
(as a percentage of age group)

Secondary School Enrolment
(as a percentage of age group)

Source: World Bank

Fig 2.12 Most African countries have now broken the barrier of primary education, with enrolment in Africa quadrupled between 1960 and 1983. Secondary education has also grown fast in countries like Nigeria and Zimbabwe, though in most of Africa it serves only a small minority.

particularly health and education, has to increase just to maintain the same level per person.

Until recently, few African governments recognised the importance of family planning. However, in 1984, at the Second African Population Conference in Tanzania, a new approach was evident. Three-quarters of African countries now endorse family planning and some (Nigeria and Kenya) have set targets for population growth rates (see Chapter 5). Family planning can reduce the

number of children born per family, as has been shown in Zimbabwe and Kenya, both of which provide good access to family planning clinics in the rural areas. But as yet there is little evidence that Africa's population growth rate is declining, although the impact of the AIDS epidemic may affect future growth rates in central and east Africa (see Chapter 5).

Family planning is only one aspect of population policy. It is more important, as we shall see later, to improve the conditions in which people live, especially health and sanitation. It is clear from population studies that economic development results in a decline in growth rates. The basic challenge of Africa's development therefore remains, and is simply reinforced by the issue of population growth.

△ The Economic Forecast

Throughout this chapter we have referred to the gap between the resources Africa needs for its economic recovery and the actual funds that are available. In the next two chapters we discuss in more detail how the gap might be closed and the efforts that are being made by both international agencies and governments. Improving the prospects for Africa depends, however, on ensuring that more resources are made available from the international community and it is by no means certain that this will happen.

On current projections of capital flows and international trends, the real wealth of Africa is expected to grow only slowly over the next five years. The IMF estimates that national income will grow by 2.5% in 1987, 3.2% in 1988 and at an average of 3.2% per year in 1989–91. Income per head will therefore stagnate, as the population is expected to increase by just over 3% a year in the same period. By contrast, average per capita incomes in Asia over the same period are expected to grow at over 3% a year.

The level of non-oil commodity prices is currently low and forecasts suggest this will remain so for the foreseeable future. In the short term, this will continue to hinder any recovery in Africa and increase reliance on external capital imports. In the longer term, low commodity prices emphasise the need for Africa to diversify its exports and move towards processing its agricultural export commodities. Yet the opportunities for an expansion of such 'value-added' exports remain limited unless there are stronger international policies to reduce trade barriers and encourage opportunities for new African exports.

An improvement in the prospects for Africa in the short term, for example over the next five years, depends largely on increasing the flow of external resources such as aid and private investment. On the assumption that an annual economic growth rate of 4% a year is an acceptable target, the IMF estimates that there is a resource gap of $2.5 billion for 1986–90. This is equivalent only to wiping out the debts of Tanzania and Senegal, but on current evidence of donor intentions, new aid flows are unlikely to be forthcoming on the scale required. In the next chapter, we consider the question of financing for Africa, and the role of official and voluntary donors and the private sector.

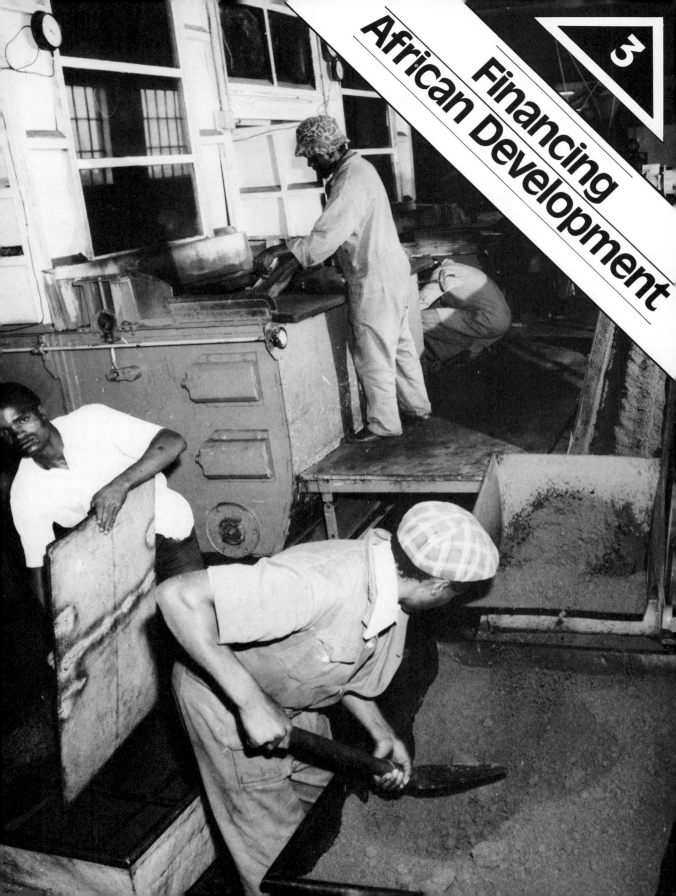

Financing
African Development

△ Investment – Where From?

One of the central arguments of this report is that Africa's people need more public and private investment in such areas as roads, hospitals, schools, factories and agriculture. The provision of investment resources from other countries plays an important role in the process of economic and social development. But why cannot African countries generate sufficient funds to meet their *own* investment needs?

In a country like Britain savings and borrowing are the primary sources of investment. Governments and companies borrow from banks and other institutions to invest. What they borrow is essentially other people's savings. The more wealth a country has the more its citizens save and the more there is to invest. The more money there is to invest, the quicker the economy will grow, providing that this investment is efficient. In Africa people are poor, so savings are very low. Over the last few years savings have fallen even further as people have been forced to spend them on food and other essentials. Gross savings in Africa fell to 4% of national income in 1986 compared with 14% in 1973. As personal incomes have fallen, so has government income (which comes mainly from taxes), with the effect of cutting expenditure on services (see Chapter 2).

Falling income and savings means that the funds available to invest also fall. The less new investment, the fewer jobs are available and the slower productivity rises. This produces further falls in income and, when this is combined with rising population levels, people's standard of living declines too. This cycle of falling income and employment can be reversed by aid and investment from outside the country.

△ Aid – Cushioning Change

The bulk of aid and foreign investment has been for projects to provide more schools, hospital and factories (see Box). Aid to help implement new economic policies is more recent: the World Bank and other donors have increasingly devoted funds to support structural adjustment through 'programme' loans, rather than conventional projects.

The Aid Business – Who Gives and How Much?

The notion of giving countries money and manpower to help them develop comes from the post-war period in Europe. It had its genesis in the Bretton Woods conference of 1944 and the Marshall Plan. Under the Marshall Plan aid was given for the reconstruction of areas of Europe destroyed in the war. The institutions created by the Bretton Woods conference included the World Bank and the International Monetary Fund (IMF), both still the major international institutions involved in economic development.

From 1944 onwards the machinery for giving aid was progressively established on a

What is Aid?

Most 'aid' is in the form of *official development assistance* (oda): the transfer of resources from governments of richer countries to governments of poorer countries either as grants or through concessional (low-interest) loans. The resources transferred are either in the form of 'technical co-operation' (training, experts, etc.) or finance.

Financial aid is often divided into 'project aid', which is for specific investments such as roads, dams or schools, and 'programme aid' which is not earmarked for specific investments. The voluntary sector, like 'official' donors, favours project aid as this fairly precisely identifies how money is intended to be spent. But many argue that this is living in an unreal world. For example, if a government receives money from abroad to deepen its harbour or to order new text books, all this means is that money that would have been spent anyway could now be switched to other uses, including military expenditure, better health services or whatever. It is this way that money flows around the system of public expenditure that economists call its 'fungibility'.

Advocates of programme aid claim that the most important contribution of foreign aid is to assist governments more generally by putting 'untied' money at their disposal. In the period after independence in Africa this was often in the form of 'budgetary aid'. In later years, many debt repayments were cancelled and the money previously due to donors was considered as aid and spread over several years. Today, programme aid is mainly in the form of providing foreign exchange. This 'balance of payments support' means that importers pay for imports in local currency and the revenue is thus available to governments to spend more or less as they please. However, what is different about programme aid today is that it is normally provided where governments have agreed on policy changes, and these changes may involve cuts in some areas of spending. This is the link with policy conditionality, or aid for structural adjustment, described in Chapter 4.

'Voluntary' aid – constructing wells for Tuareg nomads in Mali.

British aid – a workshop for Land Rovers in northern Zambia.

world-wide basis. This machinery falls into two main categories: multilateral institutions such as the World Bank, the African Development Bank and the International Fund for Agricultural Development (IFAD); and bilateral institutions such as the Overseas Development Administration (ODA) in Britain and the US Agency for International Development (USAID), which provide aid on a direct government to government basis. Now virtually every developed country and wealthy oil-exporting state has either established its own development agency or gives to a multilateral agency. Total official aid flows in 1986 were an estimated $44.1 billion or about $13 for every person in the developing world.

As well as the official institutions there are the voluntary agencies which are growing at a remarkable rate. Such agencies, including charities and church-related bodies, mobilise private funds in developed countries and also act as a funnel for some official aid through joint funding schemes. Voluntary agencies play an increasingly important role in economic development. In 1986 they channelled about $4.4 billion, or 10% of total aid, to developing countries, benefiting an estimated 100 million people. About two-thirds of this came directly from private funds; the rest came from governments. As well as money the agencies also provide personnel: in 1986 European non-government organisations provided over 10,000 experts and volunteers to developing countries.

Voluntary agencies involved in development come in all shapes and sizes, from tiny operations supporting development in just one village to the relatively large, world-wide operations of Oxfam, CARE and Catholic Relief Services in North America and Europe. In total there are about 2,200 such agencies based in developed countries, channelling money and human resources either directly to developing countries or indirectly through between 10,000 and 20,000 local organisations. In Britain, among the largest charities are those devoted to overseas aid, including Oxfam, Save the Children Fund (SCF), Christian Aid and the Catholic Fund for Overseas Development (CAFOD).

Official Finance to Africa

Finance through official channels is very important to Africa, accounting for nearly three-quarters of all external resources. Total finance from official institutions and governments to Africa in 1986 amounted to an estimated $15.9 billion, of which 86% was grant or concessionary (low-interest) loans. This aid amounted to about 10% of total national income in Africa. This equates to about $27 of assistance for every man, woman and child, over twice the world average of $13. For low-income countries like Chad, Mali and recently Zambia, official finance now accounts for nearly a quarter of total national income.

Aid to sub-Saharan Africa increased during the 1980s, rising from $9.2 billion in 1980 to an estimated $13.7 billion in 1986. Africa's share of total aid to all developing countries has also increased. It was 29% in 1980 and is expected to reach 34% in the late 1980s. On the other hand, if aid is considered in relation to the shortfall in foreign exchange, due to falling export prices and rising import prices, its value has fallen during the 1980s.

Multilateral Aid

Multilateral agencies contributed just under a third of the total official development finance made available to Africa in 1986. The World Bank contributed some $2 billion, or over 40% of total multilateral aid. The African Development Bank (ADB) contributed some $1.6 billion and the rest came from the European Development Fund, the International Fund for Agricultural Development (IFAD), the United Nations Development Programme (UNDP), the FAO and other agencies.

Over the last six years the emphasis of lending by the World Bank to Africa has shifted towards programme lending, in the form of sectoral and structural adjustment loans, intended to support the process of government policy change which, it is hoped, will lead to a more economically successful society. In 1986 20% of total lending was for structural adjustment or programme loans, compared to 8% in the late 1970s. Lending for agriculture and rural development remains the

MULTILATERAL AID TO AFRICA: WHO GIVES WHAT? (1985)

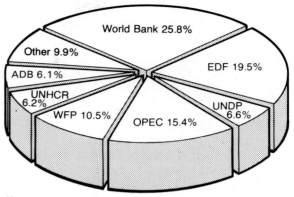

Key

ADB	African Development Bank
UNHCR	United Nations High Commissioner to Refugees
WFP	World Food Programme
OPEC	Organisation of Petroleum Exporting Countries
UNDP	United Nations Development Programme
EDF	European Development Fund (of the EEC)

Source: OECD

Fig. 3.1

most important sector, absorbing in 1986 just over 21% of the total.

In 1985 the World Bank also set up a Special Facility for Africa totalling $1.2 billion, designed to provide immediate loans to the poorest countries. During the 1985–86 financial year this fund made loans to the value of $783 million to 15 different countries. The IMF also established a Structural Adjustment Facility in 1987, which for the first time meant the IMF was lending on concessionary terms and qualified as a 'donor'.

Other Multilateral Donors

The African Development Bank was designated to play a special role in financing African development at the meeting of the OAU Heads of State in July 1985, and this impetus was kept up by the UN Special Session on Africa. In response to this call, the ADB increased its lending in 1985 by just under a third to $1.5 billion, and by a further $100 million in 1986. There are now plans under way to double the capital base of the ADB and the intention is that it will overtake the World Bank as the major lender to Africa within the next five years. The European Development Fund (EDF) is also an important multilateral donor to Africa. In 1986 the EDF made $665 million available to African countries, and this figure is expected to top $700 million in 1987.

Other donors, like FAO and IFAD, have also steadily increased their expenditure in Africa. FAO will devote some $121.7 million (41% of its total resources) to Africa in 1986–87, as compared to $45 million, or 31%, in 1980–81. IFAD have established a special programme for Africa which has a target of $300 million and is aimed at the poorest countries affected by drought and desertification. This is in addition to the existing programme worth about $50 million a year to Africa.

Bilateral Donors

The bilateral aid programme overall was worth some $10 billion to Africa in 1986, equivalent to just over 70% of all official aid to Africa and 30% of all bilateral aid to developing countries. Aid stagnated between 1982 and 1984 at $7 billion a year but since then has increased quite sharply, showing a rise of 11% in 1985 and 24% in 1986, largely due to the spending on famine relief. The largest donor to Africa is the United States, which in 1985 contributed around $1.2 billion, or 17% of the total. France is the second largest contributor, providing in 1985 about $1.0 billion. The United Kingdom aid programme to Africa came sixth after Germany, Italy and Canada.

Who Gets What?

Sudan, Ethiopia, Tanzania, Kenya, Mali, Somalia, Zambia, Zaire, Niger and Mozambique top the list of aid recipients in Africa, together absorbing just under 50% of all the aid available in 1985. In terms of aid per person, Somalia received the most aid ($66.7 per head), followed by Zambia ($66.1), Sudan ($51.7), Mali ($48.7) and Niger ($47.6).

BILATERAL AID TO AFRICA: WHO GIVES WHAT? (1985)

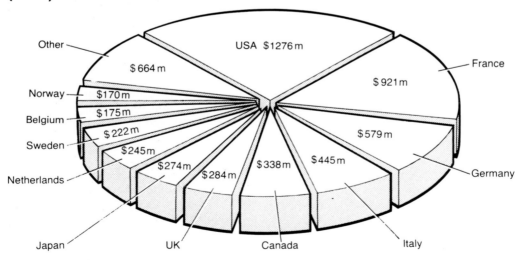

At 1984 prices and exchange rate

Source: OECD

Fig. 3.2

Rebuilding the railway to Nacala in Mozambique; a lifeline for southern Africa's trade.

In countries like Sudan and Ethiopia, relief funds – including food aid (see Box) – accounted for the high levels of assistance, and drought relief was a major component in the aid programmes of Somalia, Tanzania, Kenya, Senegal and Mali. In a normal year Sudan is likely to receive about $650 million in aid. Between 1983 and 1985, because of acute needs and the additional responsibility for refugees, the total amount of aid to Sudan doubled. Ethiopia experienced a similar increase in aid provision.

Food Aid

The volume of food aid to Africa increased sharply from 0.5 million tonnes in 1970 to over 5.4 million tonnes in 1985, worth an estimated $1.3 billion. This increase reflected the economic crisis, the general deterioration in food security, and the frequent famines in the region. It also reflected the need by Europe and the United States to dispose of surplus food. Bilateral food aid is mainly provided by the USA, Canada, and the EEC member countries. Multilateral food aid comes via the World Food Programme (WFP). The WFP obtains most of its food from the USA, Canada and EEC countries, of which in 1985 Italy and Germany were the most important. In 1986 the WFP supplied 235,000 tonnes of food to Africa compared to 336,000 tonnes the year before, reflecting improved food security.

In essence food aid is no different from any other type of aid. In normal times it can be used to support the balance of payments of a country by eliminating or reducing the need to import food. Tanzania received about 122,000 tonnes, or 35% of total cereal imports, as food aid in 1985. It is also used in emergencies, such as the recent famines in Ethiopia and Sudan, to meet the basic food needs of a section of society at risk. In 1985 Ethiopia and Sudan received over 1.3 million tonnes each, more than any other country in Africa.

Food aid nevertheless does have a number of characteristics that distinguish it from other types of aid. It tends to be additional to other types of aid, and few food donors are prepared to substitute money for food. This reluctance to exchange food aid for financial aid stems from the fact that the very origin of food aid lay in the need for the main donors to dispose of food surpluses and so reduce their own storage and/or disposal costs. Exchanging money for food would not help these objectives.

Food aid is also different because unless it is carefully planned it can have adverse effects on domestic agriculture. If a large amount of food is suddenly made available to the local market it will cause prices to fall and so reduce the incentive for local farmers to produce. Food aid must be focused on those who lack enough money to buy their own food. This can be done through food for work schemes such as road building, which effectively converts food aid into permanent assets. Selective feeding programmes for children are another way of getting food to the very poor without affecting domestic agriculture. Food aid can be a useful resource if it is part of an overall development plan. If used carelessly, it can undermine agriculture and allow governments to set other priorities above food self-sufficiency.

THE TOP TEN UK VOLUNTARY AID AGENCIES

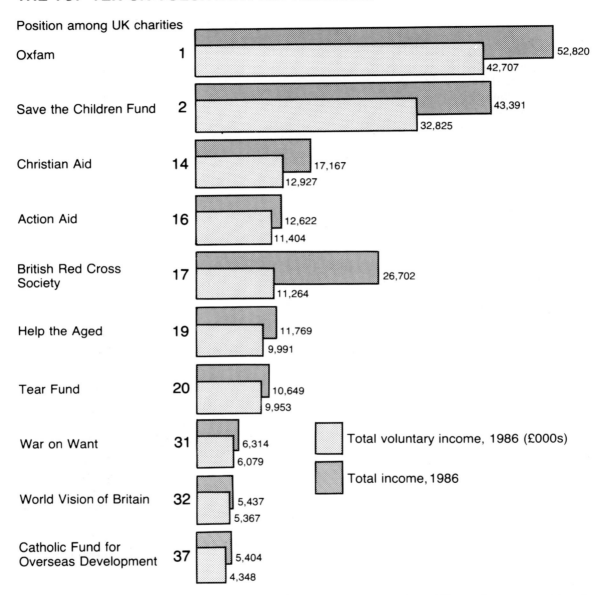

Position among UK charities

Agency	Position	Total income, 1986	Total voluntary income, 1986 (£000s)
Oxfam	1	52,820	42,707
Save the Children Fund	2	43,391	32,825
Christian Aid	14	17,167	12,927
Action Aid	16	12,622	11,404
British Red Cross Society	17	26,702	11,264
Help the Aged	19	11,769	9,991
Tear Fund	20	10,649	9,953
War on Want	31	6,314	6,079
World Vision of Britain	32	5,437	5,367
Catholic Fund for Overseas Development	37	5,404	4,348

☐ Total voluntary income, 1986 (£000s)

▨ Total income, 1986

Notes: This list excludes the Band Aid Trust, ranked 9 in 1986. Several agencies have UK as well as overseas interests, Total income includes government grants, investments and other non-voluntary sources.

Source: Charities Aid Foundation, 1987

Fig 3.4

△Voluntary Agencies

The role of voluntary agencies has changed
considerably over the last 30 years. Broadly
speaking, the emphasis has shifted from relief
work to long-term development and
campaigning to change both developed and
developing countries' policies. In terms of
funds, over 50% now goes on projects such as
small-scale irrigation works, immunisation
programmes and village water supply
schemes. Policy campaigns have included
lobbying the World Bank to incorporate
measures in structural adjustment
programmes to protect the poor, emphasising
the issue of aid and trade during general
elections, and putting pressure on
governments to increase aid during the famine
in Ethiopia.

Voluntary agency work in Africa lags far
behind that in Asia and South America.
Although about $1.5 billion (a third of the total
money distributed by agencies) goes to Africa,
this benefits only an estimated 12 million
people, working out at $125 per head in Africa
compared to $40 per head worldwide. This
1985 figure, estimated by a Dutch economist,
reflects the greater difficulty and cost of
operating in Africa and, in many areas, the
lack of local agencies to act as partners (but
see also Chapter 5). In Sri Lanka there are
over 2,000 different voluntary agencies
compared with barely 100 in Kenya. African
operations also require greater external help
because of the lack of domestic resources and
manpower.

The Agency Approach to Development – Bottom Up

Every organisation has its own goals and
objectives, but there is a common thread that
runs through the private agencies' work in
development: a 'bottom up' line of attack on
the problems of development. This means that,
instead of starting with national economic
objectives, agencies go right to the grass roots
to tackle poverty, disease and illiteracy. Funds
and human skills, through technical assistance

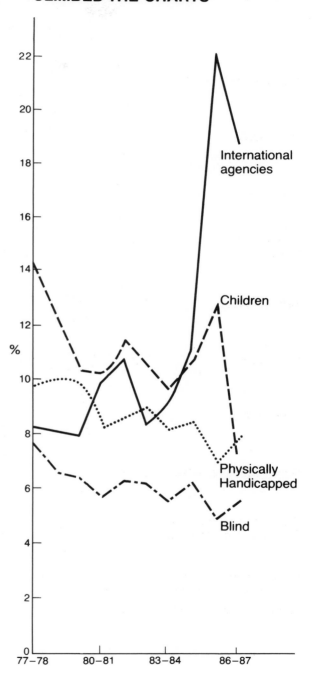

CHARITABLE GIVING IN THE UK: HOW AID HAS CLIMBED THE CHARTS

International agencies

Children

Physically Handicapped

Blind

Source: Charities Aid Foundation 1987

Fig 3.5

Save the Children in Africa

Long-Term Development

Save the Children Fund (UK) is involved in long-term health, education and child welfare programmes in 16 countries of sub-Saharan Africa. In every case its aim is not primarily to help provide a service, but to enhance the ability of the people of the country to establish and run these services themselves in a way which can be sustained with local resources. As a relatively small agency SCF cannot provide significant additional funding, but it can try out new ideas on behalf of countries unable to risk their own limited resources.

All Save the Children's activities are therefore undertaken in partnership with national governments or indigenous voluntary organisations. The kind of assistance provided depends not only on the type of programme but also on existing resources. In general the Fund aims to supply only those things which are not available locally. These may include money, equipment and supplies, but often the most valuable thing that SCF can offer is expertise.

Advisory and managerial staff are provided to support government departments responsible for health and child welfare services in a number of countries, some working at national level, others with regional authorities. In Uganda, for instance, SCF personnel occupy key medical, technical and managerial posts in the Ministry of Health's national immunisation programme, which aims to reach some three million children every year. In Mozambique the Fund provides a social worker to advise the government department responsible for the welfare of all children abandoned, orphaned or separated from their families. Often these individuals work alongside local counterparts and hand over responsibility to them when they leave. For example, SCF was actively involved in the establishment of immunisation programmes in Lesotho and Swaziland, but its role in these is now largely confined to advice and financial support.

To promote this process SCF also offers scholarships not only to its own local staff but also to employees of government or local organisations whose work would benefit from a period of study abroad. But the emphasis on enhancing indigenous resources means that training within the country is an important element in most Save the Children programmes. An integral part of SCF's support for health services in Gambia, Somalia and Zanzibar, for example, is training nursing staff, village health workers and traditional birth attendants.

Despite its increasing role at national or regional level in several African countries, Save the Children continues to initiate and support new programmes with smaller communities. In Port Sudan, for instance, health care and community development schemes have been established recently for some 10,000 Beja nomads who settled in the city during the 1984–85 drought; and funds are currently being provided for a local organisation which is setting up a primary health care programme in a poor suburb of the Ghanaian capital Accra.

The lessons of such small-scale projects are often useful in planning services at a national level. In Zimbabwe, a primary health care system established by Save the Children to serve workers on commercial farms in one district is now being used as a model for similar communities throughout the country. It is in this kind of innovative work, trying to discover more cost-effective methods of providing health care and other services, that Save the Children can make the greatest contribution to Africa's development.

Emergency Relief

SCF's policy is to respond to emergencies primarily in areas where it is already working on long-term development programmes. During the current crisis in Mozambique, for example, all SCF assistance (amounting to over $3 million so far in transport and relief supplies) is being channelled into Zambezia province, which is not only one of the areas worst affected but also the centre of a long-term SCF programme for training government health workers.

The benefit of this approach is that SCF is able to use its resources in the most cost-effective way. Concentrating on areas where SCF staff are already in place means that needs can be identified accurately and at an early stage, and that the response is both quick and appropriate.

There are occasions, of course, when this general rule is worth breaking, particularly where no other agency is better placed to lend the kind of relief assistance needed. A recent example of this came in western Sudan in 1984–86, when SCF agreed to mount a major relief transport and distribution operation in Darfur province, despite the fact that its long-term commitments lay elsewhere in Sudan.

Co-ordination with other agencies is another important aspect of SCF's approach to disaster relief. At its simplest, this prevents the Fund becoming involved in relief operations where other agencies are in a better position (whether geographically, financially or in terms of expertise) to provide the necessary help. More positively, as SCF has found through its experience in Ethiopia, Sudan and Mozambique, it means more effective assistance to those in need.

Disaster Preparedness

SCF has long recognised the importance of disaster preparedness, and in particular of reliable systems to give early warning of crisis. In Ethiopia SCF has been running a nutritional surveillance programme in some of the drought-prone areas since 1974, and in 1987 this network was providing valuable information both for the national early warning system and for targeting relief aid in affected areas during periods of famine. A similar programme is under way in Mali and Burkina Faso where, in conjunction with the London School of Hygiene and Tropical Medicine, SCF is aiming to supplement the information available to government and donors by providing a series of reports on the causes of food insecurity in drought-prone rural areas.

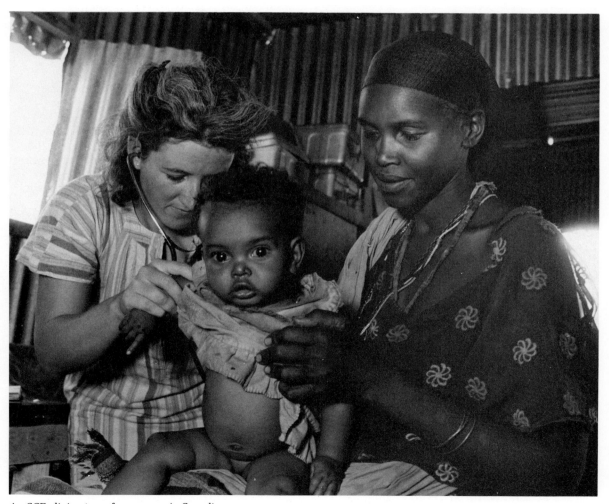

An SCF clinic at a refugee camp in Somalia.

and training, are provided at the village level. An important aspect of working at the village level is getting ordinary people involved in the design, implementation and evaluation of assistance programmes. By ensuring that the beneficiaries are involved in the project, agencies aim to achieve immediate impact and at the same time to improve co-operation and development awareness in the communities. Such involvement and the relatively small scale of operations – less than 10% of official aid from the UK, for example – enable much of the charities' work to be more flexible and innovative than the work of governments and official donors.

Agencies and Official Donors

There has been increasing co-operation between agencies and official aid bodies, shown by the fact that the agencies now draw up to a third of their resources from official institutions. Aid donors recognise that agencies can provide considerable understanding of the needs of the poor and how to tackle them. Organisations like the International Fund for Agricultural Development (IFAD) have made specific efforts to use the experience of agencies in designing and implementing programmes, particularly in getting credit to small farmers.

In designing the 1983 rural water supply project in Mali, the World Bank drew on the experiences of CARE (US), Pères Blancs (France) and Helvetas (Switzerland) to plan the project and encourage community participation. Other examples of successful or innovative voluntary agency work have been Oxfam's restocking of herds in northern Kenya; Save the Children Fund's use of solar technology for refrigeration of vaccines to serve pastoral groups in Somalia; and a Norwegian church project in Zambia which provides training in handling ox-ploughs in an area where peasant farmers traditionally cultivated the land by hoe.

Agencies and African Governments

Governments in Africa often have very mixed feelings about supporting the operations of agencies in their countries. Some provide positive assistance through funds, helping to co-ordinate the work of agencies with their own ministries; others are unsupportive and have tried to control their operations. In some cases governments have made it difficult for agencies to obtain permits for their activities and work permits for overseas staff. In Sudan stringent registration requirements have been imposed and agencies have found it difficult to import their needs. On balance there has been increasing co-operation in recent years, with governments now recognising that agencies can make a substantial contribution to their own development efforts.

Emergency Relief

Whether agencies are better than official bodies at getting assistance to the poor depends on what the programme is trying to achieve. However, few would deny that agencies have an advantage in relief aid. Agencies can work in politically sensitive areas such as Eritrea which would not be diplomatically possible for a government or official body. They can also respond more quickly to calls for aid in a crisis.

As channels of international aid, agencies in their present form have limitations when the scale of relief operations becomes very large. Despite this, the use of agencies by governments in emergency relief is increasing, especially in countries where the political climate is less favourable to foreign assistance. For example, in Mozambique, Ethiopia and Sudan, foreign governments wishing to help but without programmes of their own have, in some areas, operated solely through voluntary agencies.

In a crisis agencies are sometimes the only means of providing an emergency service and donor governments often support them for this purpose, recognising their crucial role. A joint evaluation by the Save the Children Fund and Britain's Overseas Development Administration (ODA) of the work of the SCF medical team in Mulago Hospital, Kampala, during the civil war in Uganda showed that such work in highly adverse conditions could never have been undertaken by a conventional aid programme. Such examples of high-risk projects in Africa can be cited many times over.

Reaching the Poor

Perhaps the most important advantage of voluntary organisations is that they are better at reaching the poor and identifying with them than government agencies. Again, the record is mixed and the evidence limited: the number of evaluations of non-government projects, though increasing, is still too small for any overall assessment. But the fact that governments and multilateral agencies have strengthened their links with the voluntary agencies speaks for itself.

Another important claim by voluntary agencies is that they can carry out programmes more cheaply than officially aided programmes. This is often, but not always, the case. For example, in Zimbabwe, the cost of voluntary agency-assisted family planning programmes appears to be lower than the equivalent government programmes, while in Senegal and Burkina Faso agency-supported programmes appear to be more expensive.

A related issue is 'project replicability', whether an assistance programme can be repeated elsewhere. The record is again mixed. An American evaluation of agency-funded projects in Africa showed that the replication of many projects was not possible without continued external support, due to the high cost of the programmes. In Tanzania, on the other hand, agencies demonstrated the effectiveness of an animal immunisation programme that was taken up by the government and successfully repeated elsewhere.

Co-ordination or Fragmentation?

Agencies tend to work through many small projects in a lot of different countries covering a wide range of activities, from immunisation programmes to irrigation schemes. Such diversity leads us to ask whether agencies are too fragmented and if they can be better co-ordinated. There are arguments for specialisation, as this enables lessons learnt from one area to be incorporated elsewhere. It is difficult to measure the extent of proliferation but recent examples of co-operation indicate that agencies have

recognised the problems of spreading themselves too thin. Over the last few years five charities from Belgium, France, Germany, Italy and the Netherlands have created a European Consortium for Agricultural Development, aimed at co-ordinating and sharing development experience. This trend is accelerating, with other initiatives taking off and leading to greater co-operation and programme evaluation.

One positive area of co-operation has been in campaigning. In Britain, for example, Oxfam and Save the Children Fund have demonstrated a common front in Ethiopia and Mozambique, sharing on-the-ground experience and concerns with each other and with British government officials. These agencies also joined Christian Aid, CAFOD and several others in an effective lobby of Parliament on African development organised by the World Development Movement in October 1985. WDM itself has helped to influence the British government on important issues affecting Africa, such as food aid, debt, and providing more finance for Africa through the special funds set up by the World Bank and IFAD.

△Private Overseas Investment

The other main source of outside finance in Africa is investment by private companies based overseas. Unilever, Tate & Lyle, Heinz, ICI, Lonrho and many more household names all have investments in Africa. They own plantations, mines, management companies, fertiliser and chemical plants, newspapers, banks, shipping companies and supermarkets. Such 'transnationals' are not the only forms of private overseas investment; others include loans, and the purchase of shares in existing local companies. Over the years there have been criticisms of external private investment in Africa, the most severe claiming that companies have driven farmers off their land, distorted production within countries, and made excess profits. The companies, on their side, claim they have created factories, dug mines, and built up businesses that would not otherwise exist.

Private investment is now a high priority for Africa.

Overseas private investment in Africa has fallen dramatically during the 1980s, from about $1.5 billion (over 8% of external funds) in 1981 to about $300 million (1.5% of external funds) in 1986. Yet private investment clearly remains very important to Africa because in the short term it has great room for expansion and can bring with it other benefits, such as technical and management skills. But how can transnationals be encouraged to provide the sort of investment Africa needs?

Much has already been done to improve incentives, but other conditions need to be met before investment will be made. The overriding concern of most transnationals is the security of their investment. This security is determined as much by the legal and political framework as by economic policies. Many overseas companies regard Africa as the last alternative for investment because they see little protection against expropriation or interference by some future government.

Transnationals bring with them additional benefits, other than access to capital, that are not easily replicated by domestic companies or governments and aid agencies. They tend to be much more effective at identifying and exploiting commercial opportunities; they have access to specialist technical and commercial skills; they provide new technologies and management skills; and they can more easily develop markets for exports.

Yet these strengths can raise problems for governments. Transnational investment requires a profit for its shareholders, who are usually in developed countries. This profit must be paid in the form of dividends that must be exported from the country where they are earned. This often leads to charges that transnationals exploit a poor country's resources for the benefit of shareholders in rich developed countries. Yet without that profit, the transnational would not be there in the first place. The issue is one of balance: of what percentage of profit will be reinvested in the country and how much will be exported as dividends for shareholders.

Kenya's Soap Industry

This balance depends on a wide variety of factors. The soap industry in Kenya illustrates many of the issues. In 1975 Kenya's soap industry produced 18,000 tonnes of soap products. It was labour-intensive, used wood from all over the country to fire the boilers and locally grown coconut oil to produce the soap. In contrast, Unilever established soap factories that were highly mechanised, used imported oils to make the soap and imported oil to heat the furnaces. According to its critics, the Unilever product, by using imports in its manufacture, increased the burden on the balance of payments. It also reduced employment not only in the soap industry but also among wood-cutters in the countryside. Because it was packaged and marketed very effectively, it gradually eroded the market share of the locally manufactured product.

Botswana's Diamond Mines

If the Kenya soap industry example illustrates some of the problems of transnational involvement in Africa, the case of Botswana's diamond mines illustrates another side of the coin. In 1968 Botswana's government negotiated a deal with the Anglo American group to exploit the Orapa diamond mine. The mine was entirely financed and run by Anglo American through a local subsidiary in which the government received a 15% free shareholding. Orapa turned out to be the second biggest diamond mine in the world and more profitable than anyone expected. The government renegotiated the deal and now receives about 70% of the profits from the enterprise. It is the mainstay of the economy and, along with another huge diamond mine recently discovered, called Jwaneng, produces over three-quarters of Botswana's foreign exchange earnings.

A tea estate in Cameroon. Tea has been one of the few successes among Africa's exports. Most commodity prices have fallen drastically.

Diamonds may be a special case but it is evident from elsewhere that successful foreign investment in the export sector can make a major contribution to foreign exchange earnings and, in the case of tea and coffee, for example, to the incomes of small farmers.

△ Future Financing Needs in Africa

The most recent official estimates of Africa's need for external funds were made by the World Bank in 1986. These estimates are based on the very limited objective of halting the decline in incomes and by about 1990 achieving some small measure of positive growth. Simply to achieve this, the World Bank estimated that imports will have to return to the levels achieved in 1980–82 and that Africa will need capital inflows from all sources of about $15.5 billion a year between 1987 and 1991. Of this, $12.8 billion will have to be in the form of grants or very soft loans. It is possible that these levels could be achieved during the rest of the decade *if* international interest is maintained.

More important, the Bank's estimates are based on a 10% improvement in the relative prices of African exports. This is most uncertain: indeed, export prices relative to import prices fell by a staggering 26% in 1986. This means that the gap between available and necessary capital has already gone up from $15.5 billion to nearer $20 billion.

So what are the chances that the additional funds required for Africa will be forthcoming? It depends where you look. The World Bank, a major lender in Africa, expects to be able to continue the trend of increased lending to the continent, although its 1987 report was candid about the results so far. In the previous year it had increased its lending to African countries, and its Special African Facility had forged ahead. But World Bank loans overall to Africa 'barely maintained the level of lending in real terms'. As a result, over half of the African countries involved in borrowing for structural adjustment were considered to be unable to meet their loan conditions without further financial support. (See also Box on p. 7.)

Despite this, World Bank lending to Africa presents a relatively optimistic picture when compared with the IMF and several important bilateral donors. Pressures are being brought to bear on the IMF to change its policies and be more responsive to the long-term needs of low-income African countries. Some bilateral aid programmes, including ODA, have responded to the crises in Africa. However, whether this rate of increase can be sustained is an open question. In particular, the US seems to be on a path towards actually cutting its aid to Africa. As the largest donor to the continent, once multilateral and bilateral aid is taken into account, such a move would be a major setback to meeting projected financing requirements.

Government Policies

△ The World Picture

'Reaganomics' in America, 'Thatcherism' in Britain, the 'Gorbachev revolution' in the USSR – all of these are descriptions of attempts to restructure economies. The emphases of the policies vary but all are attempting to revitalise their economies through a process in which the market plays a leading role. The process of what is termed 'structural adjustment' in developing countries is no different in principle. The common element in all the policies is the notion of economic liberalism. This 'ism' is the starting point for all programmes of structural adjustment.

Economic liberalism has at its core a belief that the market place is the most 'efficient' means of determining prices and that 'efficient' prices are the key to a successful economy. All the measures introduced under structural adjustment programmes, from devaluation to privatisation, have this one core belief. Yet to examine what the terms 'successful economy' and 'efficient prices' mean is to open a Pandora's Box, as neither can be explained without reference to prevailing political and social values.

Adjusting to changes in the economic climate is a continuous process. Normally this process goes on almost imperceptibly; new industries are created and old ones die, the exchange rate is devalued or revalued, prices alter, government policies are changed. The need for structural adjustment of the sort involved in African economic programmes arises when the changes in the economic climate are drastic or sudden and the mechanisms to cope with them do not exist, do not work properly or simply cannot cope with the scale of change required.

△ Structural Adjustment in Africa

In Africa, there are two basic stages to structural adjustment; stabilisation and structural change. Stabilisation typically tries to put right major imbalances in the economy and to control the level of inflation. One measure is to reduce the amount of spending by people and governments. This requires cuts in real incomes which, among other things, reduces the demand for imports. This demand can then be further reduced by making imports relatively more expensive through devaluation.

Structural change tries to maintain these new balances and encourage a more efficient allocation of resources within the economy. This is attempted through various policy measures:

▲ expanding exports, so increasing foreign exchange earnings
▲ altering prices so that domestic production is increased
▲ improving the productivity of public enterprises, for example through privatisation
▲ ensuring that investment is allocated to key areas of the economy.

The IMF in Africa

The International Monetary Fund lent heavily to Africa during the early 1980s in response to the call of African governments for help to lessen the disruptive effects on their economies of the balance of payments deficits caused by falling commodity prices and rising oil prices. The Fund extended substantial balance of payments assistance to over 30 countries in Africa and by the end of 1986 the region's outstanding debt to the IMF totalled over $6 billion. The problem for these countries, however, is that, unlike their bilateral debts, which are open to renegotiation, IMF loans cannot be rescheduled. This is part of the condition of the loan.

The Fund was in the vanguard of attempts to redirect policy in Africa under its balance of payments adjustment programmes. As repayments became due, in 1985 the net flow of funds to Africa from the IMF rapidly declined to virtually zero and in 1986 Africa paid back more to the Fund than it received by about $400 million. A withdrawal of the IMF from support for structural adjustment, at a time when many African countries were struggling with mounting debt and continuing balance of payments problems, promised to increase their difficulties and also risked destabilising their recovery efforts altogether. However, the new Structural Adjustment Facility introduced in 1987 has been just large enough to result in a net flow from the Fund to Africa – and the Fund has proposed a tripling in the size of the Facility.

△ The Role of the IMF and the World Bank

The sort of changes described on p. 50, as we shall see, would make any government unpopular. Structural adjustment programmes tend to be adopted by governments only as a last resort, when there are no more normal sources of credit to support the balance of payments. At that point, governments feel compelled to turn to the IMF (see Box) in the knowledge that IMF support depends on the governments concerned facing up to the fundamental weakness of their economic policies.

The IMF has given balance of payments support to over 30 countries in Africa and by the end of 1986 the region's outstanding debt to the IMF was over $6 billion. The IMF mandate involves sorting out immediate balance of payments problems. Long-term development investment is more the responsibility of the World Bank. But the distinctions between the IMF and the World Bank have become rather blurred over the last few years. In the 1980s the World Bank has also become involved in balance of payments support linked to policy reform through its Structural Adjustment Loans; and in 1986 the IMF established a new concessionary loan programme (mainly for African countries) called the Structural Adjustment Facility.

These loans are designed to support the second phase of adjustment, which is altering the structure of the economy. This move, particularly emphasising a more market-orientated approach, has been to some extent a new departure, as 'redistribution with growth' was the favoured approach in the 1970s.

Conditionality

The common feature of the IMF and World Bank programmes is that loans are made only if governments agree to make the required changes to their economies. These are often very wide-ranging and affect most areas of government policy. Governments are given specific targets, such as how much credit should be available, what wage increases are allowed, or what the interest rates should be. This is known as 'conditionality'.

There is a general consensus that major economic policy changes are required in much of Africa. Yet the adjustment programmes have caused and continue to cause enormous controversy. In Nigeria the prospect of accepting the IMF's package of reforms in 1985 led to a national debate that dominated the media for months and was discussed in every bar and street corner. In May 1987 Zambia broke off negotiations with the IMF

Stacking bags of maize at a farmers' co-operative in northern Zambia. This is a British aid project which aims to strengthen existing resources rather than dependence on imports.

after four years of meeting more or less every requirement for reform. The basis of the controversy emerges when one looks at the detailed nature of the programmes, the principle of conditionality, and particularly the rapid time-scale in which many policy reforms have been implemented. The cases of the Ivory Coast and Zambia illustrate this.

△ Adjustment in Practice

The Ivory Coast

Until the early 1980s the Ivory Coast was one of the success stories of Africa. Throughout the 1960s and 1970s national income grew at an average of over 6% per annum and the country was seen as a land of economic miracles. In the early 1980s the situation changed dramatically. In 1981 national income grew by only 1.2% and for the second year in succession the overall balance of payments deficit exceeded 20% of exports. In response to this economic and financial crisis the government introduced a structural adjustment programme, with the help of the IMF and the World Bank.

The first step was to reduce government expenditure and increase revenues. Regular spending was reduced by freezing public employees' salaries, reducing fringe benefits to government employees such as housing subsidies, and suspending promotions. Capital expenditure was reduced by cutting programmes for new roads, schools and hospitals. Fertiliser subsidies were abolished. Government revenues were increased by raising taxes on a host of consumer items such as petrol, tobacco, alcohol, vehicle taxes, insurance and property.

The second step was aimed at rationalising the public sector. New management controls, such as quarterly performance reports, were introduced. Public enterprises were examined with a view to possible privatisation.

The third step was focused on restoring profit margins to rural producers who had been the backbone of the economic miracle. Between 1981 and 1984 prices received by the producers for major crops were increased by 25%–35% and consumer prices for bread, rice and palm oil were increased in line with world prices. The private sector was given incentives to produce more goods for export and cut local production costs.

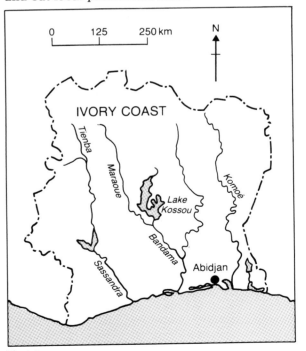

Fig 4.1

How did incomes and the economy fare under these reforms? After registering a small growth in 1981, gross real income fell by about 4% a year for the next three years. Agricultural production stagnated in 1981 and 1982, and then fell by 11% in 1983. Industrial output achieved a growth rate of 10% in 1981 but fell by 15% in 1982 and again by a staggering 24% in 1984.

The effect of cuts in government spending was particularly dramatic. Public expenditure was reduced by over 50%. As intended, the government budget deficit was reduced from 13.1% to 1.5% of national income. The balance of payments situation improved substantially over the period, moving from a deficit of over 5% of national income in 1980 to a surplus in 1984. Yet this was achieved primarily by cutting imports rather than expanding exports.

The respite from recession has proved short-lived. Economic growth slowed to 2% in 1986, production was down to 1979 levels, the slide in the Ivory Coast's terms of trade continued, and acute balance of payments problems returned. This was largely because of a fall in the value of the country's principal exports, showing how critical a factor they are in a structural adjustment programme.

In 1987 the Ivory Coast was forced to suspend payments on its international debts and seek a further round of rescheduling. Income per person had declined by about 20% since 1979. Has this period of hardship and change under structural adjustment led the Ivory Coast back on a course towards self-sustained growth? World Bank forecasts are discouraging. They suggest that real income per person will not increase over the rest of the 1980s. Imports are expected to remain at a low level and total investment is not expected to grow at more than 4% a year. What cannot be calculated accurately is what might have happened *without* structural adjustment.

Zambia

Zambia depends on exporting copper for about 95% of its foreign exchange earnings. Until 1974 Zambia ran a surplus on its balance of payments, but in 1974–75 disaster struck. The price of copper halved. The position continued to deteriorate and by 1983 the income from Zambia's exports could buy only a quarter of the imports it could buy in 1970. Reserves of ore have also declined and have become more difficult to exploit so that total production has fallen.

By 1983 Zambia was in a deep economic crisis. Per capita income had fallen by about 1.5% a year and was 44% lower in 1983 compared with 1974. Zambia was in a continuous balance of payments crisis having run a deficit every year since 1974. The government budget deficit had become too large to handle as revenues fell from 34% of total income in 1970 to 25% in 1983. Expenditures, though cut to 60% of 1975 levels, were still far higher than income. This led to a budget deficit of 21% of national income.

Total external debt amounted to $4.5 billion and debt servicing was taking up over 50% of total foreign exchange earnings. In 1983 the Government of Zambia tentatively introduced a structural adjustment programme under the auspices and with the support of the IMF. The programme involved controls on domestic credit, freezing promotions and salaries in the civil service, cutting back capital expenditure, and deregulating prices for basic products such as soap, beef and rice. Many controls remained, including price controls on maize meal (the staple foodstuff) and fertiliser.

But it was only in late 1985, in response to the worsening economic crisis and pressure from aid donors, that the government began to make drastic reforms. An auction system for foreign exchange was introduced to establish a more realistic exchange rate for the extremely overvalued Zambian currency, the Kwacha. The exchange rate under the auction system moved very rapidly from K2 = $1 up to levels of K21 = $1. Producer prices for maize were raised by over 90% and by a further 42% in 1986.

Public enterprise price controls were abolished and prices were raised in response

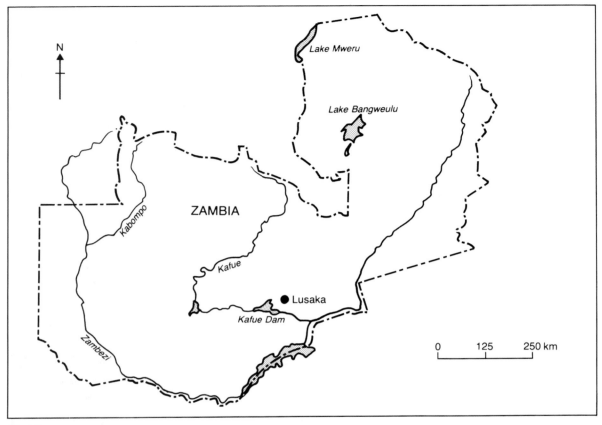

Fig 4.2

to increased import costs. The monopoly of the National Agricultural Marketing Board was ended so that anyone could now buy or sell maize, seed and fertiliser. In an attempt to encourage private investment, the government also relaxed restrictions on foreign investors sending profits out of the country.

The effects of these policy changes are difficult to disentangle. At first there were signs of improvement on the economic front: but by 1986 Zambia's domestic and external economy began to deteriorate. The government budget deficit continued to grow and in 1986 totalled 35% of total national income; a level unacceptable to the IMF. In response to this deterioration, Zambia could not draw on IMF stand-by credit. The IMF wanted greater reform and ruled that Zambia's access to credit was conditional on removing the subsidy on maize meal.

The subsidy was duly removed in late 1986 and the price of maize more than doubled from 37 to 82 Kwacha per bag. In the food riots that followed, 15 people died.

These events led to President Kaunda taking the first step away from the reforms imposed by the IMF by withdrawing the price rises and nationalising the private milling companies. In May 1987, after months of strikes and simmering unrest, President Kaunda finally broke with the IMF and ceased to implement the policies of structural adjustment. The government introduced a series of economic measures that amounted to a return to the old ways, including fixed exchange rates, the restoration of government subsidies, and controls on prices and imports.

△ Is Structural Adjustment Working?

Structural adjustment in Africa, as propounded by the World Bank and the IMF, has provoked much debate and criticism.

It is evident that in straightforward economic terms the evidence for success is slight. The main objective of structural adjustment policies is to improve a country's balance of payments position. An analysis in 1987 by the Overseas Development Institute indicated that less than half of those countries in Africa implementing IMF stabilisation policies achieved their balance of payments targets. Furthermore, these targets were met mainly by reducing imports and economic growth, and balance of payments targets alone are a poor measure of success.

But leaving aside the complex question of economic indicators and their validity, there are more specific aspects of government policy under structural adjustment that are worth reviewing.

▲ How important is 'getting the prices right'?
▲ Is privatisation workable?
▲ Can exports grow?

Getting Prices Right

Getting prices right is a crucial aspect of adjustment and one of the most important factors is the exchange rate. Devaluation has been a major tool in adjustment programmes and rapid devaluations have taken place throughout Africa during the 1980s. The effects of devaluation have been very varied. In Zimbabwe, which has the most sophisticated economy in Africa (excluding South Africa) the response has been to increase exports, but in Tanzania there has been little improvement in exports. In Zambia the manufacturing sector responded favourably to devaluation, while in Zaire there was a poor response. The key factor appears to be the ability of the industry concerned to respond to the potential opportunities devaluation presents. This ability depends on a wide range of factors including access to funds to expand or start a business, and

reliable roads and railways.

In agriculture, 'getting the prices right' is not only a matter of the exchange rate and a freer play of market forces. Many farmers have become richer under adjustment policies as governments have improved incentives. This has been done directly, by increasing prices to farmers, or indirectly, by removing any constraints on the market for the sales of produce. But governments and donors are finding that pricing policy in agriculture is not always so straightforward. For example, in Malawi the increase in maize prices in 1985–86, under a World Bank structural adjustment programme, boosted production to such an extent that there were serious difficulties in storing and disposing of a sudden surplus. Meanwhile, production of important foreign exchange earning crops, such as cotton and tobacco, declined.

But the major limitation in relying on the price mechanism is that most African farmers remain barely above the subsistence level and

Cotton from the Gezira project in Sudan, a country suffering from acute debt problems because of falling world markets and prices for cotton.

do not normally sell their small surpluses in government-regulated markets. Their main difficulty in increasing production, and thus incomes, is the low productivity of their land and labour. It requires a major technical breakthrough for such farmers substantially to increase their output, and this in turn seems to require major, long-term investment in research and development. Such investments, in hybrid maize in Kenya and Zimbabwe, for example, have led to large increases in yields. Africa's small farmers have shown themselves to be innovative and hard-working where the production opportunities are available.

Is Privatisation Workable?

An important part of the adjustment process is changing the role of public enterprises in the economy (see Box). Most parties agree that some change in this area is long overdue and change in this context means some version of privatisation. Yet the obstacles to effective privatisation are daunting and progress has been slow. It is estimated that only 5% of public enterprises in Africa have been shut down or sold since 1980.

Plans for privatisation abound. The government of the Ivory Coast has drawn up a list of 100 businesses in which it wishes to sell its holding. Zambia, Nigeria and Tanzania are also considering privatisation. However, there are no easy ways of bringing these plans to fruition; stock markets and a relatively sophisticated class of investors do not exist in

Africa. Organised capital markets function in only a handful of countries (Nigeria, Kenya, Zimbabwe) and most of the markets are relatively tiny. Potential buyers are few and often politically unacceptable: businessmen who are likely to belong to non-African communities (Asians in East Africa, Lebanese in West Africa).

As well as control by outsiders there is also fear that a small clique of local businessmen will gain control of the domestic economy. In Sierra Leone, for example, the government divestiture programme allowed business interests to acquire extensive trading concessions and a temporary hold over most foreign exchange dealings.

As well as the practical problems there are also doubts that privatised enterprises are much more efficient in practice. In many countries the small size of the market leaves little room for competition, and privatisation could mean a private monopoly which would be difficult to regulate. Furthermore, most export markets are highly competitive and the know-how to develop these markets is scarce. Often only governments are in a position to tap the overseas skills and capital markets that are essential to build new industries.

Can Exports Grow?

Increasing exports is an important key to the economic future of Africa. Adjustment programmes emphasise export generation but give very little idea of how this can be

Public Enterprises in Africa

It is estimated that there are between three and four thousand public enterprises in Africa, ranging from breweries to sawmills, cattle ranches to banks. In many African countries state enterprises dominate the economy. This domination stems not so much from the contribution that they make to the national income but to their importance in the 'modern' part of many African economies and the claim they make on financial and human resources.

The share of national income contributed by public enterprises varies widely between countries: in Kenya it is only 8% while in Zambia it is 37%. This compares with a worldwide average of about 10%. However, these figures understate the importance of public enterprises. They typically control many of the export industries and are responsible for a major section of the manufacturing industry (50% in Zambia, 90% in Ethiopia). They also take a disproportionate share of funds available for investment (61.2% in Zambia, 17.3% in Kenya) and borrow a greater share of funds available in the economy than the contribution they make to national income.

It is precisely this gap between the contributions public and private enterprises make to national wealth and the claim each has on resources that lies at the centre of the debate on their role.

A rubber factory in Liberia – the type of agricultural processing which will boost Africa's exports.

achieved on a big enough scale to compensate for the fall in commodity prices. Over the last 20 years Africa's share of the commodity markets has declined by 50% in value. Even if Africa can regain its share of the market, the likely result will be falling prices as countries compete for a limited market, despite the cushioning effect of schemes designed to stabilise such prices. Africa has shown that it can enter new world markets and British supermarket shelves testify to increased exports of agricultural produce (see p. 60). But it is totally unrealistic to expect the export of commodities such as winter vegetables or cut flowers to bridge the major foreign exchange gap of African countries that traditionally export commodities such as oil palm, coffee, cocoa and tea.

That gap can only be bridged, in the long run, by new markets for new products. Africa needs to expand and develop its processing and manufacturing industries, and add value to its agricultural commodities before export. Africa urgently needs to improve its agricultural production but this alone will not solve the core problem of insufficient export earnings. Diversification away from primary commodities into export-based processing and manufacturing is possible only if sufficient capital is made available and markets in the developed world are opened up to allow African exports to compete.

△ The Effects of Structural Adjustment

Structural adjustment policies carried out so far in Africa have resulted, as intended, in wage incomes being held down, declining government expenditure, and prices to consumers rising. The effects of these changes

Adjustment 'with a human face' – a safe water supply to avoid long journeys by children like these in Mozambique.

are not uniform across different groups in society and it is not always the case that the poor have been most seriously affected. Some of the rural poor, for example, have benefited from these changes, obtaining higher prices for their marketed crops without all of the increased income being absorbed by higher prices for goods they consume.

But one of the most contentious of adjustment policies is removing food subsidies, as it is clearly the urban poor who are most affected. From an economic perspective, across the board food subsidies are a very expensive and inefficient way of helping the poor, as the rich also benefit. But the effect on nutrition of large price increases can be dramatic and can significantly affect poverty levels. Furthermore, the welfare of a household consists not only of income but also of other benefits such as health care and education. These services have been significantly reduced by cuts in public expenditure intended to release funds for use in the directly productive sectors of the economy. These concerns about the social and welfare consequences of structural adjustment have led many donors to look for less harsh programmes of adjustment.

A New Approach

The aim of a new approach to adjustment is to combine change in the economies of Africa with protection for those who are at the mercy of change: this is 'adjustment with a human face'. Some progress has already been made. Many international institutions no longer accept that it is enough simply to adjust the exchange rates, privatise public enterprises, remove price controls and subsidies, and cut expenditure.

It is increasingly recognised that structural adjustment is not simply a matter for the productive sectors of the economy. The social services in most African countries also need restructuring. For example, there is much scope for reallocating resources from high cost investment, such as urban hospitals, to low cost activities, such as rural health clinics dealing with basic needs. Many of SCF's primary health care programmes in Africa assist in this process.

There is also now seen to be a need to use special programmes to alleviate some of the effects of adjustment on vulnerable groups: for example, by measures to maintain nutrition levels when subsidies are taken off foodstuffs.

Adjustment with a Human Face

A recent study by UNICEF set out the principles of a new approach to structural adjustment designed to protect the poor during economic change and reform. The proposed new approach has six major elements.

▲ A more expansionary emphasis in national economic policies. This means implementing policies that sustain the levels of output, investment and basic services over the adjustment period. Such an approach typically requires that imports are kept at a level high enough to maintain investment and employment. This, in turn, means a greater injection of funds in the short and medium term and a more gradual approach to economic reform.

▲ Adopting policies within each sector of economic activity that meet, as a priority, the needs of vulnerable groups in society while at the same time promoting economic growth.

▲ Restructuring agricultural and small-scale industrial policies to increase employment and the incomes of poor households. Such policies involve providing improved technological packages to small farmers, providing credit to small-scale entrepreneurs and focusing programmes on women.

▲ Introducing policies that increase the spread and efficiency of social services. Such policies include directing health care expenditure to primary health care in the rural areas, ensuring that clean water is widely available, and shifting education expenditure away from universities and colleges towards primary schools and vocational colleges.

▲ Establishing feeding programmes, food for work schemes, and public works programmes to maintain nutritional levels.

▲ Creating systems for monitoring and evaluating the effects of policy changes on the more vulnerable groups in society so that policy makers can determine what has been happening and why.

Meeting basic needs. These mothers are attending a monthly health clinic in Zimbabwe.

African Supermarket

The British are among the lowest European consumers of fresh fruit and they are generally highly conservative in their preferences: apples, pears, oranges and bananas remain the staple fruit for most families. But over the past decade the demand for grapes, easy-peel citrus, and what are termed 'exotics' has increased. The main bulk of these exotics, such as mangos, pineapples, pawpaws, lychees and passion fruit, come from tropical or sub-tropical regions and several African countries are now entering the UK market.

It is a difficult market for African producers. Countries such as Israel, Brazil (and South Africa of course) are already well-established and have experience of dealing with the formidable packaging and transport problems associated with perishable goods. Yet there are some real successes for African exporters. The fresh pineapple market has more than doubled since 1978 and most of this increase has been for medium-size Cayenne varieties grown in the Ivory Coast, which now has 80% of the UK market. The greener varieties grown in Ghana and Uganda are less popular, though Ghana now has an 8% market share.

There has been an even more spectacular increase in mango imports to the UK: up 340% since 1978. Countries such as Venezuela and Mexico (and India, which exports small green mangos for chutney and pickle) have done especially well but there are also some African successes. Mali, for example, now has 3% of the UK market, and several African countries are now producing the fibreless 'Florida' varieties popular in the UK.

Such market opportunities are most unlikely to transform the economic prospects of individual African countries. But these successes – and others, such as passion fruit from Kenya, popular among immigrant communities for flavouring – demonstrate the opportunities open to African countries for creating and meeting new demands.

△ The Politics of Structural Adjustment

Few African governments are eager to institute major policy reforms of the sort often requested as a condition of structural adjustment loans. This is because of the effect structural adjustment can have in changing the social and economic order of a country. Many African governments owe their support to the urban population and many of the policies pursued in the past (low food prices, industrial protection, burgeoning bureaucracies) were aimed at maintaining that support.

The exact balance of support tends to vary depending on the original source of power. In countries such as Kenya and the Ivory Coast, the core of pre-independence nationalism lay in the countryside, and policies since independence have not discriminated too severely against agriculture. In Nigeria and Zambia, on the other hand, governments have relied more upon support from the towns and in these countries policies have often discriminated against the small farmer. Under structural adjustment policies the changes proposed tend to benefit most rural producers at the expense of civil servants and workers in urban industries. Opposition to these policies therefore often implies a desire to maintain the current distribution of wealth.

As well as these domestic political realities, there is also a feeling in many African countries that the imposition of wide-ranging conditions on loan programmes is an infringement of sovereignty. The IMF and the World Bank in particular are often accused of behaving in a high-handed manner and of forcing policies without awareness of the realities of government in borrowing countries. This opposition to the principle of imposed 'conditionality' can threaten the process of structural adjustment. Unless there is a meeting of minds it is unlikely that policy prescriptions will stick or that the aims of adjustment will be achieved.

Three
African Challenges

△1 The Debt Problem

In trying to understand Africa's debt situation the first point to keep in mind is that most countries' debt problems are largely a symptom of *other* sources of economic difficulty, and it is these difficulties which make loan repayment so burdensome. A shortage of foreign exchange, and of the imports it can buy, is at the heart of many of these difficulties. This problem featured prominently in the debates of the 1986 UN Special Session.

The Economic Context

The crucial variable is the balance of payments (BoP) – a record of a country's trading and financial transactions with the rest of the world. Most developing countries can expect to run deficits on their trade with the rest of the world, financing these by external grants and loans. These capital receipts enable them to buy imports in excess of the value of their export earnings. In effect, they allow countries to augment their own savings with some of the savings of the outside world. But for it to make sense to borrow from abroad at least two conditions must be satisfied: (1) the returns from the activities financed by the loan should exceed the rate of interest on the loan; (2) the country should be able to expand its foreign exchange earnings sufficiently to be able to service the loans in hard currency as the obligations become payable. Neither of these conditions has commonly been satisfied in many African countries.

A major source of difficulty for many African countries is that BoP current deficits have grown beyond the limit of prudent borrowing and to unsustainably large amounts. In 1981 the average deficit for Africa as a whole was equal to over a third of the value of export earnings. Even though this ratio had fallen to 22% by 1986 it was still the highest deficit ratio of all developing country regions. Underlying this has been a weak external trading position. For Africa as a whole and for most individual countries within Africa, the value of export earnings has tended to expand only sluggishly and considerably less rapidly than the demand for imports. This has been the result both of adverse world economic conditions and of structural weaknesses and policy mistakes in debtor countries. These have already been described in earlier chapters.

There has been a reduction in Africa's BoP deficits in recent years: for sub-Saharan Africa as a whole the deficit fell from a peak of $13.0 billion in 1981 to 'only' $6.9 billion in 1985. Unfortunately, much of this improvement was a result of cuts in the volume of imports, due both to economic depression and to restrictions on imports. In many countries these cuts have themselves tended to hurt: starving industries of needed imported supplies and forcing major reductions in investment levels, thereby reducing the countries' capacity to expand and diversify exports and to produce import-substitutes. In Nigeria, for example, imports of industrial inputs had by 1984–85 been slashed to a bare half of the 1982 level. Small surprise, therefore, that industry was unable to operate at full capacity in the same period. During 1986 African countries expanded their imports a little and the deficit promptly rose again, to $9.8 billion.

Expanding Africa's natural resources and exports – one way out of the debt crisis.

The need to cut back on imports was not merely the consequence of poor export performance, however. It also reflected a very sharp decline in the *net* volume of finance flowing in from the outside world. If we take total capital inflows, minus the cost of debt servicing, the net inflow to low-income African countries moved as follows (in billions of US dollars):

1980	3.3	1984	1.0
1981	2.7	1985	0.8
1982	2.3	1986	0.8
1983	2.1		

While the cost of debt servicing has been rising and aid has remained static the commercial banks have been leaving Africa, with substantial *return* flows to the banks since 1983. It is possible to make too much of this, however. While the withdrawal of commercial bank support has certainly heightened a financing crisis, it would not make sense for most African countries to take on extra debts on the commercial terms available from banks when they are little able to afford those they already have.

The gravity of this problem becomes clear if we consider once more what has been happening to saving and investment. The World Bank estimates that gross domestic saving had fallen to just over 4% of gross domestic product (GDP) by 1984, compared with 23% for all developing countries taken together (and 17% for the UK). Gross investment (which includes depreciation) was down to under 12%, approaching three-quarters of that financed by inflows of capital from the rest of the world. In order to protect already miserable living standards Africa has been consuming almost all the income it generates and is saving or investing very little. Levels of investment are too low to secure growing incomes in the future, and to service debt and keep trading account in credit. An expansion seems essential but that implies cutting further on consumption standards already far below expectations.

To sum up, what is suggested is that 'the debt problem' is to a considerable extent a symptom of a BoP weakened by adverse world economic forces and domestic policy shortcomings, as well as of reduced access to new capital inflows. Let us turn next to a comparison of the nature of Africa's debt with that of other developing countries. At this point we need to set out some of the basic facts about Africa's debt.

Characteristics of Debt

Figures 5.1, 5.2 and 5.3 set out some of the key comparative statistics of Africa's debt. It is necessary to begin by saying that even now, after several years of improving the data base, statistics on the debt of many African countries are suspect and incomplete. The official data understate the true amounts because they do not adequately cover obligations to the IMF or payments arrears, and because knowledge of the private sector is seriously deficient. A country's indebtedness invariably turns out to be much larger than the expected figure. Nevertheless, the diagrams are based on the best available data.

Figure 5.1 highlights a number of contrasts with other developing country debtors. It shows the modest size of Africa's debt in absolute terms and by comparison with other developing countries. Note that a far higher proportion of sub-Saharan Africa's debt is owed to official creditors than to the private capital markets. Note also that a higher, though still modest, proportion of the total is owed to the IMF. This is a fact of some importance given that until recently the Fund has been trying to reduce its exposure in Africa: there was a net return flow from Africa to the Fund in 1986 (see p. 51).

Figure 5.2 shows that a much higher proportion of Africa's debt has been obtained on concessional terms, mainly in the form of aid. This contrast is also brought out in the comparison between interest rates and maturity terms. Viewed from this perspective, it may seem surprising that Africa should have a debt servicing problem at all.

The debt-export ratios in Figure 5.3, comparing what Africa owes to what it earns, help to explain why there is a problem. Furthermore, the total outstanding debt of the poorest African countries (see p. 27) relative to exports is much larger than for developing countries as a whole.

However, there are enormous variations between countries: so large as to reduce the usefulness of any averages. At the one

THE STRUCTURE OF DEBT, 1985

DEVELOPING COUNTRIES

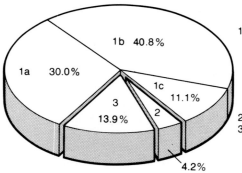

SUB-SAHARAN AFRICA

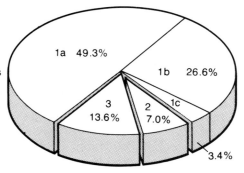

1. Long-term debt
   of which:

   a) Official loans
   b) Commercial loans
      to governments
   c) Loans to private
      sector
2. Liabilities to IMF
3. Short-term debt

Source:- World Bank

Fig 5.1 Most of Africa's long-term debt is to official creditors, reflecting the loss of confidence in Africa by the private sector.

AFRICA'S DEBT, 1985: WHAT ARE THE TERMS?

	Least Developed Countries	Sub-Saharan Africa	Low-income Africa
Interest (%)	8.0	5.8	3.0
Maturity (years)	16.1	24.2	32.9
Concessional debt as % of total debt	21.7	37.9	53.4
Total value of out-standing debt ($bn)	892.4	85.6	45.9

Source: World Bank

Fig 5.2   Africa's debt problem is minute by comparison with that of the rest of the world, although its effects may be felt more.

extreme there are some countries with large debts relative to their exports and whose interest payments absorb a high proportion of current export earnings. These include Burundi, Kenya, Madagascar, Mali, Niger, Somalia, Togo and Zaire. According to World Bank data these countries in 1985 had total recorded debts equivalent to more than twice the value of annual exports, and interest payment obligations equivalent to more than 10% of exports. At the other extreme there is a more numerous group of countries – including Botswana, Cameroon, Gabon, Mauritius and the Seychelles – with debt-export ratios of around or less than 100% and interest-export ratios of less than 5%. As Africa's largest and best-known debtor, Nigeria is in an intermediate position, with a total debt at the end of 1985 of $18.3 billion, a debt-export ratio of 141% and an interest-exports ratio of under 10%.

These country comparisons give a clear warning against generalising too readily about the debt situation of Africa. Three-quarters of Africa's total debt is accounted for by ten countries and probably a rather smaller number have a really severe debt problem. Most confront a generally weak BoP situation, which makes almost any level of debt servicing difficult.

It is also helpful to examine trends between 1982 (when the 'debt crisis' first broke upon the world) and 1985, the latest year for which such data are available. *In all cases the ratios worsened in this period.* This is a measure of the inability of developing countries to do more than buy time. The world is still further from,

PAYING OFF AFRICA'S DEBT: THE EXPORT-DEBT RATIO, 1985

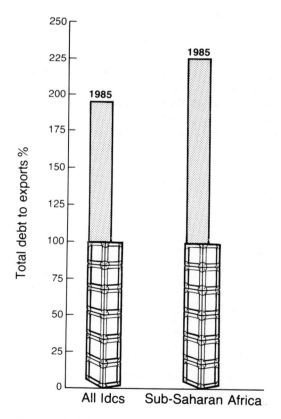

Source: World Bank

Fig 5.3   Africa's debt is now running at more than twice the value of its exports – higher than the ratio of developing countries as a whole. (See also Box on p. 7.)

rather than nearer to, any basic solution. This is true also of sub-Saharan Africa as a whole and the poorest countries within the region. Africa's total-debt and debt-servicing ratios have deteriorated substantially. This is not only because the debt and the cost of servicing it have been growing, but also because average incomes and export earnings have been performing poorly.

As a result, many African countries have found it impossible to make interest and amortisation payments on the due dates and have had to reschedule. In 1975–86 African countries negotiated no fewer than 88 separate reschedulings of their official and private debts, including 17 in 1986 alone.

Towards a Solution

Two factors increase the difficulty of finding a solution to the African debt problem. The first is the weakness of the BoP and savings position of African debtors, where there are few grounds for optimism about a rapid recovery. The second is the fact that such a high proportion of Africa's debt is already held on concessional terms, with much of it owed to 'preferred lenders' such as the IMF and World Bank, whose credits cannot be renegotiated. This feature of Africa's debt situation puts the continent on a different footing from that, say, of the major Latin American debtors. Conventional debt reschedulings can only bring very limited relief to Africa.

A weakness of most past reschedulings has been their short-term nature, typically covering 12 to 18 months (although in 1986 the Ivory Coast negotiated reschedulings over three to four years). Since 1975 Zaire has had eight successive agreements covering just over 12 years. Under the terms usually negotiated repayments begin to fall due on rescheduled debts after four or five years, when the breathing space has elapsed. Creditor countries have tried to refuse further relief on debt already rescheduled but its sheer impossibility has forced exceptions to be made in several cases. Because they charge interest on the deferred amortisation and interest payments, these reschedulings increase the size of future debt servicing obligations and the burden on the next generation.

But if past reschedulings have offered no solution, it would be wrong to think that there has been no progress on any front. First, the situation has been eased, by Britain and certain other aid donor countries, through 'debt forgiveness' or the conversion of past aid loans into grants. Second, 1986 saw the creation of the Structural Adjustment Facility (SAF) in the IMF, which was designed to provide medium-term, low-interest relief to the poorer developing countries. This has proved a useful new source of finance, with total credit commitments from the SAF to Africa amounting to $343 million as at May 1987. In 1986 the eighth replenishment of the International Development Association (IDA) – the soft-aid window of the World Bank – at a level above $12 billion for a three-year period, was also a better outcome than many had feared, and an increased share of it is earmarked for Africa.

Perhaps the most encouraging development, however, is that the governments of the West increasingly accept that there is a need for further special action to reduce the plight of African debtors. Several proposals were put forward during 1987. First was a three-point proposal by the British Chancellor of the Exchequer, Nigel Lawson. This envisages agreement among the creditor countries to make concessions to African countries, undertaking programmes of policy reform that would (1) convert aid loans into grants; (2) reschedule other official credits over a longer period, including longer grace periods; and (3) reduce interest rates on these debts 'to well below market levels'.

At about the same time the IMF's Managing Director, Michel Camdessus, proposed a tripling in the size of the SAF; soon after that the World Bank announced a programme combining features from the Lawson plan, an enlargement of the SAF, increased lending by IDA and greater co-financing of debt-related adjustment programmes from the aid programmes of creditor countries, the European Community and other sources.

Taken together, these were fairly radical proposals and would certainly bring substantial relief to African debtors, or at least those willing to swallow the policy conditions that would be attached. Sadly, they have so far made limited progress, particularly against objections from the US and Germany. It was hoped that agreements could be reached at the annual meeting of the IMF and World Bank in October 1987, but no more could be agreed at that meeting than to study the proposals further.

There was, in any case, the risk that debt was being over-emphasised in the efforts of the international community to help African countries, and that some governments might be either unable or unwilling to comply with the policy conditionality to which assistance would be tied. As regards the former, the position is quite simple: there are a number of African governments confronting grave economic difficulties but which do not have a particularly heavy debt problem. Uganda and the countries of Southern Africa are examples. Their needs are in danger of being neglected because of a narrow preoccupation in the West with debt.

Concerning the question of policy conditionality, there are countries in Africa – such as Uganda and Sudan – which simply do not have the necessary political stability to implement demanding and wide-ranging policy reforms. There are others (such as Benin and Ethiopia) whose left-wing orientation makes them unwilling to implement the market-oriented policies which would be required of them. It is doubtful whether conditionality can be flexible enough to accommodate these differing situations. Another question, yet to be convincingly demonstrated, is whether there are any satisfactory alternatives to the conventional adjustment programmes of the IMF and World Bank. Countries which have tried to go it alone with unconventional approaches – Brazil is a recent example – do not have a very impressive record.

To return to the main theme: if Africa's debt problem is best understood as a symptom of a fundamentally weak BoP position, it follows that what we think of as the debt problem is likely to persist until the trading positions of African countries can be strengthened and until they can rely upon larger and sustained inflows of aid and investment. Equally important will be domestic policies to raise the volume of saving and the productivity of investment. This is a formidable twin challenge to donors and governments, but the most encouraging aspect of the 1987 proposals

for dealing with Africa's debt was that, at least in desperate situations, internationally co-operative solutions are still sometimes possible, even in a world that has seemed to move towards more nationalistic values.

△2 Population and Health in Africa

In the summer of 1987 the five billionth person in the world was born – a baby which had a one in twelve chance of being from sub-Saharan Africa. In 1985, 418 million lived in sub-Saharan Africa, and this number is increasing annually by 3.3%, much faster than any other region or the low-income countries as a whole. By 2000, one-tenth of the world's population will live in sub-Saharan Africa and one-eighth in all of Africa. Africa has already

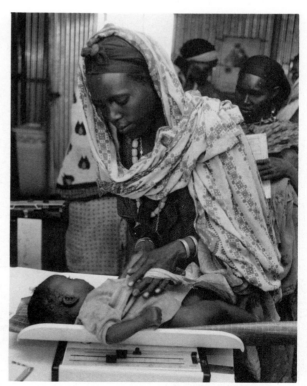

Population growth is a concern at both national and international level. For the mothers of newborn babies, it is much more a question of survival.

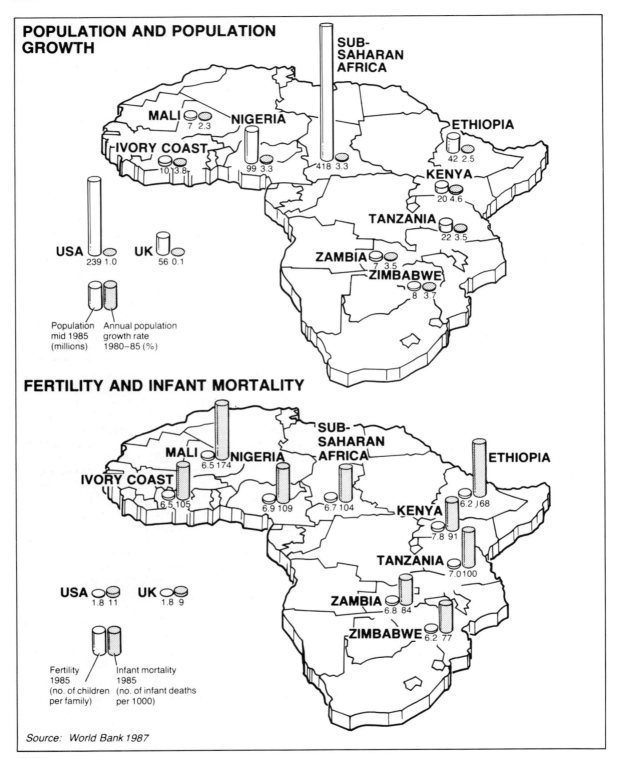

POPULATION AND POPULATION GROWTH

SUB-SAHARAN AFRICA

MALI
7 2.3

NIGERIA

IVORY COAST
10 3.8

99 3.3

418 3.3

ETHIOPIA
42 2.5

KENYA
20 4.6

TANZANIA
22 3.5

ZAMBIA
7 3.5

ZIMBABWE
8 3.7

USA
239 1.0

UK
56 0.1

Population mid 1985 (millions)   Annual population growth rate 1980–85 (%)

FERTILITY AND INFANT MORTALITY

MALI
6.5 174

NIGERIA

IVORY COAST
6.5 105

6.9 109

SUB-SAHARAN AFRICA
6.7 104

ETHIOPIA
6.2 168

KENYA
7.8 91

TANZANIA
7.0 100

ZAMBIA
6.8 84

ZIMBABWE
6.2 77

USA
1.8 11

UK
1.8 9

Fertility 1985 (no. of children per family)   Infant mortality 1985 (no. of infant deaths per 1000)

Source: World Bank 1987

Fig 5.4

overtaken Europe as the region with the largest population outside Asia.

Are these facts encouraging or threatening to Africa? Should Africa be more concerned about her population growth, or should others on her behalf? If so, what is being done, and by whom? These questions touch international issues, but they first have to be addressed to Africa.

This section will be concerned mainly with the relation between population and aspects of development, especially health. It will also describe perhaps the most serious current threat to Africa's population – the AIDS epidemic, which may prove to be the greatest challenge of all for African governments.

Is Africa Over-Populated?

People concerned about the population increase in developing countries often think in terms not of absolute numbers but of more and more poor people, adding to the existing threat of the 'starving millions'. In fact, the figures overall show an encouraging general trend in the opposite direction. Studies by the World Bank show that in most poor regions of the world – Asia, Latin America and the Middle East – the steady rise in the average income of the poor, together with the gradual slowing of fertility rates, will inevitably mean a big reduction in the number of poor between 1980 and 2000.

However, in sub-Saharan Africa, where economic growth has declined quite sharply, the number of poor (defined as people with annual incomes below $135 in 1980) is likely to have increased by nearly 70% during the same period. This increase could be reduced to below 20% if health and development programmes were able to achieve a rapid fall in the fertility rate.

The problem for Africa is not 'over-population' but that the increase in population is unmatched by increases in incomes, production and welfare. Some, in fact, would go even further and say that Africa is actually under-populated and needs more, not fewer, citizens to generate wealth and assure family security.

In much of Africa, the concept of a large, healthy family is highly developed, based on ancient traditions and only thwarted by chronic poverty and disease. Most African governments have paid lip service to family planning and many support it: 29 countries attended an all-Africa parliamentary conference on population held in Zimbabwe in 1986. But some countries still firmly believe in the right to increase and take a positive 'pro-natalist' line.

In apparent sympathy with African views is the argument used by the United Nations agencies, voluntary agencies and churches, and echoed by the Brundtland Commission in 1987, that people are a country's most important resource and cannot be a 'problem' in themselves. This is not an argument for encouraging population increase. Many voluntary agencies support family planning programmes but, as SCF's own medical officer points out (see p. 70), family planning must be seen in the wider context of community development. Most development agencies regard economic development as being closely related to family planning, and they point to evidence that families have fewer children once incomes rise, welfare improves and confidence grows that more of their children will survive.

Even this approach has been criticised by some African writers. Journalist Herbert Ekwe-Ekwe reminded readers of *West Africa* magazine in May 1987 that Europe's population had also increased dramatically in 1650–1850 from 103 million to 274 million, while Africa's remained static at 100 million, drained of her manpower by transportation and slavery. No wonder, he argued, that Africa needed to build up her population today to make up for this scandal.

The European Comparison

The history of rapid population growth elsewhere is a poor guide for Africa. In England during the eighteenth century, for example, there was both a high growth rate in population and at the same time an 'agricultural revolution' – involving enclosure, especially – which squeezed many small farmers and farm labourers out of their livelihoods. But unlike Africa today, the English economy was simultaneously creating large numbers of jobs in manufacturing and even in small industries based on wood and leather-working, which developed with

Family Planning in Africa

△ Interview with Dr John Seaman, Save the Children Fund

How important is family planning to the poorest people in Africa?

In the sense of limiting family size by using modern contraceptive methods, family planning is not a priority for poor people. Birth spacing and other traditional family planning methods are still of considerable importance in Africa, but these are more to increase the chances of the survival of children than to limit family size. Indeed, for much of Africa there is no concept of an 'ideal family size'.

From the individual poor family's point of view, a larger family means more labour, and consequently the possibility of increasing and diversifying family income and increasing family security.

On the population level the importance of family planning is mostly over-emphasised. Even in areas of Africa such as highland Ethiopia, where population levels are such as to cause severe land shortage, the absolute population density is often low. The immediate problem is low productivity from primitive agricultural technology and poor systems of pricing, distribution and marketing. At the time of Malthus, Britain was thought to be grossly overpopulated, but it easily supports more than twice the population today at a much higher economic level.

But the problem should not be entirely dismissed. Some countries such as Kenya have real population problems in that even with a highly developed agriculture they are now net food importers.

Is it the lack of funds which is the problem?

A lot of money is spent on family planning projects. The problem is not primarily one of resources but of the practical problems of getting people to use contraception to limit their family size. What limits the use of family planning methods is not always certain but it is clear that the provision of contraceptives is not enough. People must want to limit their families. If this is to occur they must be sure that having a small family will not lead to a loss of economic security. And where child mortality is high, they must be sure that it is possible to aim for a small family and know the children will survive.

How would money be better spent?

It would be better spent on securing the conditions necessary to change behaviour. The first line of investment must be in effective health and education services and in the development of the necessary infrastructure – such as roads, markets – to establish at least the preconditions for improved welfare and economic performance.

Although in discussions of overseas aid the need for population control in places like highland Ethiopia is often emphasised, it is perhaps not sufficiently realised that in many regions only a tiny fraction of the population can be reached with any services. Even if contraceptive supply was an issue of primary importance, this could not currently be guaranteed in many areas.

What is SCF itself doing about family planning?

In Africa very little; we give much more support to family planning projects in Asia. Our priority is to concentrate on the development of effective and sustainable health services for large populations. We have published one report arguing for the wider acceptance by governments of long-acting injectable contraceptives. These have been the subject of much misinformation and they are banned in some countries. This is a pity, as in a village setting they are often the only effective contraceptive technology available.

agricultural change. Africa is not experiencing a similar industrial revolution to absorb labour, and much of its new agricultural industries are based on imported steel and plastic products rather than those of local artisans.

Similarly, there were exceptional population growths in countries such as Sweden, Italy (and Scotland and Ireland) around the turn of the century. In this case there was massive migration to the USA, with the populations of some European countries declining by 25% between 1900 and 1914. Although numbers of Africans – particularly from the Mediterranean and northern parts of the continent – have migrated to Europe, this has been on nothing like the scale of the European migrations. Even so, the small African migrations have led to measures controlling any future flow of African labour to European services and manufacturing industries.

Africa's population problem is twofold: low agricultural production and pressure on the environment; and the problem of urbanisation and employment. These are compounded by the major difficulties of improving family planning, health and health education. Let us take these in turn.

Population and Agriculture

Agriculture provides one-third of the average national income of sub-Saharan Africa and three out of four people still live in rural areas. But their number is gradually falling, as farming on over-cultivated land becomes more difficult and poverty drives subsistence farmers into the towns. Between 1980 and 1985 the food supply per head fell in many African countries, including Ethiopia, Mozambique, Niger and even Kenya. Drought in these countries, leading to famine and food imports in many regions, is only the sharp end of a crisis on the land which, without agro-forestry and soil conservation measures of the kind described below, will drive more and more people into urban shanty towns.

By European standards few people live on the land. Sub-Saharan Africa has only 19 per square kilometre, compared with 230 in the UK and India, and more than 300 in Belgium and Japan. But the proportion of fertile land is much smaller in Africa and rainfall is often low and erratic.

Many voluntary organisations in Africa are engaged in smallholder agriculture projects aimed at soil and water conservation. More health and family planning workers are recommending self-help schemes and small-scale development projects which will create alternatives to subsistence farming. Governments have also emphasised rural development and resettlement schemes, many of them controversial, as an alternative to rural poverty or urban overcrowding. But in the food deficit areas such efforts may be too feeble and too late to save already degraded land and pasture, or to prevent growing numbers from seeking solutions elsewhere.

The Drift to the Towns

Urbanisation in Africa is often seen as a problem in itself because of urban over-crowding, but it is the natural result of agricultural decline as well as the growth of a more consumer-oriented society based on imports and innovations from abroad. Largely owing to migration from the land, about 25% of Africans now live in urban areas compared with 13% in 1965. This is only a fraction of the proportion in the UK (over 90%) or of industrialised countries as a whole (75%) but the rate of urbanisation is a major problem.

This is not because urbanisation itself is damaging. After all, the most successful economies in recent decades – Japan and East Asia – have high rates of urbanisation. But for Africa the problem is housing the new town-dwellers and providing them with jobs and welfare services.

Health and family planning services, still unknown to millions of rural Africans, are more accessible to the urban poor, but they are not given the same priority as housing and jobs. Primary health care, which focuses on the basic needs of the poor, is paradoxically not as advanced in cities as in rural areas. Often, as in the voluntary agency HUZA self-help housing project in Lusaka, Zambia, health and nutrition are taken seriously only when a development programme is already established. Non-government and church

One in four Africans now live in urban areas, twice as many as 20 years ago. Overcrowded settlements here contrast with modern office blocks in Kampala, Uganda.

Kenya, the Most Quoted Country

The country which seems to carry the can for all Africa's population problems is Kenya, where the average family size of 7.8 in 1985 was the highest after Rwanda. Kenya's national family planning programmes – the first in Africa – have been highly publicised for their scandals as much as their high acceptance rates. But the population continues to rise. Kenya's health successes have also helped to keep fertility up because of a dramatic fall in infant mortality rates and in death rates generally. Kenyans today can expect to live to 54 and they receive more health care per person than most other Africans.

Kenya's population growth rate is 4.1%, which means that it will double its present number of 20 million by the end of the century. The population may even quintuple before levelling out, a situation which Vice-President Mwai Kibaki has called a 'catastrophe'. Apart from a coffee boom in 1986 Kenya's economy has been trailing and there are fears that neither the land nor the new urban developments will contain the population increase.

KENYA'S POPULATION STRUCTURE

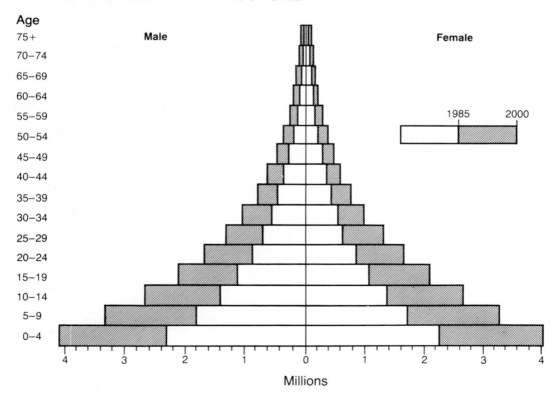

Source: United Nations

Fig 5.5

organisations play a crucial role, but they have limited funds.

In 1977 the National Christian Council of Kenya opened a nutrition and family centre in the Mathare Valley, Nairobi's vast shanty town with a population of over 150,000. The centre has had notable successes in reaching the most destitute with nutrition, health, family planning and job creation projects. But its work also demonstrates the vast unbridged gap between the services offered and the reality of poverty and misery in the home.

Slums and squatter settlements in Africa are growing faster than populations as a whole, and they will therefore need even more urgent solutions. Yet the signs during 1987, declared the UN International Year of Shelter for the Homeless, were that the urban poor will continue to be neglected.

Cultural Obstacles to Family Planning

In Africa's more rural and less developed regions, family planning and primary health

Family Planning Targets

Certain countries in Africa with high population growth rates, such as Kenya, Zimbabwe, Rwanda and Burundi, have long been seen to take family planning seriously, though with mixed results. But there are many others whose campaigns have not yet shown the same interest and whose governments have followed a more popular, arms-length view of birth control. Others still firmly defend a pro-natalist policy.

Nigeria's population is now over 100 million, growing at 3.3%, the same rate as the sub-Saharan average. This means that if, as predicted, it reaches 300 million in about 2020, it will still represent about one-quarter of Africans south of the Sahara. What Nigeria does is significant, not only because of the numbers involved, but also because of its influence on the rest of traditional Africa, the hinterland where fertility is the norm and where amulets and healers are much more trusted than paramedics or contraceptive salesmen. Unfortunately some of the positive traditional restraints on childbirth, such as child spacing, have declined to make way for more urban lifestyles.

The initiative for family planning in Nigeria has come from the voluntary sector, mainly through the Planned Parenthood Federation of Nigeria. The PPFN has provided education and training as well as family planning services, and in 1984 it was in touch with over 442,000 young men and women through its community education project. In the same year it also started a male motivation project in industrial centres, aimed at reducing male resistance to family planning by promoting a sense of shared responsibility.

The government of Nigeria has recently decided to tackle the population issue head-on and has adopted some ambitious new targets. It plans to reduce fertility from 6 to 4 children per mother by 2000, and simultaneously to bring the population growth rate down to 2%. To do this, it aims to extend family planning services to reach 80% of women of child-bearing age (a long way ahead of the present 5–6% of married women) and to concentrate more educational effort on men. During the same period, it also hopes to bring infant mortality down from about 100 to 30 per 1000.

Africa should be impressed by this latest burst of activity in Nigeria. The trouble is that the government already knows it does not have the resources to achieve these targets, however commendable. Much, too, will depend on the will to bring about a change of attitude in the local community, and the ability to make the best possible use of the voluntary sector.

Zimbabwe's recent achievements, meanwhile, will be an encouragement to countries like Nigeria. Its high fertility rate has fallen below 6.0 and its acceptance of contraception is 40%, the highest in Africa. With USAID backing it has recently more than doubled the number of family planning community workers. Adequate funding and skilled organisation have shown that family planning targets can be met, although Zimbabwe still has a lot further to go.

At the other end of the scale there are several countries that have declared themselves in favour of high population growth. Guinea has a policy of high fertility and low mortality, and forbids contraception. Gabon, with one of the lowest growth rates of 1.6%, hopes to double this rate by 2000. Francophone countries like Chad have continued to operate old French anti-contraception law. The Ivory Coast replaced it with a penal code in 1982 but still restricts birth control, hoping to improve on its already high growth rate of 3.4%. Sterilisation is still a capital offence there unless performed under certain strict conditions.

care programmes are still treated with caution, even by governments. In the poorest communities, as in Europe until comparatively recently, the practice has been to have large families to ensure the survival of the fittest. God and the older generation seem to smile on any number of new-born children. Modern contraception offends against the dignity of nature and the traditional order. Health workers may intrude into the privacy of the family, introducing modern concepts which can threaten social patterns and the power of men over women in particular.

These attitudes are often reinforced by organised religion and by superstition. Family planning has been better received in Christian communities where the intrusion of missions and churches is already well established, although Roman Catholicism has also been a restraint on contraception and abortion. In Muslim countries, such as Nigeria and most of Francophone West Africa, the Koran expressly forbids any compulsory limits to child-bearing. But it also encourages families to have only the number of children they can look after, and thus is not a guide to population increase.

Social and religious customs such as polygamy and circumcision, however frowned on internationally, are still openly practised in rural Africa. It is arguable that, like infanticide and child-dumping, female circumcision leading to sterility has been a crude traditional restraint on population growth. Polygamy, which is still common all over West Africa, can improve child care and encourages birth spacing, but it appears to lengthen the period of fertility.

The strongest traditional influence is the stereotype of the woman as procreator, which sets her role of child-bearing above every other activity, even food-gathering, though the two usually have to co-exist. This role is easy to criticise in the West, but in Africa it is proudly defended.

Family Planning and Women's Development

Family planning has for a long time been an aspect of maternal and child health care in Africa, the responsibility of health workers

Improving village water supplies and sanitation will have a lasting effect on community health, family life and women's development.

and midwives trained to advise women on family health, maternity and nutrition. As health has become more associated with sanitation, clean water and the wider community background, family planning has been seen as a more integral part of social and economic development.

The last decade has seen the growth of a completely new approach to family planning: women's development, or the direct involvement of women in community-based, income-generating projects to help raise their economic and social status. Such projects can give women a greater say in decision-making and help them to achieve more independence. For practical purposes they can bring women together, strengthen their common concerns and help to circulate new ideas about child health.

The International Planned Parenthood Federation's programme, called Planned Parenthood and Women's Development, is designed for those normally out of reach of family planning services – an admission that development might be more important than the family planning services themselves. Women's groups in Kenya, for example, have become successfully involved in handicrafts, poultry-rearing and building. They also provide a workplace away from the family home where ideas of family planning and women's development can be discussed.

Health and Fertility

Health and population are two sides of the same coin. The major cause of population increase in Africa, as in Europe in the last century, has been a decline in the mortality rate due to improved standards of health. Kenya and Ethiopia are the classic examples. Kenya's death rate in 1965 was only one point above Ethiopia's, at 21 per 1,000; 20 years later it had fallen to 13, while Ethiopia's (on the figures available) remained almost the same. Meanwhile, owing to natural and man-made disasters, Ethiopia's population has recently grown at a rate of only 2.5%, well below the African average of 3.3%. Infant

Ethiopia – The Population Crisis

Until the first population census was carried out in 1984 planners could only guess at the number of people living in Ethiopia. The 1984 census revealed that the population was 8 million above the official estimate of 34 million and had been growing at over 2.9% per annum. If that growth rate continues the population will double in 24 years, and in 30 years will reach 114 million. Even if the size of the average family begins to fall the population will still total 81 million.

This means that simply to keep pace Ethiopia will have to achieve a growth rate in national wealth in excess of the 1974–84 average of 2.5%. More important, Ethiopia is currently able to feed its population only in a good year, and even then nutritional levels are only three-quarters of the recommended minimum. Agricultural output will have to grow at 4.5% per annum for the next 30 years (a rate achieved only twice in the past eight years) if Ethiopia is not to be increasingly dependent on food imports.

Most of the energy consumed in Ethiopia comes from wood, crop residues and dung. As the population and hence the demand for fuel increases, within 10 or 20 years there may be few trees left in the highlands. Fuel prices will rise, making poor people poorer still, and using dung for fuel instead of wood could reduce crop yields by more than one million tonnes a year as soil fertility declines.

Another serious effect of these population levels and growth rates is likely to be in social spending. At current rates of population growth universal primary education will not be achieved until the year 2000. Health coverage is now only 35%, rather than the 45% assumed under the pre-census plan of 1984, and only 60% coverage will be attainable by 1994, rather than the planned 78%.

mortality there has actually risen to 168, one of the highest in the world.

Health workers are still relatively scarce in countries like Ethiopia – there is only one for every 5,000 people. But how far the availability of health services helps to reduce infant and child deaths is still a matter for debate. The World Fertility Survey of 1972–84 proved that proper sanitation was a much more significant factor, even more than a clean water supply. Health care and education, together with family planning counselling, play a vital supporting role. High infant mortality often coincides with the low proportion of women aged 15 to 49 who are responding to or have access to family planning. The figures for Mali are one in five babies and one in 100 women respectively. A World Bank Study showed that child spacing at intervals of more than two years could lower infant mortality in a developing country by as much as 25%.

High fertility in Africa has been seriously affected by sexually transmitted diseases such as syphilis and gonorrhea. Infertility results from an infection of the pelvis or of the Fallopian tubes, which can also be caused by a miscarriage or an improperly performed abortion. In a survey of 10 villages in eastern Cameroon, 35% of the women interviewed suffered from secondary infertility, the more common form which occurs after at least one pregnancy. Southern Sudan and parts of Zaire, Congo and the Central African Republic are similarly affected.

Mother and child health and family planning services are restricted by the funds available from central government, especially in areas with poor communications where delays are inevitable. Aid agencies, from USAID to small but effective voluntary agencies such as the African Medical & Research Foundation in east Africa, help to plug the gaps, but the needs are immense. Average government spending on health services in sub-Saharan Africa has fallen, as shown in Chapter 2, and the emphasis now is on self-reliance and low-cost primary health care in the absence of, and as a substitute for, formal health services (see Box on Primary Health Care in Africa).

Health Education and Young People

The pace of population growth is such that more than half the people of sub-Saharan Africa are under 20. Schoolchildren today are the major target of family planning education,

Primary Health Care in Africa

The government health services of most countries in Africa, in their present form, will not be able to provide acessible, effective services for all of the people all of the time.

Many people living in rural areas have virtually no contact with health services at all. For others, any contact is fleeting through health campaigns, mobile health team visits or after a long journey by the patient to a distant health centre. It is unlikely that such contact will have a general impact on health in the community.

The most important reasons for this are:

▲ There is not enough money to pay for such services, and when money is short, the health service is the first to suffer from cuts. Currently, expenditure per head on health care in Africa is around $3.4 per annum.

▲ Many areas are almost inaccessible. Communications are poor, roads often impassable, and delivery systems and support frequently lacking. Fixed health centres can provide a service only to their immediate neighbourhood. Though many do undertake outreach programmes, these are expensive, time consuming, and still leave large gaps in coverage.

▲ Lack of management skills at all levels often means that even existing health facilities are inefficiently run. Limited funds are wasted through inappropriate prescriptions, expensive medicines, and unco-ordinated resources, both human and financial. Too many health programmes are 'vertically' run, with inevitable duplication of effort.

Most communities care for their sick and dying in their own way, as they have for centuries. This traditional form of care may be beneficial (physically, spiritually or both), or it may be harmless, but in some cases it may actually be detrimental to health. In no case is it free.

One way to make better use of available resources is to improve and increase the involvement of the community in its own health care by providing appropriate training for people chosen from the village to act as village health workers. These health workers must then be continuously supplied and supported after their basic training. This is the basis of primary health care. By this means, it is hoped that the coverage of health services will be extended, and that the quality of health care will improve.

Most deaths in Africa occur in young children, and are usually due to diarrhoeal diseases, respiratory diseases or other communicable diseases. Many of these can be prevented by vaccination or providing a safe water supply, adequate nutrition and good sanitation. Many are curable, for example by using oral rehydration for diarrhoea and simple, cheap antibiotics for severe respiratory infections.

Health workers are trained to recognise common diseases and to apply standard treatments from a basic drug supply. At the same time they have an important role to play in passing on information about disease prevention to the community, and this knowledge can be used to improve health through better use of available resources. Better birth practices, better weaning habits, better use of available water and the sanitary disposal of human waste are all examples of simple, realistic ways to improve health.

The Save the Children Fund is involved in the development of primary health care in several African countries including Gambia, Mali, Burkina Faso, Ethiopia, Somalia and Zimbabwe. Villagers are usually enthusiastic and there are no real difficulties in selecting and training village health workers. The major problem is short- and long-term financing of the support and supply of primary health care workers.

According to SCF professionals, there are several ways to plan for the recurrent funding of health services.

▲ Existing government health services must be efficiently and economically run and properly managed so that scarce resources are not wasted. In this way funds may be made available to extend services. SCF has a role to play here by providing additional training in management skills to all levels of health care staff.

▲ Up to 80% of total health budgets are being used to finance hospital-based services in large cities. These services are often available to under 10% of the population. It may be possible to shift expenditure within existing budgets from urban to rural services. However, this is often impracticable because most countries have low health budgets.

▲ All or part of the cost of services may be recovered by imposing charges on patients at all levels of service delivery. These charges are usually acceptable to people who are already used to paying for health care in the traditional or private sectors. In addition, paying for a service that provides medicines, vaccines and care is better than having a free service that can seldom provide any of these.

▲ SCF has shown that providing relatively small recurrent budgets can greatly improve the success of small-scale primary health care projects. At national level, the financing of recurrent expenditure by the larger donor agencies may well be a more cost-effective way of improving health than spending money on large-scale capital health projects.

The concept of primary health care requires some profound changes in the thinking of the leaders within a country, including politicians, local community chiefs, and doctors who may have received medical training in an industrialised country.

The development of primary health care in any community cannot be created overnight. It will take much time if it is to be developed alongside the community and with a sensitive appreciation of the needs of all sectors of that community.

Unfortunately many donor agencies measure success in terms of the amount of money spent. They need to disperse funds over defined periods of time, even if the progress of the project being funded may not require or benefit from spending money at that rate.

There is also considerable pressure on donors, including SCF, as well as on politicians and health workers, to demonstrate progress in terms of diseases cured and deaths prevented as soon as possible. This is important, but it is likely that the impact on death and disease will be far greater in the long term if the project is developed in a way that will ensure its continuation. This takes time, patience and money.

It has been SCF's experience that primary health care can work if properly funded. Coverage of immunisation and the uptake of other services has been shown to improve. The support and supply of health workers is, however, not done for nothing. Any truly committed government must recognise that it is not necessarily the cheapest option, but if properly managed it is the most cost-effective.

Teaching village health workers to make their own posters – part of a health education campaign in Uganda.

with the proportion of children in school increasing fast. Primary education is one of Africa's success stories, with the average number of girls enrolled up from 30% in 1965 to 68% in 1984. The figure for Tanzania is now 84% and for Zambia 95%.

Family planners now recognise that young women, and boys too, need to be given practical advice during adolescence, well before they contemplate marriage or a regular relationship. Studies in Swaziland show that pregnancies are more frequent among teenagers under 19 than in any other age group. The pressures of family tradition requires courage from girls who may need to explain their attendance at clinics or family planning sessions. Here, the voluntary agencies and accepted associations such as mothers' unions are as important as schools and health services, spreading ideas through literacy schemes and cultural events as well as posters and wallcharts. Young men are increasingly being involved in family planning education and in decisions previously left to women alone.

A key factor, underlined by the International Population Conference of 1984, is that young women need to be offered alternatives to child-bearing. Secondary education and first jobs tend to delay first pregnancies, and research has confirmed that mother and child death rates and family sizes both fall when first pregnancies are delayed. With more and more young people growing up in towns, factories and companies are becoming an important channel of education for those in employment, once schools – and indeed families themselves – have ceased to have a strong influence.

The Impact of AIDS

No discussion of population growth, health, social or economic development can have any relevance today unless considered in the light of the current epidemic of infection with the virus that causes the Acquired Immune Deficiency Syndrome (AIDS). The primary health care needs of children and the community will become all the more important as AIDS places additional burdens on already over-stretched health services and budgets.

The knowledge we have gained in the seven years or so since AIDS was first identified strongly suggests that we are in the early stages of a global epidemic of an almost invariably fatal disease which mainly affects the sexually and economically active groups within society.

Most diseases have relatively short incubation periods, and the association between infection and disease can be made easily. Smallpox was a good example of this. This is not the situation with AIDS. Infected persons may remain well for months, even years, quite unaware that they are infected and therefore infectious to others.

The burden of most other infectious diseases falls upon the very young and the very old. The AIDS virus, however, infects young adults, and in this group there are also parents, leaders and politicians. The loss of a high proportion of people from this group would have a destabilising effect in any country.

There is no vaccine, nor any effective treatment. It will be several years at least before a commercial vaccine is available. Drugs are available in developed countries but they are expensive and at best can only prolong life. The cost of treatment in the UK, from diagnosis to death, has been estimated at about $26,000 per patient. The only way to contain the disease at present is through changes in sexual behaviour.

For transmission of the virus to occur there has to be an exchange of blood between individuals, which occurs most commonly during heterosexual intercourse. The risks increase with the frequency of intercourse and of the number of partners.

Anything that disrupts the family unit may mean an increased number of sexual partners. The reasons for such disruptions are common enough. They include poverty, migration in search of work or food, civil unrest and warfare. For some, for example long-distance lorry drivers, politicians, migrant workers and soldiers, opportunities for different partners increase as their work is often away from home and families. It has been shown that infection follows travel routes such as main highways, tourist resorts and trading routes. Soldiers are well known to be a source of transmission of sexually transmitted diseases. The deployment of troops may also spread AIDS beyond the main travel patterns.

Research indicates that the presence of other sexually transmitted diseases may facilitate the transmission of AIDS. This may in part explain the speed of the spread of the epidemic in parts of Africa. This factor could be particularly relevant in a continent where relatively few facilities exist for the treatment of these diseases, even of those people most at risk, such as prostitutes.

Other routes of transmission include the transfusion of infected blood, and the use of contaminated needles and other surgical equipment. So far the numbers infected in this way are few, and this type of transmission should be easy to eliminate by screening donated blood and ensuring that equipment is sterilised.

Perinatal transmission from mother to unborn child is another important route, and is on the increase. About 50% of children born to infected mothers will be infected themselves, and most will die in their first few years of life. They themselves are not a major source of infection.

Infection in Africa is far from uniformly distributed. Central and eastern countries have reported the highest levels of infection, ranging from 0.5% to 18% in samples from the general population, and 8% to 88% in high risk groups. In one small village in southern Uganda, a quarter of the population are reported to have died from AIDS since 1983. Southern African countries are reporting increased rates, while West African countries seem to be relatively free from AIDS at present. Most surveys in Africa, however, have been carried out in urban areas and among high risk groups.

What needs to be done?

▲ **Information sharing and presentation**
This disease has aroused anger, fear and allegations of blame world wide. Agencies have a duty to recognise these fears and prejudices and to take positive action to dispel them. All information from all sources must be shared by all agencies

involved. This will ensure that up-to-date information can be presented in a reliable, accurate and sensitive way.

▲ **Co-ordination of effort**
The World Health Organisation (WHO) has established a global Special Programme on AIDS (SPA) based in Geneva. The governments of many countries have set up co-ordinating committees. Involved agencies should be represented at these committees, and sharing of information and resources may be co-ordinated through them. Agencies like Save the Children Fund are particularly well placed to work with both village leaders and national planners.

▲ **Health education**
The most significant impact on transmission of the AIDS virus will involve a change in sexual behaviour. Ideally, this means limiting the number of sexual partners, preferably to one faithful partner. Unfortunately we know very little about behaviour in any culture. It must also be remembered that a change in knowledge does not necessarily result in a change of behaviour. The education emphasis should be on the pre-sexually active child, and the sexually active adult. Information must be provided to children at the earliest opportunity so that sexual behaviour and habits may be guided by knowledge of the risks as well as of the rewards of developing sexuality. The use of condoms is known to offer protection against many sexually transmitted diseases including AIDS, and should be recommended and made available, especially to high-risk groups such as prostitutes.

▲ **Care of the sick and the dying**
With little to offer in the way of treatment, care will usually be undertaken at home. The extended families of most African cultures will provide this care. These families will need support and this places additional responsibilities upon the Primary Health Care workers. Non-governmental organisations like SCF are well able to help with community based care of the sick, as well as of their dependants.

▲ **Protection of the non sexually active**
This group includes those who may be infected through the use of contaminated blood and injection equipment. They can be protected *now* with the help of the international community. All blood used for transfusion must be screened. The equipment for this is available, though it is expensive. The donor community must provide it together with the necessary training to use it. All injections must be given with one sterile needle and one sterile syringe for each injection. This requires a regular supply of equipment and appropriate training to ensure proper use. The international agencies can provide for this. Many injections are given unnecessarily. Additional training of health workers and their patients is necessary to ensure that injections are used only when there is no alternative.

▲ **Research**
We must know more about the extent of this infection both within a community and world wide. Diagnostic equipment is available, but is expensive. This equipment and the necessary training and support should be provided to all countries immediately.

▲ **Maintain present programmes to improve health**
With the advent of AIDS, there is an even greater need for the provision and maintenance of basic preventive and curative health services. The policy of Primary Health Care unanimously accepted by UN member states at the 1978 WHO/UNICEF Alma Ata conference, and reaffirmed every year since then, must be vigorously promoted.

△3 The African Drylands

Introduction

The drought-prone region of Africa runs through the West African Sahel and the Sudan to north-east Ethiopia and Kenya. It has experienced two periods of acute drought and crop failure over the last 20 years, causing a

THE AFRICAN DRYLANDS

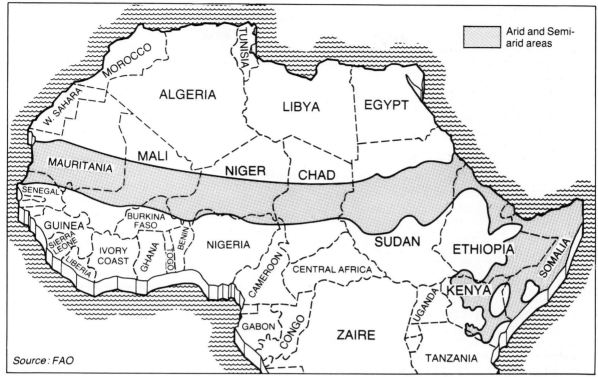

Source: FAO

Fig 5.6

large number of human and livestock deaths and widespread destitution. The region's vulnerability to drought, food shortage and human suffering has been caused by the growth in human and livestock populations, adverse rainfall patterns, poor use and management of land and, in some cases, civil war. These factors have contributed to a growing pressure on scarce natural resources and a breakdown in people's ability to grow or buy the food they need.

In response, there has been an unprecedented relief effort by voluntary agencies and donor governments in the Sahel following the droughts and famines of the last 20 years. Public awareness and pressure have been crucial for raising the necessary funds for voluntary agency activities and for prodding reluctant governments into providing tardy emergency aid. However, the success of fund-raising efforts to fight famine in Africa's drought-prone areas has one drawback. Africa is presented as a continent ravaged by

drought, with little prospect of feeding its people. In fact, as can be seen from the map, the arid drought-prone lands represent a relatively small part of sub-Saharan Africa, as do their populations. Much of Africa lies in more favourable climatic zones and represents a source of hope, enabling some arid land dwellers to settle elsewhere.

While the arid lands present particularly difficult problems, it is argued here that long-term development in this region is possible. The population of herders and small farmers does not need to be periodically racked by hunger and increasingly dependent on food aid. However, success requires a major shift in the emphasis of development work; both governments and donors will have to make environmental management their first priority and formulate programmes which, to have lasting results, will allow local populations to participate in and benefit fully from the improvements to land and resource management.

Population and Food Production

The region known as the Sahel lies roughly between the 100 and 500 mm rainfall isohyets. It borders the Sahara desert to the north and the savanna lands to the south. Of an estimated 135 million people living in the 14 states that straddle this region, some 27 million (around one-fifth of the population) are based in the arid and semi-arid zone. The drier areas of the Sahel are largely the preserve of pastoral groups, such as the Fulani and Tuareg, herding cattle, sheep, goats and camels, and following a pattern of seasonal migration in search of grazing and water. Population densities rise towards higher rainfall zones where people raise crops of millet and sorghum. Although current population densities appear very low in comparison with those of Europe, the ability of the land to support a population, given present techniques, is also low.

National rates of population growth are around 2.5% per year. Urban growth rates have often risen much more rapidly, at 5–7% per year, caused both by the general neglect of rural areas by successive governments and by waves of migration during periods of drought. In some parts of the Sahel, famine relief centres have become permanent settlements, the residual population from one famine there to greet the newly impoverished.

Grain production in Sahelian countries has grown only slowly, at 0.5% to 1.0% a year over the last 10 years, and has been far outstripped by population growth. As a result, cereal imports (much of them in the form of food aid) have risen very greatly at 12.7% a year over the period 1975–84. Figure 5.7 illustrates this growth in food aid over the period 1970–71 to 1985–86, and shows the large peaks associated with the drought years of 1973–74 and 1984–85. Most governments have a policy of self-sufficiency in grains, but

FOOD AID TO THE SAHEL, 1970–85

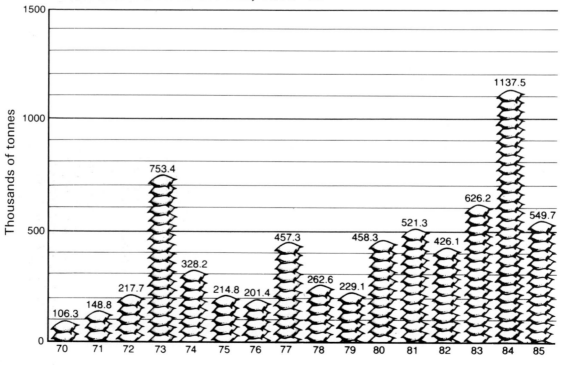

Source: CILSS/OECD

Fig 5.7   Food aid to drought-prone regions has steadily increased since 1970, rising to exceptional levels during the years of famine.

all have fallen further and further behind each year in achieving this aim. Many factors account for this, including population growth and government policies (discussed elsewhere in this review). Low farm productivity and periodic drought are other factors, and it is these that we shall discuss in this section.

Rainfall

Figure 5.8 shows data on rainfall in the West African Sahel since 1940. It shows that there has been a long downturn in rainfall since the end of the 1960s, in contrast to the better than average period during the 1950s. In the 1950s, the Sahara effectively retreated by several hundred kilometres and farmers and herders could expand their fields and herds into more northerly areas than before. Since then, rainfall zones have shifted sharply southwards again. The figure also suggests that rainfall patterns have changed in the last 40–50 years, with long time spans of above or below

average rainfall replacing a more regular swing from one year to the next of good and bad seasons.

Figure 5.9 shows that rainfall patterns are also highly seasonal. Most rain falls in a period of 2–3 months. There is also a high degree of annual variability, the total amount received commonly varying by 30–50% from one year to the next. Distribution of rainfall within the short wet season is subject to much variation; in some years the rains may start in late July and finish by early September, while in others showers may be spread out from early June to late October, with long dry patches in the middle of the wet season. Neighbouring areas often receive widely varying amounts of rain, especially at the start and close of the wet season, when heavy thunderstorms are most likely to occur.

Variability in rainfall produces a parallel variability in crop and pasture growth. Villages close together may have a first sowing date a month or more apart, while herders

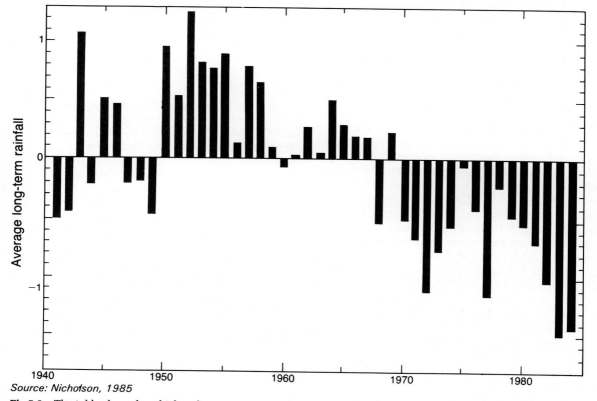

Source: Nicholson, 1985

Fig 5.8   The table shows how higher-than-average rainfall occurred during the 1950s, transforming drought areas into pasture. This trend was reversed in the 1970s and 1980s.

RAINFALL AT KALA, IN WEST AFRICA

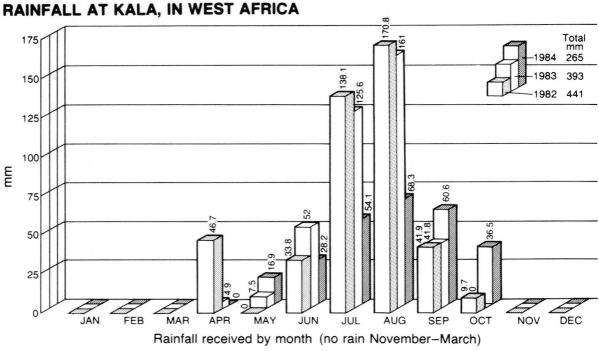

Source: Toulmin 1986 (Village of Kala, central Mali)

Fig 5.9

may hear of new grass germinating some miles to the east when their immediate surroundings are still bare. People living in these regions have developed a variety of strategies to cope with such conditions, such as moving their herds to take advantage of pastures that vary with the seasons, growing crops of different cycle length, and herding several different species of livestock. Social relations also take account of such climatic variability. It is common, for example, for people to travel from drought-stricken villages to earn money and gifts by cutting grain in a neighbouring settlement where harvests are better.

Such mechanisms for dealing with the risks of living in this region can help many households get through the hardship of one or two poor seasons. However, when large parts of the Sahel are struck by drought over a number of years, as they have been for most of the period from the late 1960s onwards, indigenous methods of providing for peoples' needs are bound to fail.

Increased Demand for Resources

To this inherent instability have been added increased demands on natural resources. These demands stem from population growth and from growing commercial interests. Although land area per person is high, all Sahelian countries are now experiencing pressure on cultivable land, since so little of their total land is good for farming. The growth in urban populations has brought a growing demand for firewood, brought by lorry from further and further away as available woodland is cleared. New roads have reduced the cost of transport and brought a wider area of the country within easy access of the major towns. New technologies, such as tractors, have meant that people can exploit natural resources on a far greater scale than before.

These rising demands and new technologies alone would not create a problem if there were clear rules governing local use of resources. After independence of the Sahel states, governments took formal control, for the first time, over their natural resources, displacing a variety of local systems. However, government administrations have rarely been able to enforce this mandate effectively. In part this is due to lack of funds and manpower. But equally important has been the way that government control has deprived local communities of their role in monitoring and regulating resource use without replacing it with an effective alternative. As a result, rights over grazing, crop land, trees and water are neither clearly defined nor enforceable.

This has led to anarchic patterns of exploitation, which rob the region of vegetation and soils of their nutrients, producing a degraded landscape less able to support crops and pasture. An example of this is seen in the 'land mining' operations of mechanised farmers in the Sudan who strip large areas of rangeland to plant one or two years' crop of sorghum, after which the land is abandoned. Having lost its topsoil and being cleared of bush and other vegetation, the land cannot return to its former state.

The danger of such patterns of land and resource use is that no one has the responsibility and incentive to control levels of exploitation. Governments are unable or unwilling to do so; indeed, some of the worst offenders may have close relations with governments. Local communities are unable to control access to these resources without both the legal framework that grants them some form of ownership and the means to monitor and restrict levels of use. In this vacuum of authority those who suffer most are communities whose long-term welfare depends on sustained productivity of these resources.

Land Degradation

Land degradation is said to be occurring rapidly in large parts of Africa. A recent study for the United Nations Environment

The encroaching desert in Burkina Faso: is it a natural cycle or are people to be blamed?

Programme (UNEP), summarised in the table below, estimates that some 90% of the rangelands and 80% of rainfed farmlands in the Sahel are affected by desertification to a moderate degree, while 30% of irrigated farmland has been damaged due to salinisation. This means that such lands have become less able to bear crops and pasture as a result of deforestation, loss of woody vegetation and soil loss.

Sahelian Areas Affected by Moderate Desertification

Type of land	Area affected (m. hectares)	% of type affected
Rangeland pastures	342	90
Rainfed farmland	72	80
Irrigated farmland	0.5	30

There is much debate about likely future trends for productivity in Africa's arid lands. The issues are of crucial importance to the future of drought-prone Africa. Is the desert actually moving south? If so, what factors are responsible? If not, what adverse environmental trends are in evidence and to what should they be attributed? Is blame to be placed on local practices such as overgrazing by livestock, or on events of global significance such as increased concentrations of carbon dioxide in the atmosphere producing a 'greenhouse effect'? What measures should be taken to reverse, or at least stabilise, losses in land productivity?

Given the rainfall pattern of recent decades, some assert that the Sahara desert is marching southwards and will soon engulf the better-watered savanna grain lands. Mankind and his animals are seen as the main agents of this process, clearing and farming land, cutting trees and over-grazing the rangelands. Strict measures are thought necessary to halt harmful forms of land use by imposing controls over use of farmland, fining those cutting wood, or preventing herders using the zone.

Other researchers think that the recent adverse conditions in the Sahel may be no more than an extreme period of low rainfall within a longer period of more favourable

In the drylands where rainfall is highly unreliable, people have ways of adapting and surviving. They have little choice.

Soil Erosion in Ethiopia

In Ethiopia, the process of land degradation is more clearly marked than in the West African Sahel. Heavy population pressure on the fertile, central highland plateau of Ethiopia has forced farmers to clear and cultivate increasingly fragile soils, on steeper slopes and in areas of lower rainfall. When there is a heavy downpour, the soils are washed down the slopes unchecked by tree cover, loading the Blue Nile with silt and leaving behind a network of gullies and gorges that nibble further each year into the remaining fields. Massive programmes of terracing have been undertaken to stem this soil erosion, and the World Food Programme has supported 'food for work' schemes since 1974. Over ten years this programme constructed 830,000 kms of terracing and protected 700,000 hectares of land either through terracing or reforestation. Despite the size of the programme, as yet only 6% of the land needing rehabilitation has been treated. Increasingly, government and agencies have tried to widen their impact by using cheaper local methods of soil conservation (such as mulching and using brushwood to prevent soils being washed off gentle slopes) and by making environmental conservation a central part of all rural development work.

weather. Local examples of degradation may be occurring, but these could be due to poor methods of land use at individual sites rather than a wider process of desert encroachment. Many ecologists have been impressed by the resilience of Sahelian soils and pastures and their capacity to return to bearing crops and grasses once rainfall conditions improve.

While few would argue that there is no environmental problem in Africa's arid lands, many question the model used and conclusions reached by those who speak of the desert moving south. Few, if any, studies have access to the kind of long-term climatic and plant data for a given area that would allow a more careful judgement of changes to be made. Most conclusions are drawn on the basis of comparing current vegetation and rainfall conditions with those of the 1950s and early 1960s, a comparison flawed by the exceptionally good rainfall of the earlier period and the drought suffered for the past 15–20 years. Most Sahelian countries have rainfall records going back at best 70–80 years and for a limited number of stations. It is hard to detect long-term climatic patterns from these records and thus to determine how far recent rainfall figures lie within the expected range of variability. We have no way of knowing whether or when rainfall will return to former levels. Neither do we know how far man's activities within his local environment relate to factors such as deforestation in coastal West Africa – which is thought to change rainfall patterns further inland.

Rehabilitation of the Sahel

'Rehabilitating' the Sahel can only mean re-establishing sustainable sources of income for local people along lines which may be very different from those pursued before the drought. Such changes are essential if people are to withstand drought better in future.

To understand the options for arid land development, we need to look at what happened after the previous drought of 1968–73 and at the responses of national governments, aid-givers and local people. Government programmes and aid projects are the most visible and best documented evidence of activity and change in the region. However, local people have also changed their own way of life to adjust to changes in climate and the economy.

Over the period 1975–84, a total of $14.7 billion has been spent by official donor agencies on the eight Sahelian countries in West Africa, much of it on irrigation, livestock development, forestry and soil conservation. Yet despite these efforts the region was hardly better prepared to cope with drought in the early 1980s than it had been some 15 years earlier. Why is this?

Irrigation

Much of the emphasis in recent decades has been on technical inputs to raise yields of crops and livestock. Constructing irrigation systems has been particularly important, accounting for 35% of aid spent on rural development, in contrast to only 16% on rainfed crops. Given the aridity of the climate and landscape, irrigation offers the vision of abundant harvests. In practice, however, irrigation schemes in Africa, whether large or small, have rarely fulfilled their promise. Farmers have still been unable to get two crops a year from their land; insecurity of tenure and the low prices paid for their crops have lowered farmers' incentive to invest; poor maintenance of canals has caused yields to decline from year to year. Farmers on many schemes prefer to spend their energy cultivating traditional rainfed crops, despite the vulnerability of such crops to drought.

The heavy concentration of population on irrigation schemes has also used local supplies of wood to provide fuel and building materials. In addition, irrigation schemes are no sure protection from drought for, in years when rains fail, the rivers and aquifers on which these schemes depend also dry up.

The often poor design of irrigation projects typify the approach of many aid-givers to the Sahel and show why so many projects go wrong. Many projects are built without consulting local people as to their needs; traditional forms of irrigation are ignored and rights to land and water forgotten. As a result, many local people lose access to valuable flood-plain land once schemes are built; and while planners assume that irrigated crops will provide a higher income to the farmer, this is often not the case. It is evident throughout the Sahel that if project planners had started by considering local people's needs and resources before designing projects, many of these costly mistakes of recent times would not have occurred.

Livestock

Developing the Sahel's livestock has also been plagued with difficulties. Eleven of the twelve projects financed by the World Bank over the period 1979–83 were reckoned by the World Bank itself to have failed. Projects have usually focused on improved range management techniques (such as setting up grazing associations or group ranches) or on raising the proportion of animals marketed from the herd. Herders have been in favour of

forming grazing associations and have thereby acquired firm rights to land through such projects, particularly in areas where they have been progressively squeezed off better grazing land in the past. However, these associations have never been strong enough to withstand the pressures of prolonged drought conditions, the need to reduce members' own herds, and demands from other groups to use the association's grazing resources. As a result, they have not solved the problem of how to protect pastures from over-exploitation and damage in time of drought.

Forestry and Soil Conservation

Only about 3.5% of official aid to the Sahel in 1974–85 was spent directly on projects to halt environmental degradation. Most of these involved forestry programmes, such as establishing plantations and distributing tree seedlings. Success rates have been very low, with appallingly high tree losses in most forestry projects.

However, governments and donors are now beginning to accept that environmental projects should not be considered separately, but as a dimension of all development activities. Forestry has to be fitted into the overall village economy and requires close participation from the local communities who will benefit from the trees and their products. Tree planting succeeds best where villagers choose the kind of trees grown and where they are given firm rights in the products (fruit, leaves cut for browse, branches for firewood, bark for rope-making) in return for the labour they spend in watering and protecting the young plants from goats and other predators.

Voluntary Agencies

In contrast to work carried out by official donors, non-government projects are often cited as demonstrating the achievements of small-scale, innovative projects in the arid lands. For example, several agencies have designed credit schemes for herders so that they can rebuild their animal holdings after drought, using their societies' traditional systems of livestock loans. For over 10 years Euro-Action Accord and several church agencies have been supporting the

Tree-planting in Burkina Faso. Success depends on the interest and participation of those who will benefit directly.

establishment in north-east Mali of multi-purpose co-operatives that provide credit, set up grain stores and help market livestock. Elsewhere in the Sahel, voluntary agencies have also worked on conservation projects, such as the Yatenga water harvesting scheme described in the Box below.

Local Participation

In some countries, voluntary agencies are foreign-based and their intervention is often tolerated, rather than encouraged, by governments. In others, like Senegal and Burkina Faso, there is now a network of local agencies which have become important in development work. Groups like the Naam Federation in northern Burkina and the Amicale des Jeunes du Walo, along the Senegal river, have become well-established among the local population.

Voluntary agencies generally operate in a different way from official donors, and their differences can make agencies more effective. Frequently, voluntary agencies can respond more rapidly to emergency situations than the larger, and more bureaucratic, official agencies. Typically, voluntary agencies have greater consultation with local people while planning a project, and are more flexible as the project proceeds and as circumstances change.

One option for rehabilitating arid lands is to promote further work by voluntary agencies by channelling an increasing share of

Conserving Soil and Water in Yatenga

The Yatenga project in the north of Burkina Faso started in 1979 as a forestry scheme, teaching farmers to dig small basins around tree seedlings to improve tree survival rates. However, farmers soon decided that these techniques could be of great value to their grain crops, particularly if low rock bunds or walls were built to prevent water and soil running off their fields. With help from Oxfam, simple techniques, such as a water-level made from a long stretch of hose-pipe, have been developed to enable farmers to design contour bunds to rehabilitate long-abandoned land. While building these rock bunds takes a lot of time and effort (many farmers manage to cover only an acre a year), they do bring marked improvements in grain harvests, with yields almost doubling in some years.

The project owes its success partly to its involvement with local farmers and the fact that the techniques promoted are improved versions of traditional practices. In addition, returns from bund construction are received in a short period of time in the form of increased food crop harvests. As a result, these techniques for reclaiming land have spread rapidly and have been adopted by the government's own extension service.

A women's co-operative garden in Yatenga, northern Burkina Faso, where a local voluntary agency, the Naam Federation, is backing hundreds of small village groups.

development aid through them. However, a number of problems may arise from such dependence on voluntary agencies, discussed in more detail in Chapter 3. These include the problems of co-ordinating the activities of a larger number of relatively small agencies, risks of duplication, conflicting approaches, and petty rivalries that unregulated voluntary agency activity can bring (though such problems are by no means limited to voluntary agencies).

Resettlement

From colonial times onwards, the movement of people out of arid areas and their resettlement in higher rainfall zones have been advocated. The success of such schemes and their underlying motivation have varied. In the 1930s, the French colonial administration hoped to attract farmers from the neighbouring dry zone to provide the work force for the cotton-growing Office du Niger irrigation scheme in central Mali. It was thought that the attractions of irrigated crop production would far outweigh their meagre living from rainfed millet production. Forcible recruitment followed when the voluntary settlement programme failed.

Governments throughout Africa have tried to settle nomadic herdsmen, claiming that nomads must be settled if their living standards are to improve and they are to take up modern livestock-rearing methods. The desire to control nomadic populations more effectively has usually blinded planners to the crucial role of mobility in using arid grasslands efficiently. Once settled, herders can no longer make good use of distant grazing areas and their livestock-based economy inevitably declines.

In particular, the resettlement programme in Ethiopia has generated controversy because of the coercion reportedly used and because of the concern that so many people have been moved so far away from their homes.

Opponents of the programme argue that many people could be resettled in neighbouring districts and that the true motive behind resettlement is the desire to destroy local support for secessionist guerilla movements in north-east Ethiopia.

Adapting to Drought

Informal settlement of individual households has taken place for centuries. This was often temporary in response to some disaster, such as drought or disease, that destroyed livestock herds. Families would farm and trade to earn enough to re-establish themselves in livestock herding, by buying a few animals each year from which the new herd could develop. The recent droughts have accelerated informal settlement of this sort, but it has become more difficult for people to replenish their herds in this way, due to the shortage of good farming land and low rainfall.

While the Fulani herdsmen of West Africa are widely known for their nomadic existence, many more Fulani now live as settled herders and farm as well as care for their animals. Similarly, the camel-owning Tuareg, who formerly guarded and raided caravans on the southern fringes of the Sahara desert, have been forced by losses of animals in drought to take up small-scale irrigated gardening. Some impoverished herders go to town to look for work while those who still own a few animals have moved their herds south to look for better grazing. It is hard to determine the scale of such migration because it happens piecemeal. However, its impact over the past 20–30 years is probably much greater than official programmes of planned resettlement.

Local people have responded to the droughts of recent years by changing their patterns of production and strategies for survival. While these changes have been forced upon some people by circumstances such as the loss of all their animals, others have chosen to adapt their systems of production (using rapidly maturing crop varieties, for example) so that they are better protected from drought. Important lessons can be learned from studying these indigenous responses to drought, as they show how flexible local people are to changing circumstances.

Development Alternatives

Heavy demands will continue to be made on the natural resources of the Sahel, with rising populations needing food, fuel and animal products. Despite their vulnerability to drought, the farmland and pastures of the Sahel are important sources of grain, milk and meat for local towns as well as farmers and herders. The traditional pastoral sector commonly provides most of the country's meat supplies for domestic and export markets. However, these resources are fragile and need careful management.

There are successful examples of sustainable rural development in this region. Some communities have been able to adapt their ways of making a living and to raise the productivity of local resources. However, there are no clear technical blueprints for such projects. The most successful projects tend to be small and specific to certain areas, involving local people themselves and providing evident benefits such as increased yields or useful products. The assurance of such benefits depends on the local population gaining firm and enforceable rights over their resources: this depends on commitment by governments to supporting these rights.

The development options of the Sahel cannot be viewed in isolation from what is happening in other regions. The causes of many of the problems in the Sahel lie elsewhere, as do some of the solutions. Given the general poverty of resources, the vulnerability of crops and pastures to rainfall failure and the absence of any obvious technical answers to raising rural incomes, the Sahel cannot sustain an ever larger population. All options must therefore involve the migration of some people from the region. History shows that people are very ready to move voluntarily and settle elsewhere when they can see that it is to their advantage. Settlement programmes need to tap people's willingness to move but must also respect their desire to control the terms of their settlement, the kind of house they want to build, etc.

Development options must also take account of the regular occurrence of drought years and the possibility of a further long period with rainfall lower than expected, as has happened since the end of the 1960s. Despite pressure from several donors to reduce government intervention in markets, attention still needs to be paid to improved marketing arrangements and temporary intervention in grain and meat markets when droughts occur. This would support livestock prices and give people access to a grain ration at prices they can afford.

Early warning systems have been established in most drought-prone countries in Africa, the aim being to monitor rainfall, nutrition levels, crops, prices and other variables, in order to detect rapidly whether a situation of shortage will turn into a potential famine. In the arid region of southern Africa, Botswana has a system that operates effectively and greatly reduces the hardship experienced during times of drought. In the Sahelian countries, much remains to be done. Thus, for example, when livestock prices start to decline drastically and grain prices rise to levels higher than normal, it should be clear that many people will soon be destitute unless they are provided with help immediately. However, for early warning systems to be effective, both local administrators and aid donors need to be in a position to respond quickly to signals of impending famine, so that measures to protect the local population, provide food rations, destock pastures and establish food for work schemes can be set in motion. The early warning system operated by Save the Children Fund in Wollo Province, Ethiopia, during the 1987–88 crop failure proved effective in alerting governments to impending disaster, and in establishing these measures.

Prospects for Africa

challenges and opportunities

▲ Sub-Saharan Africa is already seen as a priority for development aid, as proved by the growing share of world aid which is now directed to the continent. But the public still views Africa as a continent in crisis, requiring and receiving emergency help rather than long-term development, and this attitude has to be changed. The public, and even the aid agencies which support Africa, must become more aware that Africa suffers from exceptional conditions and will require much more substantial long-term aid and investment if its people are to develop benefits similar to other areas of the world.

▲ The present situation is grave largely because of a combination of inappropriate policies, the impact of world recession and deteriorating terms of trade, and not simply the lack of aid. Most African governments in serious economic difficulties have recognised the need to alter their economies to revive quickly. It is clear that too much, too soon has been expected of the 'structural adjustment' many African countries are undergoing. The sacrifices have been great, particularly for the poorest who are used to food subsidies now withdrawn, and rudimentary welfare services now severely curtailed.

▲ Africa has received substantial aid in support of these tough measures, but this aid has not kept up with the burden of inflation or the basic needs of the people.

▲ Africa needs additional resources for rural and urban development, and to direct part of these resources towards primary health care and programmes which help the poorest and most vulnerable people, including children. The voluntary agencies can play an increasingly important role in identifying and working with such groups, and in enabling governments to reach them.

▲ Even if world trade is picking up, continuing low prices for commodities hinder recovery in countries whose economies and ability to earn foreign exchange depend on a thriving export market. Many African exports have lost some of their share of world markets. The time has come for a substantial injection of capital by investors and especially by African entrepreneurs, which could in turn attract new investment from overseas. Confidence in the African economy is now a crucial factor in its long-term development.

▲ For external donors – official and voluntary – a new emphasis is required in three major areas. First, the industrialised countries must find solutions to Africa's debt crisis, which is relatively small in global terms but which now represents a major obstacle to recovery in many African countries. Relieving debt will not solve the deep-rooted economic problems in many African countries, but it is a necessary first step towards a more optimistic period when future debts can be adequately serviced by sounder investment.

▲ Second, the population issue must be seen as an issue primarily of health and human resources, concentrating on the ability of aid agencies and governments to adapt to meeting the basic needs for primary health care, proper nutrition, clean water and sanitation as well as for family planning.

▲ Third, in the drought-prone regions, urgent emphasis needs to be given to tackling environmental problems through carefully planned support for crop, livestock and forestry activities and for soil and water conservation, with more involvement of the people and of local voluntary agencies.

Such positive steps are already evident but they need to be multiplied if Africa is to escape from a financial, economic, environmental and human crisis. The outside world, which has historically contributed to this crisis, now has a responsibility to encourage those measures and to offer more assistance, while committing itself to a genuine partnership with the African people and their leaders. The voluntary agencies must help to interpret Africa's problems to a wider public, through means such as this review, while continuing to make their own particular contributions at local and regional levels.

Index